This book belongs to
Janice Kingsround 6-8-70

WHO, ME?

Books by Betty MacDonald

    WHO, ME?
    ONIONS IN THE STEW
    ANYBODY CAN DO ANYTHING
    THE PLAGUE AND I
    THE EGG AND I

Juveniles

    NANCY AND PLUM
    MRS. PIGGLE-WIGGLE'S FARM
    MRS. PIGGLE-WIGGLE
    MRS. PIGGLE-WIGGLE'S MAGIC
    HELLO, MRS. PIGGLE-WIGGLE

Who, Me?

The Autobiography

of

BETTY MacDONALD

J. B. LIPPINCOTT COMPANY
PHILADELPHIA & NEW YORK

PUBLISHER'S NOTE

Betty MacDonald wrote four books of autobiographical reminiscence: *The Egg and I* (1945), *The Plague and I* (1948), *Anybody Can Do Anything* (1950), and *Onions in the Stew* (1955). The chronology of publication does not follow that of the events related: each of the four books centers in a particular segment of the author's life—her experiences on a chicken farm on the Olympic Peninsula; her conquest of tuberculosis (and of the sanitarium where she was treated); her career in gainful employment; and her life on Vashon Island with her husband and her two daughters.

WHO, ME? presents selections from those four books in chronological sequence to form a single-volume autobiography. Nothing has been added; the words throughout are Betty MacDonald's.

CONTENTS

PART I

1	AND I'LL BE HAPPY	11
2	A FAR CRY FROM THE SMITH BROTHERS	22
3	"LOOK 'PEASANT,' PLEASE"	36
4	CHUCKHOLES AND SMOOTH PLACES	44
5	SPRING COMES, AND SO DO PEOPLE	59
6	GAME OR WHO IS	77
7	AND NOT A DROP TO DRINK	89

PART II

8	"GOING HOME, GOING HOME"	103
9	ANYBODY CAN DO ANYTHING	127
10	FINANCE CAN BE FUN, OR CAN IT?	149
11	I LOVE THE GOVERNMENT	167

PART III

12	I HAVE A LITTLE SHADOW—WHO DON'T?	183
13	I'M COLD AND SO IS THE ATTITUDE OF THE STAFF	200
14	DECK THE HALLS WITH OLD CREPE PAPER	223
15	AMBULANT HOSPITAL	248
16	"LET ME OUT! LET ME OUT!"	258

PART IV

17	ANYBODY CAN WRITE BOOKS	273
18	OWNER DESPERATE	279

Contents

19	GOD IS THE BOSS	298
20	WHY DON'T YOU JUST RELAX, BETTY?	311
21	ADOLESCENCE, OR PLEASE KEEP IMOGENE UNTIL SHE IS THIRTY	325
22	BRINGING IN THE SHEAVES	342

PART I

1

And I'll Be Happy

MOTHER'S ANCESTORS were Dutch. Ten Eyck was their name and they settled in New York in 1613. One of my father's family names was Campbell. The Campbells came to Virginia from Scotland. They were all nice well-bred people but not daring or adventuresome except for "Gammy," my father's mother, who wore her corsets upside down and her shoes on the wrong feet and married a gambler with yellow eyes. The gambler, James Bard of Bardstown, Kentucky, took his wife out West, played Faro with his money, his wife's money, and even some of his company's money and then tactfully disappeared and was always spoken of as dead.

We never saw this grandfather but he influenced our lives whether he knew it or not, because Gammy was a strong believer in heredity, particularly the inheritance of bad traits, and she watched us like hawks when we were children to see if the "taint" was coming out in any of us. She hammered on my father to such an extent about his gambling blood that he would not allow us children to play cards in any form, not even Slap Jack or Old Maid, and though Mother finally forced him to learn to play double Canfield, he died without ever having played a hand of bridge, a feat which I envy heartily.

The monotony of Mother's family was not relieved in any way until she married Darsie Bard who was her brother's tutor and a *Westerner working* his way through Harvard. This was a very shocking incident as Mother's family believed that the confines

11

of civilization ended with the boundaries of New York State and that Westerners were a lot of very vulgar people who pronounced their r's and thought they were as good as anybody. Mother's mother, whom later we were forced to call Deargrandmother, had fainting fits, spells and tantrums but to no avail. Mother went flipping off without a backward glance, to live, for heaven's sake, in Butte, Montana.

My sister Mary was born in Butte. She had red hair and to appease Mother's family was given the middle name of Ten Eyck which necessitated her fighting her way through grammar school to the taunts of Mary Tin Neck.

When Mary was less than a year old my father was sent down to the Nevada desert to examine gold property. Mother joyfully went with him and lived in a shack and rode horseback with the baby on the saddle in front of her. Both Mother and Daddy were happy in his work.

I was born in Boulder, Colorado. Gammy was with us then and the night I was born, when Mother began having pains, she called to Gammy (Daddy was away on a mining trip) and told her to phone for the doctor and nurse. But Gammy, prompted by the same inner urge which made her wear her corsets upside down, rushed across the street and pounded on the door of a veterinary and when he appeared, she dragged him bewildered and in his long underwear to Mother's bedside. Mother, very calm, sent the poor man home, but because of the delay and confusion I was born before the doctor could get there and it was necessary for Gammy to tie and cut the umbilical cord. This was very unfortunate, as Gammy, a Southern girl, had been "delicately reared" and her knowledge of rudimentary anatomy could have been put in the eye of a needle. She thought the cord had to be tied into a knot and so grabbing me like the frayed end of a rope, she began looping me through and under as she attempted the knot. The upshot was that Mother sat up and tied and cut the cord herself and I was named for Gammy and became another in a long line of Anne Elizabeth Campbells. My hair was snow white but later turned red.

When I was a few months old Mother received the following

wire from Daddy: "Leaving for Mexico City for two years Thursday—be ready if you want to come along." This was Monday. Mother wired: "Will be ready" and she was; and Thursday morning, we all, including Gammy, left for Mexico.

Díaz was serving his last term as president of Mexico then, and Mexico City was a delightful place of Mexicans, flowers and beautiful horses. My sister, Mary, because of her brilliant red hair, was much admired by the Mexicans and learned to speak fluent Spanish, but I, an outstanding dullard, didn't even begin to speak anything until almost three. There was a series of violent earthquakes while we were in Mexico but Mother, never one to become hysterical, inquired as to earthquake procedure, and when the lamps began to describe arcs in the air, the mirrors to sway and the walls to buckle, Mother sensibly herded Mary, Gammy and me into the doorway of the apartment, where the building structure was supposed to be strongest and, though the apartment building was cracked from top to bottom, we were all unharmed. A woman in the next apartment became very excited and rushed into the street in her nightgown, where, I am happy to relate, a water main burst directly under her.

From Mexico we moved to Placerville, Idaho, a mining camp in the mountains near Boise, where the snow was fifteen feet deep on the level in winter and Mother bought a year's supply of food at a time.

In Placerville, my father supervised his first large placer mining project and as the work was both dangerous and hard, Mother tore the partitions out of the crackerbox house, built a fireplace and bore my brother, Sydney Cleveland, all by herself. Cleveland had red hair. All this red hair caused a lot of comment in Placerville, as Mother was a blonde with brown eyes and Daddy had jet black hair and gray eyes. What no one knew was that Daddy had a bright red beard if he let it grow. When Cleve was born Mother's father wired her, "I trust you won't feel called upon to have a child in every state in the Union."

Our next jaunt was East to visit Mother's mother or Deargrandmother. The moment we arrived, we children were stuffed into a nursery with an adenoidal nurse named Phyllis, and at my five-year-old birthday party the children were instructed by Deargrandmother not to bring presents. My, how we longed for Gammy with her shoes on the wrong feet and her easy friendly ways. Deargrandmother was noted for her beautiful figure and proud carriage but she toed out and had trouble with her arches. She taught Mary and me to turn our toes out when we walked, say "Very well, thank you" instead of "Fine" when people inquired of our health, and to curtsy when we said "How do you do?" She tried hard to scrape the West off these little nuggets, but as soon as we returned home Daddy made us walk like Indians again, feet pointed straight ahead. I would like to remark here and now, that this walking with feet pointed straight ahead is the only thing about an Indian which I would care to imitate.

When we returned from Auburn, we moved to Butte and lived there for the next four years.

Of Butte I remember long underwear which Gammy called "chimaloons" for some strange reason of her own. We folded our "chimaloons" carefully at the ankles so as not to wrinkle our white stockings. I remember my new Lightning Glider sled and coasting fourteen blocks downhill on Montana Street and hitching a ride all the way back. I remember icicles as big as our legs hanging outside the windows, and bobsledding at night with Daddy, who invariably tipped the sled over and took us home bawling. Creamed codfish and baked potatoes for breakfast and hot soup with grease bubbles in it which Gammy called "eyes," for lunch. Walking to the post office with Daddy on Sunday night and holding bags of popcorn in our clumsy mittened hands and drinking the hot buttery popcorn out of the bag. The Christmas when we had scarlet fever and the thermometer went down and stuck in the bulb and we got wonderful presents which had to be burned. Creaking down the street through the dry snow to dancing school, our black patent leather slippers in a flowered bag, our breath white in front of us. A frozen cheek that Mother thawed with snow. A wonderful sleighride into the mountains at night with the bells sounding like tinkling glass, the runners hissing softly and our eyes peering from heaps of robes.

My first memories of being the Trilby for Mary's Svengali go

And I'll Be Happy

back to that winter in Butte, Montana, when each morning Mary marched importantly off to the second grade at McKinley School, while my brother Cleve and I, who could already read and write, shuffled despondently off to Miss Crispin's kindergarten, a gloomy institution where all the crayons were broken and had the peelings off.

The contrast between Miss Crispin's and real school, in fact between Miss Crispin's and anything but a mortuary, was heartbreakingly obvious even to four and five year olds, but the contrast between Miss Crispin's and the remarkable school that Mary attended and described so vividly to us, was unbearable. Nothing ever happened at Miss Crispin's except that some days it was gloomier and darker than on others and we had to bend so close to our coloring work to tell blue from purple or brown from black that our noses ran on the pictures; some days Miss Crispin, who was very nervous, yelled at us to be quiet, got purple blotches and pulled and kneaded the skin on her neck like dough; and on Fridays to the halting accompaniment of her sight-reading at the piano, we skipped around the room and sang. Miss Crispin taught us all the verses of "Dixie," "Swanee River," "My Country 'Tis of Thee" and "Old Black Joe," and for the bottom rung on the ladder to enjoyment, I nominate skipping around the room dodging little kindergarten chairs and singing "Old Black Joe."

Compare this then to the big brick school that Mary attended where everyday occurrences (according to Mary and Joe Doner, a boy at school called on so often to prove incredible stories that "If you don't believe me, just ask Joe Doner" has become a family tag for all obvious untruths) were the beating of small children with spiked clubs, the whipping of older boys with a cat-o'-nine-tails in front of the whole school, the forcing of the first graders to drink ink and eat apple cores, the locking in the basement of anyone tardy, and the terribly cruel practice of never allowing anyone to go to the bathroom so that all screamed in pain and many wet their panties.

Naturally Cleve and I believed everything Mary told us, but also naturally, after a while, we grew blasé about the continual beatings, killings and panty wettings that went on in the second grade at real school, so Mary, noting our waning interest, started the business about the "sausage book" and for months kept us feverish with curiosity and acid with envy.

One snowy winter afternoon she came bursting in from school, glazed with learning, but instead of her usual burden of horror stories, she was carrying a big notebook with a shiny, dark red, mottled cover, like salami. "Look at this," she announced to Gammy and Mother. "I call it my 'sausage book' and I put everything I learn in it. See!" Carefully she brushed the snow off her mittens, turned back the shiny cover and with great pride pointed to the first page. "That's what we did in school today, all by ourselves, without any help," she said.

"Why, that's beautiful, dear," Mother said. "Just beautiful!" Gammy echoed and Cleve and I crowded close to see what was beautiful. Immediately Mary grabbed the book, snapped it shut and put it behind her back. "Hey, we want to see in your sausage book," Cleve and I said. Mary, in a maddeningly sweet, sad way, said, "I'd like to show it to you, Cleve and Betsy, I really would, but Miss O'Toole won't let me. She said it's all right to show our sausage books to our mothers and fathers but never ever to our little brothers and sisters." Mother and Gammy laughed and said, "Nonsense," so Mary stamped her foot and said, "If you don't believe me, just ask Joe Doner."

Day by day Mary built up the importance of the sausage book until I got so I dreamed about it at night and thought that I opened it and found it full of paper dolls and colored pencils. But no spy was ever more careful of his secret formula than Mary with that darned old notebook. Sometimes she did homework in it but she guarded it with her arms and leaned so far forward that she was drawing or writing under her stomach; she slept with it under her pillow, she even took it coasting and to dancing school. She never was cross or mean about not letting Cleve and me see inside it, but persisted in the attitude that she was only obeying her teacher and trying to protect us, because she realized, even if Mother and Gammy didn't, that seeing into her sausage book might lift the veil of our ignorance too quickly and send our feeble minds off balance. Our only recourse was not to show her the pictures we made at Miss Crispin's, which she didn't want to see anyway.

Then one day Miss Crispin ordered her kindergarteners to draw an apple tree and as not one of us little Butte children had ever seen an apple tree, she told us each to find a picture of one and bring it the next day. We told Mother and Gammy about our kindergarten assignment and Mother found us a very nice colored picture of an apple tree in our *Three Little Pigs* book. Mary looked at it critically for a minute then said, "I'll show you a much better one," and to Cleve's and my absolute joy opened up her sausage book, flipped over some pages and showed us a large drawing of what looked like a Kelly-green Brussels sprout covered with red dots and with a long spindly brown stem. "This," said Mary, "is the way they draw apple trees in real school. Here," she said, generously tearing out the page, "take this to Miss Crispin and just see what she says." We did and Miss Crispin looked at it a long time, pulled at her doughy neck and said, "Mmmmmmm."

The next winter, when we were six and eight, I started to real school and because of a shyness so terrible that I was unable to speak above a faint whisper, it took them several months to discover that I could read and write and really belonged in the second grade.

When the terrible ordeal of reading, in my faint whisper, before the principal and writing my name and several sentences on the blackboard in front of the whole giggling class, had been completed and I had been told that I was in the second grade, my first exultant thought was "Now I'll get my sausage book." But the whole morning went by and I didn't. I peered from under my eyelids at the other children and they didn't seem to have them either. Finally in desperation I raised my hand to ask the teacher and she, misinterpreting my wants, said, in a loud voice, "Number one or number two, Elizabeth." I said, "When do we get our sausage books?" She said, "Your what?" I repeated a little louder, "Our sausage books." She said, "I don't know what you're talking about, now open your reading books to page three."

I got up and went home. I didn't even stop for my coat or rubbers but ran sobbing through the streets and burst in on Mother and Gammy who were having a cup of coffee. "We don't get them," I shrieked. "Don't get what?" Mother said. "Sausage books," I said. "I'm in the second grade and I asked the teacher and she said she didn't know what I was talking about."

Mother explained that I had a different teacher from Mary's and that she probably didn't use sausage books. I refused to be comforted. School had come to mean but one thing to me. A sausage book of my very own filled with secret things that I'd let Cleve but not Mary see. I bawled all afternoon and finally Mother, in desperation, went downtown and bought me a new Lightning Glider sled.

When Mary came home from school, I was out in the back yard, a steep slope about a hundred feet long, reaching from a woodshed and toolhouse at the very back of the lot down to a small level place behind the house, still red-eyed and snuffling, coasting down our little hill on my new sled. When I told Mary about my second grade teacher not giving us sausage books, Mary was so outraged she was going right back to school and mark on the desks and put paste in the inkwells, but to her relief I pled with her and finally talked her out of this dangerous act of loyalty. So as a reward she tried to invent perpetual motion and knocked out all my front teeth.

The back yard was a dandy place to slide and for a while, until Mary had her inspiration, we happily climbed up the little hill and coasted down again, climbed up and coasted down, on the big new shiny sled. Then suddenly at the bottom of the hill, Mary jumped off the sled, dashed into the cellar and came out brandishing the clothes pole.

"Betsy," she said. "I have a wonderful idea. We'll both get on the sled at the top of the hill, I'll hold this pole out in front of us [the pole was about eight feet long] and when we slide down the pole will hit the house and push us back up the hill again. Then down we'll go, then up, then down, then up and we'll never have to climb the hill."

It sounded like a terribly good idea to me so when we had pulled the sled back up the hill to the woodshed, I climbed on the front and put my feet up on the steering bar and Mary got on the back and we both held the pole out in front of us in a direct line with my mouth. Mary gave us a big shove to send us off and whee! how we flew down the little hill. Then everything went black and I began spitting blood and teeth onto the white hard-packed snow, for the pole, when it hit the house, had been forced well back into my mouth. "Oh, Betsy," Mary said, her face so pale her freckles looked like brown moles, "I didn't mean to hurt you. I'm so sorry," and I knew she was because she gave me her old sausage book. Anyway they were only first teeth.

My sister Darsie was born when I was in the second grade. She was small and had dark hair.

Mary and I wore white stockings to school every day and shoes with patent leather bottoms and white kid tops. Mary turned her stockings wrong side out and wore them two days which would have been all right but she told everybody and I was ashamed. Gammy made us wear aprons which she called "aperns" over our dresses while we were playing after school. She would greet us at the door with the "aperns" but if we managed to sneak out without them she would stand on the porch and call in a high mournful wail, "Giiiiiiiirls, come get your aperns" (this last a high banshee shriek).

When Cleve and I used to "rassle" to see who would get the biggest apple, the most candy, or any of the other senseless things children quarrel about, Gammy would stand over us and shout, "Get the hatchet, Cleve, and kill her now. You'll do it some day, so why not now." This infuriated us so that we would cease pounding each other and become bosom friends just to "show" Gammy. Perhaps this was her underlying motive but it used to seem to me that she was far too anxious to get rid of her little namesake.

Our summers were spent camping in the mountains. Usually we had a camp man and slept in tents and followed Daddy about while he examined mines, but other times we had cabins on a lake and stayed with Gammy while Mother and Daddy did the traveling. My still-smoldering hatred for and distrust of wild animals were implanted on these camping trips. Once we almost fell on a large bear, placidly eating huckleberries on the other side of a log.

Another time Daddy pointed out a mountain lion lying in the sun on a ledge above our heads. Bears were always knocking down our tents and eating our supplies and at night the coyotes and timber wolves howled dismally.

Mother and Daddy fished incessantly and we had Rainbow trout, which we children loathed, three times a day. Sometimes Gammy came camping with us but only when we had cabins and didn't spend our days "traipsing" through the mountains. Gammy stayed with us while Mother and Daddy took trips and fished and although they were considerate and always asked if we cared to come along, we always refused because Mother and Daddy loved danger and were always walking logs over deep terrible ravines; walking into black dangerous mine tunnels; wading into swift turbulent streams and doing other scary things. Gammy, on the other hand, carefully avoided danger and was constantly on the alert for it.

When Mother and Daddy went away from home on long trips, which they did frequently, we stayed at home with Gammy. She had us all sleep in her room on army cots and folding beds which she hastily and carelessly erected and which were always collapsing and giving us skinned noses and black eyes. Gammy kept a pair of Daddy's shoes beside her bed and when she heard any noise in the house she leaned out of bed and stamped the shoes on the floor so that the robber or killer, whichever one happened to be downstairs, would think that there was a man in the house instead of "a lone helpless woman and several small children" all huddled upstairs waiting to be killed.

Our "hired girls" often came in late and I've wondered since if this stamping of manly feet upstairs in the dead of night, when they knew that Mother and Daddy were in New York or Alaska, didn't lead them to believe that Gammy had a secret love life. To the casual eyes of a maid this idea might have been plausible, as Gammy was a very pretty woman, small with large blue eyes, delicate regular features and tinselly curly hair. But to those of us who knew her there were several good reasons why this wouldn't, couldn't be. In the first place Gammy hated men—all men, except Daddy.

In the second place, any lover of Gammy's would have had to equip himself with enduring desire and a bowie knife, for Gammy was well covered. She thought nakedness was a sin and warned us, "Don't let me catch you running around in your naked strip!" and for her own part, she merely added or removed layers of clothing as the weather demanded. On top she always had a clean, ruffly white "apern"—during the day this was covered by a large checked "apern." Under the aprons were a black silk dress, a black wool skirt, a white batiste blouse with a high collar, any number of flannel petticoats, a corset cover, the upside-down corset with the bust part fitting snugly over the hips, and at long last the "chimaloons."

In the third place, a lover of Gammy's certainly would have had a lumpy couch with her nightgowns, bed jackets and several extra suits of "chimaloons" folded under the pillow, her Bible tucked under the sheet at the top right-hand side, any book she happened to be reading tucked under the sheet on the other side, little bags of candy, an apple or two, current magazines, numerous sachets and her bottle of camphor just tucked under the blankets or scattered under the pillows within easy reach. We children thought this an ideal arrangement, for when we were lonely or frightened Gammy's bed was as comforting as a crowded country store.

Gammy was an inexhaustible reader-aloud and took us through the Bible, *Pilgrim's Progress*, Dickens, Thackeray, Lewis Carroll, Kipling, *The Little Colonel*, *The Wizard of Oz*, *The Five Little Peppers*, and all of Zane Grey, which we adored, before we left Butte. She changed long words to ones we could understand without faltering, but after an hour or two with *The Little Colonel* or *The Five Little Peppers* she would begin to doze and we would be dispatched to the kitchen to ask Mary the Cook for some black coffee. Usually this revived her completely and she would continue until lunch or supper or bedtime, but sometimes, especially during the nauseous antics of the Little Colonel or the continual bawling of the Five Little Peppers who cried when they were happy, Gammy would drink cup after cup of black coffee but would still fall asleep and when she awoke would read the same paragraph over and over. We would make several futile trys to wake her and then would give up and go out to play.

Gammy was patient, impatient, kind, caustic, witty, sad, wise, foolish, superstitious, religious, prejudiced and dear. She was, in short, a grandmother who is, after all, a woman whose inconsistencies have sharpened with use. I have no patience with women who complain because their mothers or their husbands' mothers have to live with them. To my prejudiced eye, a child's life without a grandparent *en residence* would be a barren thing.

2

A Far Cry from the Smith Brothers

WHEN I WAS nine years old we moved to Seattle, Washington, and the pioneering days were over and preparedness for the future began. At least I'm quite sure that is what Mother and Daddy had in mind when they started Mary and me taking singing, piano, folk dancing, ballet, French and dramatic lessons.

In addition to our injections of culture, we children were suddenly tumbled into a great health program. We ate no salt, never drank water with our meals, chewed our food one hundred times, got up at five o'clock in the morning and took cold baths, exercised to music and played tennis. Also, to keep our minds healthy, I guess, we were not allowed to go to the movies or to read the funny papers. One of the houses we lived in had belonged to the Danish Consul and had a large ballroom in the basement which Daddy immediately turned into a gymnasium with horizontal bars, basketball hoops and mattresses. Every night he forced us into this torture chamber for a workout. We leaped over the bar without hands, swung by our knees, played basketball, did back flips and hated Daddy. We did not want to be healthy. We wanted to go to the movies, read the funny papers and relax like all the other unhealthy children we knew. Fortunately Daddy left home on mining trips quite often and the moment the front door closed on his tweed-covered back we got out several months' supply of funny papers and settled down to a life of hot baths and blissful slothfulness until he returned. His mining trips kept him away from home about six months of the year, off and on, and it is a wonder that our muscles withstood this business of being hardened up like flints, only to squash back to jelly. Only the lessons kept on while Daddy was away, as Mother and Gammy weren't any more anxious to get up at five o'clock and take cold baths and exercises than we were.

I have been told that I was directly responsible for this dreadful health complex of Daddy's, for I was a thin, greenish child who caught everything. Up to this time I had brought home and we had all had measles, both German and Allied, mumps, chickenpox, pink eye, scarlet fever, whooping cough, lice and the itch. Every morning before sending me off to school, Mother and Gammy would examine me in a strong light to see what I had broken out with during the night, for I looked so unhealthy all of the time that they were unable to determine if I was coming down with a disease until the spots appeared.

We always lived in large houses because Daddy had a penchant for inviting people to stay with us. He would casually wire Mother from Alaska "Meet the SS *Alameda* on Thursday—Bill Swift and family coming to Seattle for a few months—have asked them to stay with you." Mother would change the sheets on the guestroom beds, heave a sigh and drive down to meet the boat. Sometimes Bill Swift and his wife and children were charming and we regretted to see them go, but other times Bill Swift was the world's biggest bore, his wife whined all the time and we fought to the death with the children. After the first day, we could tell what the guests were like from Gammy, for if they were interesting, charming people Gammy retaliated in kind and was her most fascinating and witty self, but if they were dull or irritating in any way,

Gammy would give us the signal by calling them all by wrong names.

When I was eleven and just about ready to go up on my toes in ballet, we bought a house in Laurelhurst near the water. This was a fine big place with an orchard, a vegetable garden, tennis courts and a large level lawn for croquet. We immediately bought a cow (which obligingly had a calf), two riding horses, two dogs, three cats, a turtle, white mice, twelve chickens, two Mallard ducks, several goldfish and a canary. Our animals were not very useful and too friendly and hovered in the vicinity of the back porches day and night. We had a schoolboy who milked the cow, fed the calf, curried the horses and tethered them all out, but either he was weak or they were strong, for the minute he left for school they would all come galloping home to the back porches where Gammy fed them leftover batter cakes, toast and cocoa. We loved all of our animals and apparently our guests did too, or if they didn't love them they didn't mind them, for our house overflowed with guests and animals all of the time. Guests of Daddy's, guests of Mother's, guests of Gammy's, and our friends and animals. There were seven of us, counting Daddy who was rarely home, but our table was always set for twelve and sometimes forty. Dinner was an exciting event and we washed our knees, changed our clothes and brushed our hair with anticipatory fervor. Mother sat at one end of the table and Daddy at the other, if he was home, Gammy sat at Daddy's right and we children were spaced to eliminate fighting. Daddy had made a rule and it was strictly enforced, whether or not he was home, that only subjects of general interest were to be discussed at the table. This eliminated all such contributions from us, as "There is a boy in my room at school who eats flies," and "Myrna Hepplewaite stuck out her tongue at me and I said bah, bah, bah and she hit me back and I told her mother. . . ." In fact, it precluded our entering the conversation at all except on rare occasions which I think was and is an excellent idea. I resent heartily dining at someone's house and having all my best stories interrupted by "Not such a big bite, Hubert," or "Mummy, didn't you say the Easter Bunny came down the chimney?"

As soon as we were settled in Laurelhurst, Daddy decided that in addition to Mary's, Darsie's and my singing, piano, ballet, folk dancing, French and dramatics and Cleve's clarinet lessons, we should all have lessons in general usefulness and self-reliance. His first step in this direction was to have Mary and Cleve and me paint the roof of our three-story house. The roof was to be red and we were each given a bucket of paint, a wide brush, a ladder and some vague general instructions about painting. It seems that there was a shortage of ladders so Cleve and I were on the same one—he was just a rung or two ahead of me and both of us biting our lips and dipping our brushes and slapping on the red paint for all we were worth. We weren't working hard because we liked this job; we didn't, we just thought it was another one of Daddy's damnfool notions and we wanted to get it over with as quickly as possible. Cleve and I had just finished the small area over the back porch and were moving up when something went wrong and Cleve dumped his bucket of paint over my head and down the back of my neck. Gammy cleaned me off with turpentine but she grumbled about it and said, "It's a wonder to me you aren't all dead with the ideas some Men get." We finished the roof, though, with Daddy lowering me by the heels so that I could paint the dormers of the attic, but it was a scary, slippery job and was an outstanding failure as far as a lesson in self-reliance was concerned. Daddy's next step was the purchase of a .22 rifle and a huge target. Gammy had hysterics. "*Guns*," she bawled, "Guns are for Huns and heathens. Those childen will kill each other—please, Darsie, don't give them a gun." So we learned to shoot. Mary and I were both rather nearsighted and very poor shots but Cleve was a good shot and practiced all the time. Cleve became such an expert marksman that he took up hunting when he was only ten years old and Daddy thought it was a fine idea until Cleve drew a bead and fired at a quail that was perched on the sill of a huge curved bay window of a neighbor's house. None of the neighbors was killed but the bay window was very expensive and so the gun was put away for a while and Daddy bought us an enormous bow and arrow and a big straw target.

While he and Cleve were practicing archery, Mary and I were

learning to cook. Mother supervised this herself as she was a marvelous cook and Gammy was the world's worst. Mother taught us to put a pinch of clove and lots of onion in with a pot roast; to make French dressing with olive oil and to rub the bowl with garlic; to make mayonnaise and Thousand Island dressing; to cook a sliver of onion with string beans; never to mash potatoes until just before serving; to measure the ingredients for coffee; and always to scald out the teapot.

Gammy taught us that when you bake a cake you put in anything you can lay your hands on. A little onion, several old jars of jam, leftover batter cake dough, the rest of the syrup in the jug, a few grapes, cherries, raisins, plums or dates, and always to use drippings instead of butter or shortening. Her cakes were simply dreadful—heavy and tan and full of seeds and pits. She made a great show of having her feelings hurt if we didn't eat these cakes but I really think she only offered them to us as a sort of character test because if we were strong and refused, she'd throw them out to the dogs or chickens without a qualm.

When I was twelve years old Daddy died in Butte of streptococcic pneumonia. My sister Alison, who has red hair, was born five months later. It was a very sad year but rendered less tragic and more hectic by a visit from Deargrandmother, who came out to comfort Mother and make our lives a living hell. She dressed Mary and me in dimities and leghorn hats; asked *who* our friends were and *what* their fathers did; she wouldn't let Gammy work in her garden as it was unbecoming to a lady, so Gammy had to sneak out and hoe her potatoes and squash at eleven o'clock at night; she wouldn't let our old Scotch nurse eat at the table with us and insulted her by calling her a servant; she picked her way downtown as though we had wooden sidewalks; and was "amused" by anything she saw in our shops because this wasn't New York. Our only recourse was to go out to the laundry, which was a large room built on the back of the house and connected to the kitchen by a series of hallways and screened porches, with Nurse and Gammy, where we would make tea on the laundry stove and talk about Deargrandmother.

When she finally left for New York we took life in our own

hands again and things continued much the same as they had before Daddy died except we were poorer and fewer of our guests were Mother's and Daddy's and Gammy's friends and more and more of them were friends of Mary's. As an economy measure we had stopped all our lessons but the piano and the ballet, and we were to go to public schools in the fall.

In high school and college my sister Mary was very popular with the boys, but I had braces on my teeth and got high marks. While Mary went swishing off to parties, I stayed home with Gammy and studied Ancient History or played Carom or Mahjong with Cleve. Mary brought hundreds of boys to the house but she also brought hundreds of other girls, so I usually baked the waffles and washed the dishes with a large "apern" tied over my Honor Society Pin and my aching heart. Gammy used to tell me that I was the type who would appeal to "older men," but as my idea of an older man was one of the Smith Brothers on the coughdrop box I took small comfort in this. To make matters worse I suddenly stopped being green and skinny and became rosy and fat. I grew a large, firm bust and a large, firm stomach and that was not the style. The style was my best friend, who was five feet ten inches tall and weighed ninety-two pounds. She had a small head and narrow shoulders and probably looked like a thermometer, but I thought she was simply exquisite. I bought my dresses so tight I had to ease into them like bolster covers and I took up smoking and drinking black coffee but still I had a large, firm bust, just under my chin, and a large, firm stomach slightly lower down. I am sure that Mary also had a bust and stomach but hers didn't seem to hamper her as mine did me. Perhaps it was because she had "life." "Torchy" they called her and put under her picture in the school annual: "Torchy's the girl who put the pep in pepper." Under my picture was printed in evident desperation "An honor roll student—a true friend."

When I was seventeen years old and a sophomore in college, my brother, Cleve, brought home for the weekend a very tall, very handsome older man. His brown skin, brown hair, blue eyes, white teeth, husky voice and kindly, gentle way were attributes enough in themselves and produced spasms of admiration from Mary and her friends, but the most wonderful thing about him, the outstanding touch, was that he liked me. I still cannot understand why unless it was that he was overcome by so much untrammeled girlishness. He took me to dinner, dancing and the movies and I fell head over heels in love, to his evident delight, and when I was eighteen we were married. Bob was thirteen years older than I but a far cry from the Smith Brothers.

Why do more or less intelligent people go on honeymoons, anyway? I have yet to find a couple who enjoyed theirs. And, if you have to go on a honeymoon, why pick quaint, old-world towns like Victoria, B.C., which should be visited only with congenial husbands of at least one year's vintage or relatives searching for antiques.

On the boat going up to Victoria, Bob seemed to be well established in the insurance business and held forth at some length on premiums, renewals and "age 65," and I determined to ask Mother just how much I should learn about insurance in order to be helpful but not meddlesome, and wondered what the wives of insurance men were like for friends. On the way back from Victoria, Bob talked of his childhood on a wheat ranch in Montana, his days at agricultural college and his first job as supervisor for a large chicken ranch. When he spoke of the wheat ranch it was with about as much enthusiasm as one would use reminiscing of the first fifteen years in a sweat shop and I gathered that he thought farming hard, thankless work. But then he began on the chicken ranch job, sorting over the little details with the loving care usually asociated with first baby shoes. When he reached the figures—the cost per hen per egg, the cost per dozen eggs, the relative merits of outdoor runs, the square footage required per hen—he recalled them with so much nostalgia that listening to him impartially was like trying to swim at the edge of a whirlpool. He told me at last that he had found a little place on the coast, where he often went on business, that was ideally situated for chicken ranching and could be bought for almost nothing. "What did I think about it?" What did I think about it? Why, Mother had taught me that a husband must be happy in his work and if Bob wanted to be happy in the chicken business I didn't care. I knew how to make mayonnaise and mitre sheet corners and light candles for dinner, so, chickens or insurance, I could hold up my end. That's what I thought.

The next morning after our return to Seattle, the alarm went off with a clang at six-thirty; at six-thirty-one Bob, clad in a large wool plaid shirt, was stamping around the kitchen of our tiny apartment making coffee, and demanding that I hurry. At eight-forty-five we had driven twelve miles and were boarding a ferry as the first lap in our journey to see the "little place."

It was one of our better March days—it was, in fact, one of the March days we have up here which deceives people into thinking, "With spring like this we are sure to have a long, hot summer," and into stocking up on halters and shorts and sunglasses. Then later, summer appears wan and shaking with ague and more like February. This March day, though, was strong and bright and Bob and I spent the long ferry ride walking the decks and admiring the deep blue waters of Puget Sound, the cerulean sky, densely wooded dark-green islands which floated serenely here and there, and the great range of Olympic Mountains obligingly visible in all of their snowy magnificence. These Olympics have none of the soft curves and girlish plumpness of Eastern mountains. They are goddesses, full-breasted, broad-hipped, towering and untouchable. They are also complacent in the knowledge that they look just as mountains should.

The ferry landed, we drove ashore and made a circuit of the two streets which comprised Docktown. There were a great sawmill, a charming old Victorian hotel with beautifully cared for lawns and shrubs, a company store, a string of ugly company houses, and a long pier where freighters were being loaded with lumber by an alarmingly undecided crane that paused first here, then there and finally dumped a gigantic load of planks almost on top of the longshoremen. Curses flew up like sparks from the men as they scattered to safety but in a moment or so the air cleared and they were back at work. Cranes and piledrivers can keep me at a pitch of nervous excitement for hours and hours and when I finally do tear myself away it is always with the conviction that the operator is going to find the operation very difficult without my personal supervision. I would have been content to lean on the sun-warmed railing of the ferry dock, smelling that delicious mixture of creosote, cedar and seaweed which characterizes coast mill towns, and watching the cranes for the rest of the day; but Bob warned me that we had a long drive ahead of us and if we intended to return that night we should get started.

The road out of Docktown was dangerously curved and not too wide and alive with cars, trucks and logging trucks with terrific loads and terrible trailer tails that switched and slithered behind them. Everyone drove as if he were going to a fire and on the wrong side of the road, and we were warned of approaching corners by the anguished screams of tires and brakes. Bob is an excellent driver but he was hard put to it to hold his own when a logging truck carrying three of the largest logs of the largest stand of Douglas fir in the world came winging around a curve and we had to leap the bank and scurry for the woods to avoid being smashed into oblivion by the playful trailer. The driver leaned out and grinned and waved at us and then went careening off down the road. We backed carefully onto the road again and trundled sedately off, hugging the bank nervously when we spotted another logging truck. After a while we left the woods and began skirting a great valley where emerald winter wheat, the velvety blackness of plowed fields and the tender green of new pastures checkered the bottom land. This was dairy country and the smallest farms ran to three hundred and fifty acres. The houses, for the most part unattractive boxlike abodes, close to the road and unadorned with flowers or shrubbery, were across the road from their farmlands, their back porches snuggled against the blue-black tree-covered hillsides. The barns, silos, bunkhouses and outbuildings, magnificent structures of generous proportions were on the valley side. I thought this arrangement had something to do with keeping the cattle out of the house until Bob informed me that the road had been put in after the ranches were laid out.

I had noticed wisps of smoke rising from the ground in the farthest fields. "Burning peat," Bob explained. "One of the great tragedies of this country. Years ago some of the farmers, in an effort to clear the practically unclearable peat land, set fire to some of the huge piles of logs, roots and trees unearthed during plowing. When the roots and stumps had burned the farmers were surprised to find that the land itself was burning and that ditching, plowing and wet sacks were ineffective agents in putting it out. After much experimenting they learned that by digging four-foot-deep drainage ditches around a small area at a time, they could control the fire but this was such an undertaking that in most cases they let 'er burn."

"Isn't the land arable after the fires have burned out?" I asked.

"Unfortunately, not for years and years because peat burns deep down to a light feathery ash which will not bear the weight of a horse or a tractor. Hand-cultivated, it will grow potatoes almost as big as watermelons and about as watery, too," Bob concluded dismally.

"Look at those fields," I exclaimed pointing to plowed fields as black as licorice. "That soil must be terribly rich."

"It's rich all right," Bob said, "but it's peat land and hellishly expensive to clear and drain. You clear and plant a field and the next year your plow digs up a stump every three feet and you have to clear all over again. Every acre of it has to be tile drained, too."

After that, for a time we drove along in silence while the unconquerable peat lay black and scornful in the valleys and the unconquerable forests thundered down at us from the hills.

This land resents civilization and it isn't a little futile stick-out-the-tongue kind of resentment, but a great big smashing resentment that is backed by all the forces of nature, I thought, huddling down into my coat and hoping we'd soon come to a town.

We did, and it boasted the mad confusion of four enterprises —a hotel, a barbershop, a gas station and a country store and post office. In addition there were a dear little graveyard and an imposing brick schoolhouse. Five roads led away from this small town but Bob didn't hesitate. He chose one pointing southwest toward the frosty Olympic Mountains. For the next several hours we saw no more towns, only crossroads stores; rich valleys separated by heavily wooded hills; herds of cattle and widely spaced farm houses. We had nosed our way into the foothills of the Olympics while we were still in the farming county and it wasn't until I looked from the car window and saw, far below the road, a frustrated little mountain stream banging its head against immense canyon walls that I realized that we were in the mountains proper. Yellow highway signs announcing WINDING ROAD appeared at intervals and Bob put the car in second and then low gear as we spiraled forward and upward. We were climbing but seemed to be getting nowhere for we were walled in on all sides by the robust green mountainsides and only by sticking my head clear out of the window was I able to peer up and see the sky. Two or three hundred million board feet of Douglas fir later, we turned off the main highway onto a dirt road and jounced and skidded our way at last to the "little place."

On first sight it looked distressingly forlorn, huddled there in the lap of the great Olympics, the buildings grayed with weather, the orchard overgrown with second-growth firs, the fences collapsing, the windows gaping. It was the little old deserted farm that people point at from car windows, saying, "Look at that picturesque old place!" then quickly drive by toward something not quite so picturesque, but warmer and nearer to civilization. Bob halted the car to take down the rails of the gate and I looked morosely around at the mountains so imminent they gave me a feeling of someone reading over my shoulder, and at the terrific virility of the forests, and I thought, Good heavens, those mountains could flick us off this place like a fly off their skirts, rearrange their trees a little and no one would ever be the wiser. It was not a comforting thought and the driveway, which proved to be a rather inadequate tunnel under the linked arms of two rows of giant trees, did nothing to dispel it. Heavy green branches lashed the top of the car and smaller twigs clawed at the windows and the car wheels churned and complained on the slick dry needles. We drove for perhaps a quarter of a mile like this and then abruptly the trees stopped and we were in the dooryard of the farm, where a great-grandfather of a cherry tree, hoary with bloom, stood guard over the huddled buildings.

I'm not sure whether it was the cherry tree or the purple carpet of sweet violets flanking the funny silvery woodshed, or the fact that the place was so clean, not a scrap of rubbish, not a single tin can, but it suddenly lost its sinister deserted look and began to appear lonely but eager to make friends. A responsive little farm that with a few kindnesses in the way of windows and paint and clearing might soon be licking our hands.

While I stood in the dooryard "feeling" the place, Bob was bounding around with a hammer, pounding the walls and calling happily, "Look, Betty, hand-hewn-out-of-cedar logs, and sound as a nut." The hand-hewn cedar shakes which covered the sides and roof had worked loose in several places and Bob pulled them off to show me the cedar logs and the axe marks.

The house, evidently begun as a log cabin about twenty feet by twenty and added on to at either end, was beautifully situated on a small rise of ground from which an old orchard, peering out from the second-growth fir, sloped gently down to a small lake or large pond. The original cabin was the living room with windows on the north and south sides and a thin rickety porch across the front. It faced south, across the orchard, to the pond and of course the mountains. The mountains were everywhere—I'd start to turn around, come up against something large and solid and wham! there was a mountain icily ignoring me.

Opening off the living room on the right, with windows north, west and south, we found a bedroom with roses and honeysuckle vines in heaps on the floor below the windows, as though they had climbed up to peek in and had fallen over the sills. Down three steps and to the left of the living room were an enormous square kitchen with windows east and north and a pantry the size of our apartment in town, with three windows facing east. Jutting off the kitchen toward the front was a bedroom with windows looking east and south. Up a creepy flight of stairs from the living room were two tiny slope-ceilinged bedrooms. Under the front porch we discovered a bat-hung cellar, and to one side of the kitchen, forming an ell with the living room, an entryway and wood room.

A very large, very surly and slightly rusty range was backed defiantly against the north wall of the kitchen—otherwise the place was empty. The floors were warped and splintery—the walls were covered with carefully tacked newspapers dated 1885.

At first glance the outbuildings seemed frail and useless, but closer examination revealed fine bone structure in the way of uprights, beams and stringers and so we were able to include in the assets of the place, a very large barn, two small chicken houses, a woodshed and an outhouse. The assets also included ten acres of land showing evidences of having once been cleared, and thirty acres of virgin timber, cedar, fir and hemlock—some of it seven feet and more in diameter. Scattered over the ten cleared acres, like figures in a tableau, were the dearest, fattest, most perfectly shaped Christmas trees I have ever seen. Each one was round and full at the bottom and exquisitely trimmed with brown cones. I was caressing and exclaiming over these when Bob told me that such little jewels of trees are cut by the hundreds of thousands by Christmas tree dealers, who pay the farmers two cents each for them. Incredible that anyone who professed a love of the soil would sanction such vandalism and for such a paltry fee.

At the edge of the clearing and sheltered by one of the great black firs, we found an old well. It was half full of water, but the intake was a tiny trickle instead of a robust gush which this season warranted, so Bob decided it had been abandoned and we looked elsewhere for water. We found a larger, more substantial spring at the foot of the orchard, feeding the lake, but as it had not been boxed in and showed no other signs of use, either it was a thing of recent origin or suffered from summer complaint—time would tell. It did too, and water became one of the major obsessions of my life.

We threaded our way through the orchard and found slender fruit trees bravely blossoming with frail hands pushing futilely against the dark green hairy chests of the invading firs. The firs were everywhere, big and virile, with their strong roots pulling all of the vitality out of the soil and leaving the poor little fruit trees only enough food and light to keep an occasional branch alive. These were no kin to the neatly spaced little Christmas tree ladies of the back pasture. These were fierce invaders. Pillagers and rapers.

The more we walked around, the stronger became my feeling that we should hurry and move in so that we could help this little farm in its fight against the wilderness. Bob was overjoyed when I told him of this feeling and so we decided to buy it at once.

For the forty acres, the six-room log house, the barn, two small chicken houses, woodshed, outhouse and the sulky stove, the mortgage company was asking four hundred and fifty dollars. Between us and by pooling all savings accounts, wedding presents, birthday presents and by drawing on a small legacy which I was to get when I became twenty-one we had fifteen hundred dollars. We sat in the sunny doorway under the cherry tree, used a carpenter's blue pencil and shingle and decided that we would pay cash for the farm; put seven hundred dollars in the bank to be used to buy, feed and raise three hundred and fifty pullets; and we would use the rest to fix up the buildings. Fuel and water were free and we'd have a large vegetable garden, a pig to eat leavings, a few chickens for immediate eggs and Bob could work occasionally in one of the sawmills to eke out until the chickens started to lay. Written out in blue pencil on the weathered shingle it was the simplest, most delightful design for living ever devised for two people.

We left then and hurried home to put our plans into action. The next morning Bob paid the $450, and brought home the deed. The following week we borrowed a truck, loaded on everything we possessed and left for the mountains to dive headfirst into the chicken business.

3

"Look 'Peasant,' Please"

"WHO, ME?" I asked when we were moving and Bob pointed casually to a large chest of drawers and said, "Carry that into the bedroom."

"Who else?" he snapped and my lower lip began to tremble because I knew now that I was just a wife.

"Who, me?" I asked incredulously as he handed me the reins of an enormous horse which he had borrowed from a neighbor, and told me to drive it and a heaving sled of bark to the woodshed while he gathered up another load.

"Yes, you!" he roared. "And hurry!"

"Not me!" I screamed as he told me to put the chokers on the fir trees and to shout directions for the pulling as he drove the team when we cleared out the orchard. "Yes, you! I'm sure you're not competent but you're the best help I can get at present," and Bob laughed callously.

"Hand me that hammer. Run into the house and get those nails. Help me peel this stringer. Hurry with those shakes. Put your weight on this crowbar. Stain that floor while I lay this one. You don't measure windows that way, bonehead. Help me unload this chicken feed. Run down and get a couple of buckets of water."

"If I can handle the plow, surely you might manage the horse more intelligently!"

"Go get those seeds. It's time to fill the baby chicks' water jugs. Bring me some of those two-by-fours. Cut me about twenty-five more shakes. Don't be such a baby, bring them up *here*. I'm not climbing down from this roof every time I want a nail."

And that's the way it went that first spring and summer. I alternated between delirious happiness and black despair. I was willing but pitifully unskilled. "If only I had studied carpentry or mule skinning instead of ballet," I wailed as I teetered on the ridgepole of the chicken house pounding my already mashed thumbs and expecting momentarily to swallow the mouthful of shingle nails which pierced my gums and jabbed into my cheeks.

"You're coming along splendidly," said Bob kindly and he could afford to be kind for his work was like the swathe of a shining sharp scythe. He was quick, neat, well-ordered and thorough. My efforts were more like shrapnel—nicest where they didn't hit. Bob pounded nails with a very few, swift, sure strokes, right smack on the head. I always tried to force my nails in sideways and my best efforts look hand adzed. Bob sawed lightly, quickly and on the line. Zzzzzzzz—snap and the board was through with the sawdust in orderly little heaps on either side. My saw rippled in, was dragged out, squealed back and when I got through Bob said, "How in God's name did you get that scallop in there?" He had the temperament and the experience and all I had was lots of energy.

The first day we moved all of the furniture into the house and I thought that the next day we would start putting in windows, laying new floors, painting woodwork and sheathing the walls. That's what I thought. The next day we started building a brooder house because to get started with the baby chickens was the important thing. We built the brooder house in the prettiest part of the orchard, facing the pond and the mountains, and its newness was so incompatible with the other silvery buildings that I suggested to Bob that we plant a few quick-growing vines and perhaps a shrub or two to tone it down a little. He was as horrified as though I had suggested bringing potted plants into a surgery. "Brooder houses are built on skids so that they can be moved from place to place as baby chickens must have new UNTAINTED soil," he said. This still seems an unnecessary precaution to me, for the land up there was all of it so untainted, so virginal, that I expected the earth to yell "Ouch" when we stuck a spade into it and any germ that could have survived the rigors of that life would have been so big and strapping we could have seen it for blocks.

When the brooder house was finished and the seven hundred and fifty yeeping chicks and the brooder were installed therein, I thought we would then begin on the house. The nights were very cold and it rained at least three of the seven days a week and I thought we might pamper ourselves with a few windows and doors. That's what I thought. The most important thing was to build two small pullet houses and to whitewash the walls of and lay a new floor in one of the small chicken houses so that the cockerels would be comfortable while fattening. We built the cockerels a nice yard also and then we remodeled the other small chicken house for the baby pig because the pig must be comfortable and protected from the cold night air and the damp day air. By the time we finished those buildings it was May. A cold damp May with so much rain that mildew formed on our clothes in the closets and the bedclothes were so clammy it was like pulling seaweed over us.

Now, I thought, we have all the livestock warm and comfortable, surely it is at last time to fix the house. That's what I thought. It was time to plow and plant the garden. I had read that the rigors of a combination of farm and mountain life were supposed eventually to harden you to a state of fitness. By the end of those first two months, I still ached like a tooth and the only thing that had hardened on the ranch was Bob's heart.

Right after breakfast one May morning he drove into the yard astride a horse large enough to have been sired by an elephant. Carelessly looping the reins over a gatepost he informed me that I was to steer this monster while he ran along behind holding the plow. All went reasonably well until Birdie, the horse, stepped on my foot. "She's on my foot," I said mildly to Bob who was complaining because we had stopped. "Get her off and let's get going," shouted the man who had promised to cherish me. Meanwhile my erstwhile foot was being driven like a stake into the soft earth and Birdie stared moodily over the landscape. I beat on the back of her knee, I screamed at her, I screamed at Bob and at last Birdie absent-mindedly took a step and lifted the foot. I hobbled to the house and soaked my foot and brooded about men and animals.

When the garden, about 50 feet by 350 feet, had been plowed, disked, harrowed and dragged until the deep brown loam was as smooth as velvet, it was planted to peas, beets, beans, corn, Swiss chard, lettuce, cabbage, onions, turnips, celery, cucumbers, tomatoes and squash. The preparing process was repeated on an acre or so in the back field which was planted to potatoes, kale, mangels and rutabagas.

Then I was drafted into the stump-pulling development. The scene was the orchard and my part in the activity was to try and grab the chain as the horse walked by, fasten it around the trunk of a fir tree before the horse shifted her position and it wouldn't reach, shout "Go ahead" to Bob and forget to get out of the way of the heavy sprays of damp loam. Clearing land is very satisfying work because you have something definite to show for your efforts, even if it is only a large hole. In the orchard it was wonderful to watch a little fruit tree huddle fearfully as we worked to remove a large bullying fir; then when with a last grunt the protesting fir was dragged away and the earth patted back on the fruit tree's roots, to watch the little tree timidly straighten up, square its shoulders and stretch its scrawny limbs to the sun and sky.

When the gardens were finished and the orchard had been cleared and plowed, we started on the big chicken house. Up to this time we had been buying all of our building materials from the Docktown sawmill and our groceries from the company store, but now we had to have special items like glass cloth and heavy mesh wire so we took a trip to "town."

"Town" was the local Saturday Mecca. A barren old maid of a place, aged and weathered by all the prevailing winds and shunned by prosperity. Of late years a small but gay army post and a thriving branch of the Coast Guard settled within arm's length, but the Town shunned their advances, preferring just to keep body and soul together through her little ordinary businesses. These were succored by the surrounding country and the mountain dwellers who referred to her disparagingly as the world's only lighted cemetery. All except me, that is, and to me "Town" spelled L-I-F-E!

I loved the long sweeping hill that curved down to Town: I loved the purply-green marshes we crossed at the bottom of the hill; I loved the whitecaps in the harbor and the spray lacing the edges of the streets; I loved the buildings squatting along the water on the main thorofare, their faces dirty but earnest, their behinds spanked by icy waves; and I loved the Town's studied pace, her unruffled calm, her acceptance of defeat.

We drove around her quiet streets, over her lovely hills and looked at her wonderful views, then we went into her shops, and we knew instantly that her customers were farmers and Indians. The grocery store smelled like sweat, cheese, bakery cookies and manure. The drugstore smelled like licorice, disinfectant, sweat and manure. The hardware store smelled like commercial fertilizer, sweat and manure. The only place which managed to rear its head above its customers was the small candy store catering mostly to townspeople. I breathed in great draughts of its rich fudgy smells and bought a bag of vanilla caramels (pronounced "kormuls" by the proprietress) which had evidently never hardened for they stuck to the brown paper bag and to each other so stubbornly that I had either to turn back the bag and lick the brown lumpy mass therein or to pry off little bits of candy and brown paper and eat both. Finally I threw it away en masse and watched the sea gulls scream and swoop for it and was disappointed that they didn't fly up again all stuck together by the beaks.

We had three strokes of luck in Town on that visit. One was that a check of our bank balance found that it tallied with our check stubs and was holding up surprisingly well. Another was a tip on where to buy a dozen laying pullets for ten dollars. And the last was a ranch-warming present of a gallon of moonshine from the best of the local moonshiners, of which there seemed to be hundreds. The moonshine in a gallon jug was a dark amber color and had a hot explosive smell. We had a drink before dinner that night and it went down with lights flashing like marbles in a pinball game.

The next morning we had breakfast in that filmy period just before daylight and were busily at work on the big chicken house before sunrise. The work was hard and the task large but Bob and I, or rather, Bob impeded by me, had first to remove all of the big barn's viscera; then put in nests, dropping boards, roosts and windows on three and one-half sides (the other half was the doorway); and to install Healtho-Glass in the windows. Healtho-Glass was a glass cloth which, so the advertisements said, sorted out the sunlight and let in *only* the health-giving *violet rays*. The first day we put it up I half expected to find the chicken house suffused in soft lavender light and the hens scratching around under a purple spot. Actually Healtho-Glass gave the same type and amount of light as frosted lavatory windows.

Down the middle of the old barn were log uprights. We naturally didn't jerk these out although I thought it a fine idea until Bob pointed out drily that they held up the roof. We built mash hoppers between the uprights, whitewashed the walls even unto the rafters, swept and scraped the hard dirt floor—the barn, like most things there in the mountains, had gone barefoot all of its life and the soles of its feet were as tough and smooth as leather—and it turned out to be a very useful, though unorthodox, chicken house where we kept as many as fifteen hundred hens.

The first day the chicken house was finished Bob drove to Town and bought the twelve Rhode Island Red pullets for ten dollars and we immediately turned them into the great new house, where they rattled around like beads in an empty bureau drawer and, being chickens, instead of laying in the row upon row of convenient new nests, they laid their eggs on the dropping boards at the entrance of rat holes or out in the yard.

It was late summer before we even started on our house. We laid new floors; put in windows; kalsomined the walls; fixed broken sills and sagging doors; put in a sink (without water but with a drain) and made other general repairs and, though it looked about as stylish as long underwear in its gray sturdiness, it began to feel like home. The kitchen had two armchairs and a rocking chair, a big square table, rag rugs and the stove. The kitchen was the hub of all of our activities. We kept the egg records there—we wrote our checks—made out our mail orders—read our mail—ate —washed—took baths—entertained—planned the future and discussed the past. We began the day in it at 4 A.M. and we ended it there about eight-thirty by shutting the damper in the stove just before blowing out the lamp. The rest of the house was clean and comfortable and unimportant.

We traded our car for a Ford pick-up truck. We traded a valley farmer a waffle iron and toaster (wedding presents) for a dragsaw. We traded electric lamps (wedding presents) for gasoline lanterns, kerosene lamps and sad irons. We bought tin washtubs and a pressure cooker.

We hewed a road into the virgin timber at the back of the ranch and drove the truck out there, loaded with axes, mauls, wedges, peaveys, oil and gasoline and we sawed shake bolts from fallen cedars four feet in diameter and straight grained. We sawed fallen firs, six and seven feet in diameter and conky in the middle, for wood. The dragsaw barked and smoked dangerously but its sturdy little arm pulled the blade back and forth with speed and skill and the great wooden wheels rolled off and Bob split them with the sledge hammer and the wedge, and I stacked them in the truck and gathered bark.

The woods were deep and cool and fragrant and treacherous with underbrush, sudden swamps and roots. Laden with a six-inch-thick hunk of bark and a wedge of wood I would start toward the truck, step on what I took for a hummock, go knee-deep in water, get slapped in the face by the Oregon grape and salal bushes, and peel the skin off my forearms as I fell with the wood. The next two or three trips would be without mishap, then just as I reached the truck, overconfident and overloaded, I'd catch the toe of my shoe in a root and fall flat. I learned the inadequacy of "Oh, dear!" and "My goodness!" and the full self-satisfying savor of sonofabitch and bastard rolled around on the tongue. I also learned the meaning of a great many homely phrases that first spring and summer. Things like "Shoulder to the wheel," which meant actually my shoulder to the wheel of the truck while Bob raced the motor and tried to pull it out of a hole. "Two honest hands" which were Bob's and mine, hoeing, weeding, chopping, feeding, caring for and cleaning. "Teamwork" was Bob and Birdie and me pulling stumps. "Woman's work is never done" signified the dinner dishes which I washed and dried while Bob smoked his pipe and took his ease.

I believe that long-suffering Bob learned best the meaning of the one about a wife being an impediment to great enterprise.

There were many nights when I was so tired I couldn't sleep and I tossed fitfully, and hurt in numerous places and thought, And they call this living? The next morning I would get up sore and stiff and grumpy and then suddenly the windows in the kitchen would begin to lighten a little and I knew it was time for the sunrise. I'd rush outdoors just as the first little rivulets of pale pink began creeping shyly over the mountains. These became bolder and brighter until the colors were leaping and cascading down the mountains and pouring into the pond at the foot of the orchard. Faster and faster they came until there was a terrific explosion of color and the sun stood on the top of the mountains laughing at us. The mountains, embarrassed at having been caught in their nightdresses rosy with sleep, would settle back with more than their accustomed hauteur, profiles cold and white against the blue horizon. Then from the kitchen would come the smell of coffee, that wonderful heartwarming smell, and I'd think Life is wonderful! as Bob came whistling in to breakfast.

By fall our potatoes were dug, our pullets were laying, our roosters had been fattened and sold and we were really chicken farmers keeping detailed egg records and netting around $25.00 a week from our three hundred and fifty hens. Several thousand sets of new muscles had stopped aching, the blisters on my hands were healing and one night I lay in bed beside Bob and watched a full moon come up from behind the black hills—there would be a frost before morning—listened to Bob's breathing, so deep and peaceful—heard the stove make occasional crunching noises as it ate into its nightload of bark—overheard a little mouse scratching gently and thought, This is the life, after all.

And then winter settled down and I realized that defeat, like morale, is a lot of little things.

4

Chuckholes and Smooth Places

Despite its location, I never had the feeling that our small ranch was nestled on the protective lap of the Olympic Mountains. There was nothing protective about them. Each time I looked out of a window or stepped out of doors, I was confronted by great, white, haughty peaks staring just above my head and doing their chilly best to make me realize that that was once a very grand neighborhood and it was curdling their blood to have to accept "trade." We were there with our ugly little buildings and livestock, but, by God, they didn't have to associate with us or make us welcome. They, no doubt, would have given half their timber if they could have changed the locale to Switzerland and brushed us off with a nice big avalanche.

All that first spring and summer they were obviously hostile but passive. With the coming of September they pulled mists down over their heads like Ku-Klux hoods and began giving us the old water cure.

It rained and rained and rained and rained. It drizzled—misted—drooled—spat—poured—and just plain rained. Some mornings were black and wild, with a storm raging in and out and around the mountains. Rain was driven under the doors and down the chimney, and Bob went to the chicken house swathed in oilskins like a Newfoundland fisherman and I huddled by the stove and brooded about inside toilets. Other days were just gray and low hanging with a continual pit-pat-pit-pat-pitta-patta-pitta-patta which became as vexing as listening to baby talk. Along about November I began to forget when it hadn't been raining

Chuckholes and Smooth Places 45

and became as one with all the characters in all of the novels about rainy seasons, who rush around banging their heads against the walls, drinking water glasses of straight whiskey and moaning, "The rain! The rain! My God, the rain!"

In case you are wondering why I didn't take a good book, settle down by the stove and shut-up, I would like to explain that Stove, as we called him, had none of the warm, friendly qualities ordinarily associated with the name. In the first place he was too old and, like some terrible old man, he had a big strong frame, a lusty appetite and no spirit of cooperation. All attempts to get Stove to crackle and glow were as futile as trying to get the Rock of Gibraltar to giggle and cavort. I split pure pitch as fine as horsehair and stuffed his ponderous belly full, but there was no sound and no heat. Yet, when I took off the lids the kindling had burned and only a few warm ashes remained. It was as mysterious as the girl in high school who ate enormous lunches without apparently chewing or swallowing.

Incongruously, things did boil on Stove. This always came as a delightful shock, albeit I finally stopped rushing to the back door and shouting hysterically to Bob, quietly and competently at work, "The water is BOILING!" as I had done for the first few hundred times I had witnessed this miracle.

I put my first cake into the oven with such a sense of finality that I almost added a Rest-in-Peace wreath, and I felt like Sarah Crewe when I came in from the chicken house and the air was vibrant with the warm spicy smell of baking.

On the coldest dreariest mornings Stove sulked all over his end of the kitchen. He smoked and choked and gagged. He ate load after load of my precious live bark and by noon I could have sat cross-legged on him and read *Pilgrim's Progress* from cover to cover in perfect comfort.

Stove was actually a sinister presence and he was tricky. The day we first looked at the place, I remarked that he seemed rather defiantly backed up against the wall, but such an attitude could come from neglect, I thought, and so when we moved in the first thing I did was to clean his suit, take all the rust off his coat and vest, blacken every inch of him, except his nickel which I polished brightly, and then I built my first fire, which promptly went out. I built that fire five times and then Bob came in and poured about a gallon of kerosene on top of the kindling and Stove began balefully to burn a little. I learned by experience that it took two cups of kerosene to get his blood circulating in the morning and that he would only digest bark at night. In the summer and spring I didn't care how slow he was or how little heat he gave out. Bob and I were outdoors from dawn to dark and we allowed plenty of time for cooking things and all of the wood was dry and the doors were open and there was plenty of draught. But with the first rainy day I realized that Stove was my enemy and would require the utmost in shrewd, cautious handling.

From the first rain, until late spring, across the kitchen in true backwoods fashion, were strung lines and lines of washing, only slightly less damp than when first hung up days and sometimes weeks ago. Those things directly over Stove flapped wetly against me as I cooked, but I dared not take them down for they were the necessary things like underwear and socks which had to get dry before summer. Try turning the chops, and stirring the tomatoes with someone slapping you across the back of the neck with a wet dish towel—you'll get the idea. I was cold all winter—It seemed that I moved around inside of but without direct contact with my clothes, and my skin became so damply chill that put side by side with a lot of clams I would have found them cozy.

Our spring and summer had been strenuous to the point of exhaustion and I, at least, having read many books about farms and farmers, had looked forward to winter as a sort of hibernation period. A time to repair machinery, hook rugs, patch quilts, mend harness and perform other leisurely tasks. Obviously something was wrong with my planning, for it took me sixteen hours a day to keep the stove going and three meals cooked. I leaped out of bed at 4 A.M., took two sips of coffee and it was eleven and time for lunch. I washed the lunch dishes and pulled a dead leaf off my kitchen geranium and it was five o'clock and time for dinner. Everyone else in the mountains had dinner at eleven in the morning and supper at five in the evening, but dinner at night was, to me, the last remnant of my old civilized life and I clung to it like a Southern girl to her accent. Even though we had it at five instead of seven-thirty and it was as leisurely as choking down a hot dog at a football game and our conversation consisted chiefly of "Pass the pickles," it was dinner at night.

Another misconception of farm life I had gleaned from books was that winter was a time of neighborliness. In spring and summer we were too tired at the end of the day to do anything but fall into bed, but I imagined that winter evenings would be filled with neighborly gatherings, popping corn, drinking hot coffee, talking politics and crops. How wrong I was. Winter was a time for ordinary chores which took ten times as long to perform because everything was cold and wet and dark and the neighboring farmer's one idea was to get the damn things done so he could go in where it was warm and stay put. The farmer's wife followed the same pattern for winter working that I did, which occupied her for twelve to eighteen hours a day and was roughly as follows:

Monday—Washday! Washing was something that the mountain farm women had contests doing to see who could get it on the line first Monday morning. All except me. I had a contest with myself to see how long I could put off doing it at all. I attacked my washing with the same sense of futility I would have had in attempting to empty the ocean with a teaspoon. Bob had been a Marine in World War I and instead of being shell-shocked he carried home a fixation that a helmetful of water was enough to wash anything, including blankets, and on Monday morning he would say cheerfully at breakfast, "Going to wash today?" and I would answer hopefully, "Yes, and it's going to be a HUGE ENORMOUS washing!" And so Bob would go whistling down through the orchard to the spring and bring back about four tablespoonfuls in the bottom of each bucket and then disappear into the woods where he remained incommunicado until lunch.

Tuesday—Ironing! Ironing with sad irons has nothing at all to do with preconceived ideas about ironing. It is a process whereby you grab a little portable handle and run over to the stove and plug it into an iron which is always covered with black. Then you run back to the ironing board and get black on your clean pillowcase. You take the iron over to the sink and wipe it off and it is of course too cool, by now, to do any good to the dirty pillowcase so you put it back on the stove and repeat the process until your husband comes in and wants to know where in HELL his lunch is.

Wednesday—Baking Day! Each Wednesday plunged me headlong into another, great, losing battle with bread-baking. When I first saw that fanatically happy look light up Bob's face when he spoke of chickens and realized that this was his great love, I made up my mind that I would become in record time a model farm wife, a veritable one-man-production line, somewhere between a Grant Wood painting, an Old Dutch Cleanser advertisement and Mrs. Lincoln's cookbook. Bread was my first defeat and I lowered my standard a notch. By the end of the first winter, in view of my long record of notable failures, I would probably have had to retrieve this standard with a post-hole digger.

My first batch of bread was pale yellow and tasted like something we had cleaned out of the cooler. I tried again. This batch had the damp elasticity of the English muffin that tasted like something we had intended to clean out of the cooler but was too heavy.

At Bob's gentle but firm insistence I took a loaf, still quivering from the womb, to a neighbor for diagnosis. Unfortunately, the neighbor, Mrs. Kettle, was just whipping out of the oven fourteen of the biggest, crustiest, lightest loaves of bread I had ever seen. I put my little undernourished lump down on the table and it looked so pitiful among all those great bouncing well-tanned beauties that I had to control a strong desire to jerk it up, nestle it against me protectively and run the four miles home.

Mrs. Kettle had fifteen children and baked fourteen loaves of bread, twelve pans of rolls, and two coffee cakes every other day. She was a very kind neighbor, a long-suffering wife and mother and a hard worker, but she was earthy and to the point. She picked my stillborn loaf from the table, ripped it open, smelled it, made a terrible face and tossed it out the back door to her pack of mangy, ever-hungry mongrels. "Goddamn stuff stinks," she said companionably, wiping her hands on her large dirty front.

She moved the gallon-sized gray granite coffeepot to the front of the stove, went into the pantry for the cups and called out to

Chuckholes and Smooth Places 49

me, "Ma Hinckley had trouble with her bread too when she lived on your place." I brightened, thinking it might be the climate up there on the mountains, but Mrs. Kettle continued. "Ma Hinckley set her bread at night and the sponge was fine and I couldn't put my finger on her trouble till one day I went up there and then I seed what it was. She'd knead up her bread, build a roaring fire and then go out and lay up with the hired man. When she got back to the kitchen the bread was too hot and the yeast was dead. Your yeast was dead too," she added.

Having quite obviously been given the glove, I hurriedly explained that we had no hired man and the barn was now a chicken house. Mrs. Kettle heaved a sigh for all good things past and poured our coffee. With the coffee she served hot cinnamon rolls, raspberry jam and detailed accounts of the moral lapses of the whole country. It was almost noon when I left for home, clutching a loaf of Mrs. Kettle's bread, two pocketfuls of anecdotes for Bob and a few hazy instructions for myself.

Tuesday and Wednesday were also optional bath days. Saturday was a must bath day but because of fires all day for ironing and baking we also took baths on Tuesdays and Wednesdays. This cutting down from daily bathing to a maximum of two complete baths a week wasn't at all hard for me nor for anyone else who has ever taken a bath in a washtub. Washtub baths are from the same painful era which housed abdominal operations without anæsthetics, sulphur and molasses in the spring, and high infant mortality. Both Bob and I are tall—he six feet two inches—and even with conditions right, Stove going, the water warm and scented, towels large and dry (always large and slightly damp in winter) the fact remains that the only adult capable of taking a bath in a washtub in comfort is a pygmy.

A sponge bath in the sink was no sensual orgy either but it was quicker and got off some of the dirt.

Thursday was SCRUB Day! Window washing, table leg washing, woodwork washing, cupboard cleaning in addition to the regular floor scrubbing. I indulged, somewhat unwillingly, in all of these because Bob, whom I accused of having been sired by a vacuum cleaner, was of that delightful old school of husbands who lift up the mattresses to see if the little woman has dusted the springs. I didn't dare write this to Gammy; she would have demanded that I get an immediate divorce. I didn't really object too strenuously to Bob's standards of cleanliness as he set them for himself as well, and you could drop a piece of bread and butter on his premises, except the chicken houses, and I defy you to tell which side had been face down.

Friday—Clean lamps and lamp chimneys! I have heard a number of inexperienced romantics say that they prefer candle and lamp light. That they purposely didn't have electricity put into their summer houses. That (archly) candle and lamp light make women look beautiful. Personally I despised lamp and candle light. My idea of heaven would have been a ten million watt globe hung from a cord in the middle of my kitchen. I wouldn't have cared if it made me look like something helped from her coffin. I could see then, and candles could go back to birthday cakes and jack-o'-lanterns and lamps to the attic.

Saturday—Market Day! In winter Bob left for "Town" while it was still dark, to sell the eggs, buy feed and groceries, get the mail, cigarettes and some new magazines. In spring and summer I joyfully accompanied him, but in the winter driving for miles and miles in a Ford truck in the rain was not a thing of pure joy and anyway, in view of the many ordinary delays such as flat tires, broken springs, plugged gas lines, ad infinitum, I had to stay home to put the lights in the chicken house at the first sign of dusk.

Some Saturday mornings, as soon as the mountains had blotted up the last cheerful sound of Bob and the truck, I, feeling like a cross between a boll weevil and a slut, took a large cup of hot coffee, a hot water bottle, a cigarette and a magazine and *went back to bed.* Then, from six-thirty until nine or so, I luxuriated in breaking the old mountain tradition that a decent woman is in bed only between the hours of 7 P.M. and 4 A.M. *unless* she is in labor or dead.

Along about three-thirty or four o'clock on Saturday I had to light the gasoline lanterns—the most frightening task on earth

Chuckholes and Smooth Places 51

and contrary to all of my early teachings that anyone who monkeys around gasoline with matches is just asking for trouble. I never understood why or how a gasoline lantern works and I always lit the match with the conviction that I should have first sent for the priest.

Bob patiently explained the entire confusing process again and again, but to me it was on the same plane with the Hindu rope trick, and it was only when he was not home that I would tolerate the infernal machines in the same room with me. I used to take them out into the rain to pump them up, then crouching behind the woodshed door I reached way out and lit them. Immediately and for several terrible minutes they flared up and acted exactly as if they were going to explode, then as suddenly settled back on their haunches to hiss contentedly and give out candle power after candle power of bright, white light. With two lanterns in each hand I walked through the complete dejection of last summer's garden, ignoring the pitiful clawings and scratchings of the derelicts of cornstalks and tomato vines shivering in the rain, and hung the lanterns in the great chicken house which instantly seemed as gay and friendly as a cocktail lounge. When the frightened squawks of a few hysterical younger hens had died down, I stood and let some of my loneliness drip off in the busy communal atmosphere.

The floor was covered with about four inches of clean, dry straw, and the hens sang and scratched and made little dust baths and pecked each other and jumped on the hoppers and ate mash and sounded as if they were going to—and did—lay eggs. They were as happy and carefree in November, when the whole outside world was beaten into submission by the brooding mountains and the endless rain, as they were on a warm spring day.

Then I gathered the eggs. Gathering eggs would be like one continual Easter morning if the hens would just be obliging and get off the nests. Cooperation, however, is not a chickenly characteristic and so at egg-gathering time every nest was overflowing with hen, feet planted, and a shoot-if-you-must-this-old-gray-head look in her eye. I made all manner of futile attempts to dislodge her—sharp sticks, flapping apron, loud scary noises, lure of mash and grain—but she would merely set her mouth, clutch her eggs under her and dare me. In a way, I can't blame the hen—after all, softshelled or not, they're her kids.

Sunday! In the country Sunday is the day on which you do exactly as much work as you do on other days but feel guilty all of the time you are doing it because Sunday is a day of rest.

Sunday mornings I cleaned Stove's suit, taking all of the spots off his vest and coat, and it evidently pleased him for he stewed chickens and roasted meat and even exuded a little warmth. Excited by his compatibility, I would mull over recipes for popovers, cupcakes and other hot oven delicacies but would eventually slink back to deep apple pie, as I could use automatic biscuit mix for the crust and our apples were delicious no matter what I did to them.

Also because of Stove's Sunday attitude I washed my hair on that day and guided by the pictures in Saturday's magazines would try the latest hair-dos. Unfortunately my hair is heavy and unmanageable and my attempts at a pompadour usually ended up looking like a Tam o'Shanter suspended over one eye. It made little difference, though, except as a diversion for me, because presently Bob would come in from the chicken house and look hurt and I would put my hair back the old way. I believe that Bob's mother must have been frightened by a candy box cover while she was carrying him, because he wanted me to wear long hair done in a knot, the color blue and leghorn hats, all of the time.

By one o'clock on winter Sundays the house was shining clean, my hair was washed, Bob had on clean clothes and dinner was ready. Usually, just as we sat down to the table, as if by prearranged signal, the sun came out. True it shone with about as much warmth and lust as a Victorian spinster and kept darting behind clouds as if it were looking for its knitting and sticking its head out again with an apologetic smile, but it was sun and not rain. The mountains, either in recognition of the sun or Sunday, would have their great white busts exposed and I expected momentarily to have them clear their throats and start singing "Rock of Ages" in throaty contraltos.

Whatever my original attitude was, I became reconciled to certain things as unavoidable chuckholes in my road of living on a chicken ranch and grew to accept placidly certain other things, which at first had called for hyperboles of enthusiasm, as just everyday smooth places.

Definitely a smooth place was the food. I accepted as ordinary fare pheasant, quail, duck, cracked crab, venison, butter clams, oysters, brook trout, salmon, fried chicken and mushrooms. At first Bob and I gorged ourselves and I wrote letters home that sounded like pages ripped from a gourmand's diary, but there was so much of everything and it was so inexpensive and so easy to get that it was inevitable that we should expect to eat like kings. Chinese pheasant was so plentiful that Bob would take his gun, saunter down the road toward a neighbor's grain field and shoot two, which were ample for us, and come sauntering home again. At first under Bob's careful guidance I stuffed and roasted them, but finally I got so I ripped off the breast, throwing the rest away, and sautéed it in butter with fresh field mushrooms. It made a tasty breakfast. The blue grouse were also very plentiful, but the salal berries which they gorged on gave them an odd bitter taste which neither Bob nor I cared for. Quail were everywhere but they are such tiny things that we finally passed them up for the ruffed grouse and the pheasant. There were literally millions of wild pigeons in the valleys. They descended in white clouds when the farmers planted grain and in actual self-defense they shot them even though they were protected by Federal law. Our neighbors gave them to us by the dozens and they were simply delicious, all dark meat and plump and succulent from eating the farmer's wheat, barley, oats and rye. I regret to state that their illegality didn't taint the meat one iota for me. Bob is a fine hunter and a good sport and he, at first, lectured the farmers and their sons on the seriousness of their offense in shooting the pigeons, but the first time he was present at grain planting time and saw what they did to the crops, he told me he thought there should be a bounty on them. He never shot one, however, nor admitted that he enjoyed eating them.

Venison we had twelve months a year, both canned and fresh. To the Indians, who comprised a great part of the population of that country, and to the farmers, who were part Indian, deer meat was meat and game laws were for the city hunters who came in hordes every fall to slaughter all of the bucks. Our local any-season-hunters said they killed only the barren does, which were easily distinguished by their color and which were a nuisance. True or false, the Indian hunters went through the woods without as much disturbance as a falling leaf and the only game warden able to catch them would have been another Indian, and so we had an Indian game warden and the other Indians and the farmers continued to hunt whenever they needed meat and we, in the heart of the deer county, had venison the year round.

Mushrooms grew profusely around the barns of all the neighboring farms and in our fields. Those around the barns reached a diameter of six inches and the buttons were the size of a baby's fist. Those in the fields were smaller but just as sweet and nutty.

The seafood in the Pacific Northwest is superb. The Dungeness hardshelled crabs are the largest, sweetest most delicately flavored crabs obtainable. We bought them from the Indians for one dollar a gunnysack full. We'd go on regular crab sprees—eat cracked crab with homemade mayonnaise well-flavored with garlic and Worcestershire, until it ran out our ears. Have deviled crab, crab Louis and crab claws sautéed in butter and served with Tartar sauce. We never tired of crab and in summer we went often to Docktown Bay, an exquisite little cove below Docktown which was emptied and filled by the tide, and leaned over the sides of a flat-bottomed boat and with long handled nets scooped the scuttling crabs from under seaweed. They didn't compare with the Dungeness crabs, which are gathered from deep icy water, but they were wonderful when boiled on the beach and eaten warm.

This small bay also supplied us with clams—either the large delicately flavored butter clams, which we dipped in flour after removing the neck and stomach, and fried in butter, or the tiny but stronger flavored littlenecks, which we steamed and ate by the bushel.

Another form of seafood of which we were fond and which we could get for nothing was the oyster. By driving fifty or so miles we could gather both the large soup oysters and the tiny cocktail oysters by the bucketful. The first time we went oystering I was sure there was something wrong and we would all end up in the penitentiary. It didn't seem reasonable to me that oysters, particularly the exquisite little oysters, should be scattered over the countryside free for the picking, and I feared that the shifty-eyed Indian friend of Bob's who was leading the way would probably next tell us that he knew where there was a great big patch of filet mignon that nobody owned. We drove and drove and drove and took logging roads and cow trails and sometimes seemed to cut right through the brush, but finally we came to a stretch of beach obviously known only to God and that Indian and the oysters were as thick as barnacles. We went there again and again and never saw another soul.

Brook trout could be caught in the irrigation ditches—about ten an hour and from seven to nine inches long. The trout were so thick in the mountain streams that the men in the logging camps caught them with strings, bent pins and hunks of bologna.

The steelhead salmon came up the irrigation ditches and by trolling near Docktown Bay we caught silvers, king and dog salmon. We also caught sole, cod, red snapper and flounder. Like a true squaw I learned to clean, skin and fillet fish while Bob smoked, looked on and criticized. I really enjoyed it though. I had a knife with a saw edge and a pair of pliers and I could clean, skin and fillet five flounder and two cod while Bob was putting the boat away. It was fun to straddle a log in the warm sunlight, throw the entrails to the gulls and wipe my hands on seaweed. Seaweed reminds me that I suffered one bitter disillusionment in regard to seafood. I had heard for years that clams, freshly dug and steamed in seaweed were the last word in gustatory delight. Accompanied by sweet corn and hot coffee they were too marvelous to bear description. This is a lie. Clams freshly dug and steamed in seaweed are full of sand and unless you are bent on polishing your own fillings there is nothing you can do with them but throw them away. Corn steamed in seaweed is all right if you don't mind boiling juice and seawater oozing up your sleeves. I think that the whole thing should be dispensed with and the food cooked at home. Anyway clams should be soaked overnight in fresh water with corn meal in it, so that they can open up and expel the sand.

We had fried chicken for breakfast, lunch and dinner. We had chicken roasted, fricasseed, stewed and in soup and salad. We did not tire of it nor of eggs, but we got damn sick of sowbelly, which is the only meat the local stores ever carried. It was white and fat and could be eaten when seasoned with garlic, salt and sage, but to eat it every day, fried with potatoes, boiled with cabbage or lying sluggishly in a heavy milk gravy as did most of the farmers was not within our capabilities.

Our garden, also, produced lavishly. The soil, a deep brown loam, and the continual rain made holding back rather than forcing the problem. It seemed to me that things sprouted, bloomed, bore, withered and died before I could run into the house and get a pan to pick them in.

With all of the natural resources in the way of food and the ease with which you could grow anything and everything, I never in all of the time I lived on the chicken ranch tasted salad in anyone's house but my own; nor did I see meat cooked any way but fried or boiled, nor did I ever catch anyone but the Indians eating fish. Sowbelly, fried potatoes, fried bread, macaroni, cabbage or string beans boiled with sowbelly were the fare day in and day out. They grew heads of lettuce the size of cabbages and fed it to the chickens or the pigs, they grew celery as crisp and white as crusted snow and they sold every single stalk. They grew beets like balloons and rutabagas as big as squashes, but they fed them to the cows. They grew Swiss chard three feet high, so they cut off all of the green part and fed it to the pigs and boiled the white stems with sowbelly for hours and hours and hours, until it was a greasy strangled mass which they relished with fried potatoes and boiled macaroni.

We could have kidneys, sweetbreads or liver for the asking—

Chuckholes and Smooth Places   57

"We don't eat guts," the farmers said. We did whenever we could get them. Lamb's kidneys or veal kidneys sautéed in butter, then simmered gently with fresh basil, marjoram, and a wineglass or two of sherry didn't taste like guts to us. Sweetbreads creamed with fresh mushroom bore little resemblance to guts either. But sowbelly looked and tasted exactly like its name.

Another smooth place, which I came to expect as my just deserts, was the scenery. I watched mornings turn pale green, then saffron, then orange, then flame colored while the sky glittered with stars and a sliver of a golden moon hung quietly. I watched a blazing sun vault over a mountain and leave such a path of glory behind that the windows of mountain homes like ours glowed blood red until dark and even the darkness was tinged and wore a cloak of purple instead of the customary deep blue. Every window of our house framed a vista so magnificent that our ruffled curtains were as inappropriate frames as tatted edges on a Van Gogh. In every direction, wherever we went, we came to the blue softly curving Sound with its misty horizons, slow passing freighters and fat waddling ferries. The only ugliness we saw was the devastation left by the logging companies. Whole mountains left naked and embarrassed, their every scar visible for miles. Lovely mountain lakes turned into plain ponds beside a dusty road, their crystal water muddy brown with slashings and rubbish.

I loved the flat pale blue winter sky that followed a frosty night. I loved the early frosty mornings when the roofs of the chicken houses and the woodshed glowed phosphorescently and the smoke of Bob's pipe trailed along behind him and the windows of the house beamed at me from under their eaves and Stove's smoke spiraled thinly against the black hills. I loved those things but there were the others:

Reading by the wick when I forgot to order kerosene.

Hurling myself headlong through the nearest aperture at the sound of a car but never being in time to tell who it might have been.

Telling time by the place where the sun should have been when I forgot to wind the clock.

Knowing that if I forgot to order matches I would darn well

have to learn to rub two sticks together or walk four miles on the loneliest road in the world to a neighbor.

Being asked in the same trustful I-know-you-will-do-it way to split shakes, help fell a tree, dissect a dead chicken, help castrate a pig, run and get the .30-.30 or the shotgun or the .22, flush a covey of quail, retrieve a grouse, wind a fish pole, or make another try at the damned lemon pie which I know that neither Bob's nor any other mother ever made.

Knowing that it was stupid but excusable to run out of food, toilet paper, matches, wood, kerosene, soap or water but that there was *no excuse ever* for running out of shotgun shells or chicken feed.

Being lonely all of the time. I used to harbor the idea, as who has not, that I was one of the few very fortunate people who was absolutely self-sufficient and that if I could just find myself a little haunt far from the clawing hands of civilization with its telephones, electric appliances, artificial amusements and people—people more than anything—I would be contented for the rest of my life. Well, someone called my bluff and I found that after nine months spent mostly in the stimulating company of the mountains, trees, the rain, Stove and the chickens, I would have swooned with anticipation at the prospect of a visit from a Mongolian idiot. And if the clawing hands of civilization could only have run a few telephone and light wires in there they could have had my self-sufficient right arm to chop up for insulators.

As I am so nearsighted I cannot see anything unless it is perched on my shoulder, I endured long painful periods of "There he is on that first limb." "What limb?" "The one on top of that big snag." "What snag?" "The one east of that tallest fir." "What fir?" And on and on until at last I learned to say with my eyes shut and before I had reached the window, "Oh, yes, I see him plainly," and then I'd run for my bathrobe and my coat and my wool socks.

Owls were worse than hawks for killing chickens and it was fortunate for us that Bob was a crack shot with eyes like telescopes, but it was unfortunate for me that I was not imbued with the thrill of the hunt instead of a hatred for night air and loud noises.

While I jounced and eased my way along from day to day, Bob sailed along in front of me never once touching the rough spots. He never seemed to be lonely, he enjoyed the work, he didn't make stupid blunders and then, of course, he wasn't pregnant.

5

Spring Comes, and So Do People

UNTIL I MOVED to the ranch, the coming of spring had been a gradual and painless thing, like developing a bust. In Butte the snow melted and made torrents in the gutters, the streets didn't freeze at night, we found our first bluebell and it was spring and we could take off our "chimaloons." In Seattle the seasons ran together like the stained-glass-window paintings we did at school where we wet the drawing paper first, all over, then dropped on blobs of different colors which ran into each other so that it was impossible to tell where one began and the other left off. Seattle spring was a delicate flowering of the pale gray winter—a pastel prelude to the pale yellow summer which flowed gently into the lavender autumn and on into the pale gray winter. It was all very subtle and, as we wore the same clothes the year around and often had beach fires in January but found it too cold for them in June, we were never season conscious.

Things were certainly different up on the ranch. Spring stopped there with a screech of brakes. Somewhere someone blew a whistle and all hell broke loose. We awoke one morning to a new Sears, Roebuck catalog; baby chickens, thousands of them; a new little red-haired baby girl; little yellow goslings; two baby pigs; a puppy; two kittens; a little heifer calf; fruit trees snapping into bloom all over the place; a newly plowed plot for the biggest garden in the world; streams and lakes brimming; trilliums, wild violets both purple and yellow, camas and starflowers carpeting the woods; fences to mend; seeds to plant; seed catalogs to dream through; Government bulletins to choke down and digest; and no rest ever any more.

The spring sun, a bold-faced, full-blooded little wench, obviously no kin to the sallow creature who simpered in and out occasionally during the winter, bestowed her warm caresses impartially on the handsome virile timber, the tender plowed land and the ugly impotent burn. Every place she touched throbbed hopefully and there was a rapidly spreading epidemic of pale green mustaches and beards. The mountains' noses began to run and though they tied veils over their heads they seemed less formidable.

I was so ebullient from the sun and warmth that even the fact that I had to dog trot through the long days, in order barely to scratch the surface of my thousands of new duties, failed to dampen my ardor.

I had read of beauty-starved farm wives standing for an hour on their back stoops absorbing the glory of a sun-drenched branch of forsythia; walking in the orchards and burying their noses in the fragrant boughs; standing motionless in the warm spring sun and thanking God for the miracle of fertility. What I wanted to know was, where they got the time for such ethereal pursuits. I saw the forsythia, I saw the apple blossoms, I saw the sun glancing over the emerald-tipped firs and pointing up the chartreuse maples and alders on its way. I saw those things but I had about as much chance to linger and appreciate as I would have had riding a motorcycle through an art gallery.

It all began with the baby chickens—they came first, while I was still very pregnant, and getting down on my hands and knees to peer under the brooder at the thermometer was a major undertaking. Bob and I scrubbed the brooder house, walls, floors, even the front porch with Lysol and boiling water. The brooder house

Spring Comes, and So Do People 61

had two rooms—the brooder room and the cool room. In the brooder room we had two coal-oil brooders which we lit and checked temperatures on, a week before the chicks arrived. The brooder room floor was covered with canvas and peat moss and had drinking fountains and little mash-hoppers scattered here and there. The cool room also had peat moss on the floor and buttermilk and water fountains and mash hoppers here and there. At last the chicks arrived and Bob drove down to Docktown and returned with ten cartons with air holes along the sides, in each of which yeeped one hundred chicks. We stacked the cartons in the cool room and then one by one we carried them carefully into the brooder room, took off the lids and gently lifted out the little chicks and tucked them under the brooder, where they immediately set to work to suffocate each other.

From that day forward my life was one living hell. Up at four—start the kitchen fire—put the coffee on—go out to the baby chicks—come back and slice off some ham and sling it into the frying pan—out to the baby chicks with warm water—put toast into the oven—out to the baby chicks with mash—set the breakfast table—out to the baby chicks with chick food—open a can of fruit—out to the baby chicks and on and on through the day. I felt as if I were living in a nightmare, fleeing down the track in front of an onrushing locomotive. I raced through each day leaving behind me a trail of things undone.

Of course, I chose that most inconvenient time to have the baby and her arrival quite typified the tempo of our life. I rode the fifty-odd miles to town sitting on her head, and the moment I reached the hospital she popped out, red-haired and weighing eight and a half pounds. When I came home from the hospital after two weeks of blissful rest, everything on the ranch had been busy producing and I was greeted by the squealing of baby pigs, the squeaking of baby goslings, the baaing of a heifer calf, the mewing of tiny kittens, the yelping of a puppy and the stronger louder yeeping of the chicks. All of the small eat-often screamers were assigned to my care and I found that feeding of them all and Bob and me was a perpetual task. I relegated my ironing to something I would try and finish before small Anne entered college—

my washing I tried to ignore, although it assumed the proportions of a snowball rolled from the top of Mt. Olympus—and I closed my eyes to Spring who was imploring me from every side to do something, anything, about my garden.

Bob's life was as harried, and our marriage became a halloo from the brooder house porch to the manure pile; a call for help when pulling a stump or unrolling some wire; a few grunts at mealtime as we choked down our food and turned the leaves of seed catalogs and Government bulletins. One night after dinner as I sat at the kitchen table industriously making my baby chick "feed and death" entries for the day, Bob unexpectedly kissed the back of my neck. I was as confused as though an old boss had chosen that means of rewarding me for a nice typing job. "Another year or two and we probably won't even use first names," I told Bob.

That first year no one, or very few, knew that we were up there in the mountains on our ranch and so we were skipped by the door-to-door sellers. I didn't learn about that delight of country living until one drear day late the first fall. Bob was out in the woods usefully and gainfully employed cutting shingle bolts and I was rattling around in the house longing for my lovely big noisy family and hating the mountains, when a little black truck sidled into the yard, a small man alighted and crept to the back door, where he scratched like a little mouse. I rushed to the door and he was so heartened by my greeting, not knowing that I was glad to see anybody, that he hurriedly scrambled back into the truck and came staggering back under four great black suitcases. He opened the first one and I realized that at last I was face to face with the creator of the knitting book outfits. The coat sweater made like a long tube with an immense shawl collar. The tatted evening dress. The lumpy crocheted bed-jacket tied with thousands of little ribbons. The great big tam. The slipover sweater with the waistline either crouching in the armpits or languishing just above the knees. Jack the Knitter had them all and mostly in maroon, a pink so bright it could have given a coat of tan, and orchid.

Spring Comes, and So Do People

As I turned down offering after offering, Jack's little watery eyes grew sadder and his little black suit shinier and shabbier, and we were both pretty desperate when he brought out the socks—the really superior wool socks. I immediately ordered twelve pairs for Bob and begged Jack to stay for dinner. He, however, seemed to have revived considerably under the stimulus of the order and briskly declined, packed his wares and left in the direction of Mrs. Kettle's, where he undoubtedly had dinner after selling all of his sweaters.

Then came spring and the Stove Man. Along in January, Stove developed virulent digestive trouble. In fact, where his grate had been there was a gaping hole and I had to build my fire like a blazing fringe around the edge. Stove was "taken" in January, but it was March before anything was done about it. We of the mountains didn't dash into town for a new grate. We wore our already taut nerves to within a hair of the snapping point trying to cook on the circle of fire or that faint warm draught that wafted from the ash pit down around Stove's feet, where the pieces of grate and all of the wood had fallen, and waited for a mythical character known as the Stove Man who was supposed to make rounds in the spring.

One morning I had reached the stage where I was craftily planning to chop up a chair or two and build a fire in the sink in an effort to drive Bob to some immediate action, when the Stove Man arrived. With him also were a truckload of stove parts and tools, his wife and three-year-old daughter. Stove Man quickly disemboweled Stove, something which I had been longing to do to that big black stinker all winter, spread the entrails all over the kitchen floor and went out to the chicken house to point out to Bob the many opportunities for failure in the chicken business.

This black-future attitude was not from any manic depressive tendencies on the part of Stove Man, but was the reflected attitude of the farmer. The farmers wanted to be sad and they wanted everyone who called on them to be sad. If your neighbor's chickens were each laying a double-yolked egg every single day, all of his cows had just had heifer calves, his mortgage was all paid, his wheat was producing a bushel per stalk and he had just discovered an oil gusher on the north forty, you did not mention any of these gladsome happenings. Instead, when you looked at the chickens, you said, "A heavy lay makes hens weak and liable to disease." The neighbor, kicking sulkily at the feed trough, would reply, "Brings the price of eggs down too."

When you went into the barn you looked over the heifer calves and said, "Lots of t.b. in the valley this year. Some herds as high as 50 per cent." The neighbor said, "Contagious abortion is around too." Leaning morbidly on the fence around the groaning wheat fields, you said, "A cloudburst could do a lot of damage here." The neighbor said, "A heavy rain in harvest time would ruin me." I learned that our farmers were like those women who get some sort of inverted enjoyment out of deprecating their own accomplishments—women who say "This cake turned out just terribly!" and then hand you a piece of angel food so light you have to hold it down to take a bite.

Our farmers were big saddos and our farmers' wives were delicate. Farmers' wives who had the strength, endurance and energy of locomotives and the appetites of dinosaurs were, according to them, so delicate that if you accidentally brushed against them they would turn brown like gardenias. They always felt poorly, took gallons of patent medicines and without exception they, and all of their progeny, were so tiny at birth that they slept in a cigar box and wore a wedding ring for a bracelet.

For several weeks after the visit of the Stove Man the weather was clear and bright and we worked like maniacs to get caught up with Spring, which raced ahead of us each day, unfolding new tasks for us to do and cautioning us about leaving the old ones too long. Each night Bob drove the truck down into a small valley below the house and filled ten ten-gallon milk cans with water, and the next morning as soon as I was dressed I filled Stove's reservoir and my wash boiler, and between chores I washed all day long. The clothes billowed and flapped whitely against the delphinium blue sky and the black green hills, and at night I brought in armloads of clean clothes smelling of blossoms and breezes and *dry*.

For three weeks I washed all day and ironed every night and

felt just like the miller's daughter in Rumpelstiltskin, for there was always more. After all, I had been heaping dirty clothes in the extra bedroom ever since September and only washing what we had to have and what I could dry over Stove. After the baby came, I had to wash for her every day, so I threw everything into the extra bedroom. Finally one morning I found the room empty. I tottered back to the kitchen and emptied the wash boiler into the sink and collapsed by Stove. Immediately the sun was obscured by a heavy dark cloud, a wind came swooshing out of the burn; there was a light patter of rain and I fell asleep.

Like coming to the surface after a deep, deep dive, I came at last to the top of my sleep and heard hammering at the back door. I drifted through a heavy mist to the entryway and opened the door. It was the Rawleigh Man, who burst in and snapped me to attention by looking deep into my eyes, and saying, "I heard you got a new baby, organs all back in place OK?"

The Rawleigh Man sold spices, hand lotions, patent medicines, coffee, soap, lice powder, flea powder, perfume, chocolate—all kinds of dandy things—and in addition he fancied himself a self-made physician and asked the most intimate and personal questions as he opened his truck and brought out his wares. After I had put his mind at rest about my organs he told me all about his hernia and I'm sure would have showed it to me if I had been a customer of a little longer standing. He told me about a bad ovarian tumor up north, a tipped uterus near "Town," some incurable cases of constipation in the West Valley and a batch of ringworm down near Docktown which had resisted every salve he had.

I made him a cup of coffee and a ham sandwich and he asked me every detail of Anne's birth. He was pleased that I had gone to the "Town" hospital instead of going to the city. He couldn't have been any more pleased than I, for never in my life have I spent such a delightful two weeks.

The "Town" hospital, run by Sisters, was on a high bluff overlooking the Sound. My room had a ceiling about sixteen feet high, inside shutters on the four tall windows, which faced the sound, old-fashioned curly maple furniture, a bathroom with a chain pull toilet, and pale yellow walls. The Sisters had their own cows, chickens, turkeys, and garden. They baked all of their own bread and thought nothing of bringing a breakfast tray with home-canned raspberries that tasted so fresh I could almost see the dew on them, a thick pink slice of home cured ham, scrambled eggs, hot rolls so feathery I wanted to powder my back with them, hot strong coffee and cream I had to gouge out of the pitcher. They further spoiled me for any other hospital by having homemade ice cream and fried chicken on Sundays and by bringing me tea and hot gingerbread or chocolate cake or rock cookies in the middle of the morning. In the evenings the dear little Sisters brought their sewing to my room and we talked and laughed until the Mother Superior shooed them out and turned out my light. The prospect of two weeks in that heavenly place tempted me to stay pregnant all the rest of my life, but in spite of the coziness of our relationship I did not tell this to the Rawleigh Man.

Other door-to-door sellers were the nursery men, who identified our fruit trees for us and sold us English walnut, filbert, chestnut, apricot and peach trees; the shoe salesmen, who carried no samples, only pictures, and when the brown moccasin-toed oxfords I ordered came, I found out why. The shoes were sturdy—thick-soled—heavy stiff leather—strong sewing—(Gammy would have said they were "baked" together)—firm lining—but they were never intended to be worn.

There were also a Corset Lady and a Housedress Lady. They traveled together ond one squeezed me into a corset and the other jammed me into a housedress. The Corset Lady had piercing black eyes and a large bust and stomach apparently encased in steel, for when I brushed against her it was like bumping into our oil drum. She was such a high-pressure saleswoman that almost before she had turned off the ignition of her car I found myself in my bedroom in my "naked strip" being forced into a foundation garment. First she rolled it up like a life preserver, then I stepped through the leg holes, then she slowly and painfully unrolled it up over my thighs, hips and stomach until she reached my top—then she had me bend over and she slipped straps over my arms and then snapped me to a standing position. My legs were squashed so tightly together I couldn't walk a step and I had to hold my

Spring Comes, and So Do People

chin up in the air for my bust was in the vicinity of my shoulders.

"Look, Ella," the Corset Lady called to the Housedress Lady, "Don't she look grand?"

The Housedress Lady, who looked just like the Corset Lady except that she had piercing blue eyes, said, "That's a world of improvement, dear. A world!"

I inched over to the mirror and looked. At that time I was thin as a needle and, encased in the foundation garment, I resembled nothing so much as a test tube with something bubbling out the top. Even if I had looked "grand," I had to walk and I wanted to lower my head occasionally, so I took off the foundation garment much more quickly and not nearly so carefully as it had been put on me. The Corset Lady was furious and made no effort to conceal it. While the Housedress Lady was showing me her wares, the Corset Lady sat in a kitchen chair, legs wide apart—but stomach in, bust up—and gazed stonily out the window. Some of the housedresses were quite pretty although electric blue and lavender were the predominating colors, and they were very reasonably priced. I ordered four and two pairs of silk stockings which turned out to be outsize, so I gave them to Mrs. Kettle.

The most important people in a community are usually the richest or the worthiest or the most useful, unless the community, like ours, happens to be scattered thinly over the most rugged mountains and the largest stand of Douglas fir on the North American Continent. Then the most important people are the closest. Your neighbors. Our neighbors were the Hicks' and the Kettles.

My first brush with the Kettles came about two weeks after we moved to our ranch and before we had bought our dozen Rhode Island Red hens, when I in my innocence thought I would walk to a neighbor's and arrange to buy milk and eggs. Bob had gone to Docktown after lumber or I probably never would have made that fruitless voyage.

I remember with what care I donned a clean starched housedress and pressed my Burberry coat. How carefully I brushed my hair and fixed my face and composed little speeches of introduction. "So, you're Mrs. Kettle! Bob has told me so much about you!" or "I'm your new neighbor up on the mountain and I thought it about time to come down out of the clouds and make myself known!" (Ha, ha.)

My first disappointment was a little matter of distance. It was possible to keep my spirit of good will and neighborliness whipped to a white heat for about a mile, then it began to cool slightly and by the fourth mile the whole thing had become a damned bore and I wondered why I ever had the idea in the first place. It had rained hard the night before and the road, normally pocked with holes and pits, was dotted with little lakes and pools, which reached clear across the road and oozed into the salal along the edges. In order to traverse these it was necessary to make detours into the soaking wet brush so that by the end of the first mile my neatly pressed coat slapped wetly against my legs and my hair and shoulders were full of twigs and stickers.

The day was clear and blowy with clouds like blobs of thick white lather sailing along on the wind, which was so strong and so playful that incredibly tall, spindly, snags leaned threateningly toward me, particularly when I was trying to edge around an especially large puddle and couldn't have got out of the way if the snag had shouted *"Timbah!"* before it fell. This fear of falling snags wasn't just idle terror on my part either, because every once in a while there would be a big blundering crash to the right or left of me. As the snag was usually just about to hit the ground by the time I had it located, I finally gave up and decided that if God willed it, God willed it, and there was nothing I could do about it.

On either side of the road were dense thickets of second growth, clear green and bursting with health and vigor. Back of these thickets rose the giant virgin forests, black and remote against the sky. Occasionally a small brown rabbit flipped into the brush just ahead of me and little birds made shy rustling noises everywhere. The mountains looked down scornfully at my skip, hop and jump descent and when I saw their unfriendly faces reflected in the puddles I felt the resisting power of that wild country so strongly that I was almost afraid to look back for fear the road would have closed up behind me and there would be noth-

Spring Comes, and So Do People 69

ing but trees, sky and mountain and no evidence that I had ever been there.

Lost in these gloomy thoughts I trudged on until I turned a bend and suddenly came on the Kettle farm. First there was a hillside orchard, alive with chickens as wild as hawks, large dirty white nuzzling pigs and an assortment of calves, cows, horses and steers. Wild roses laced the fences and dandelions glowed along the roadside and over and above the livestock arose the airy fragrance of apple blossoms.

Below the orchard were a large square house which had apparently once been apple green; a barn barely able to peep over the manure heaped against its walls; and a varied assortment of outbuildings, evidently tossed together out of anything at hand. The pig house roof sported an arterial highway sign and the milkhouse had a roof of linoleum and a wooden Two Pants Suit sign. All of the buildings had a stickery appearance, as any boards too long had been left instead of sawed off. The farm was fenced with old wagons, parts of cars, broken farm machinery, bits and scraps of rope and wire, pieces of outbuildings, a parked automobile, old bed springs. The barnyard teemed with jalopies in various stages of disintegration.

I turned into a driveway that led along the side of the house but there arose such a terrific barking and snarling and yapping from a pack of mongrels by the back porch, that I was about to leap over the fence into the orchard when the back door flew open and someone yelled to the dogs to "stop that goddamn noise!" Mrs. Kettle, a mountainously fat woman in a very dirty housedress, waddled to the corner of the porch and called cordially, "Come in, come in, glad to see you!" but as I drew timidly abreast of the porch my nostrils were dealt such a stinging blow by the outhouse lurking doorless and unlovely directly across from it that I almost staggered. Apparently used to the outhouse, Mrs. Kettle kicked me a little path through the dog bones and chicken manure on the back porch and said, "We was wonderin' how long afore you'd git lonesome and come down to see us," then ushered me into the kitchen, which was enormous, cluttered and smelled deliciously of fresh bread and hot coffee. "I'll have a pan of rolls baked by the time the coffee's poured, so set down and make yourself comfortable."

The Kettles' kitchen was easily forty feet long and thirty feet wide. Along one wall were a sink and drainboards, drawers and cupboards. Along another wall was a giant range and a huge woodbox. Back of the range and woodbox were pegs to hang wet coats to dry but from which hung parts of harness, sweaters, tools, parts of cars, a freshly painted fender, hats, a hot water bottle and some dirty rags. On the floor behind the stove were shoes, boots, more car parts, tools, dogs, bicycles and a stack of newspapers. In the center of the kitchen was a table about nine feet square, covered with a blue and white oilcloth tablecloth, a Rochester lamp, a basket of sewing, the Sears, Roebuck and Montgomery Ward catalogs, a large thick white sugar bowl and cream pitcher, a butter dish with a cover on it, a jam dish with a cover on it, a spoonholder, a fruit jar filled with pencil stubs, an ink bottle and a dip pen. Spaced along other walls were bureaus, bookcases, kitchen queen, worktables and a black leather sofa. Opening from the kitchen were doors to a hall, the parlor, the pantry (an enormous room lined with shelves), and the back porch. The floor was fir and evidently freshly scrubbed, which seemed the height of useless endeavor to me in view of the chicken manure and refuse on the back porch and the muddy dooryard.

While I was getting my bearings, Mrs. Kettle waddled between the pantry and the table setting out thick white cups and saucers and plates. Mrs. Kettle had pretty light brown hair, only faintly streaked with gray and skinned back into a tight knot, clear blue eyes, a creamy skin which flushed exquisitely with the heat, a straight delicate nose, fine even white teeth, and a small rounded chin. From this dainty pretty head cascaded a series of busts and stomachs which made her look like a cooky jar shaped like a woman. Her whole front was dirty and spotted and she wiped her hands continually on one or the other of her stomachs.

But never in my life have I tasted anything to compare with the cinnamon rolls which she took out of the oven and served freshly frosted with powdered sugar. They were so tender and delicate I had to bring myself up with a jerk to keep from eating

Spring Comes, and So Do People 71

a dozen. The coffee was so strong it snarled as it lurched out of the pot and I girded up my loins for the first swallow and was amazed to find that when mixed with plenty of thick cream it was palatable.

Mrs. Kettle began most of her sentences with Jeeeeesus Keyrist and had a stock disposal for everything of which she did not approve, or any nicety of life which she did not possess. "Ah she's so high and mighty with her 'lectricity," Mrs. Kettle sneered. "She don't bother me none—I just told her to take her old vacuum cleaner and stuff it." Only Mrs. Kettle described in exact detail how this feat was to be accomplished. As Mrs. Kettle talked, telling me of her family and fifteen children, she referred frequently to someone called "Tits." Tits' baby, Tits' husband, Tits' farm, Tits' fancywork. They were important to Mrs. Kettle and I was glad therefore when a car drove up and Tits herself appeared. She was a full-breasted young woman and, even though Mrs. Kettle had already explained that the name Tits was short for sister, I found it impossible to hear the name without flinching. Tits was a Kettle daughter and she had a six-month-old son whose name I never learned as she referred to him always as "You little bugger." Tits fed this baby pickles, beer, sowbelly and cabbage and the baby ungratefully retaliated with "fits." "He had six fits yesterday," Tits told her mother as she fed the baby hot cinnamon roll dipped in coffee.

Then there were Elwin Kettle, a lank-haired mechanical genius, who never seemed to go to school, although he was only fifteen, but spent all of his time taking apart and putting together terrible old cars; and Paw Kettle whom Bob aptly described as "a lazy, lisping, sonofabitch." The other Kettles were shiftless, ignorant and non-progressive but not important.

On that first visit Mrs. Kettle told me that she had been born in Estonia and had lived there on a farm until she was fourteen; then she had accompanied her mother and father and sixteen brothers and sisters to the United States and, somewhere en route to the Pacific Coast, had been unfortunate enough to encounter and marry Paw. Immediately thereafter she began having the fifteen children who were all born from ten to fourteen months apart and all delivered by Paw. Mrs. Kettle was plunging into a detailed recital of the conception and birth of each, when I hurriedly interrupted and asked about the milk and eggs. She was shocked. Sell milk? They had never even considered it. They separated all of their milk and sold the cream to the cheese factory. Nope, selling milk was out of the question. "What about eggs?" I asked. "Well," said Mrs. Kettle, "Paw just hasn't gotten around to fixing any nests in the hen house and so the chickens lay around in the orchard and when we find the eggs some are good and some ain't." I hurriedly said that that was all right, I could get the eggs in town, took my leave and went home, and there learned that Bob the efficient, Bob the intelligent, had already arranged with the Hicks' for milk and eggs.

The Hicks', our other neighbors, lived five miles down the road in the opposite direction from the Kettles. They had a neat white house, a neat white barn, a neat white chicken house, pigpen and brooder house, all surrounded by a neat white picket fence. At the side of the house was an orchard with all of the tree trunks painted white but aside from these trees there was not a shrub or tree to interfere with the stern discipline the Hicks' maintained over their farm. It made me feel that one pine needle carelessly tracked in by me would create a panic. Mrs. Hicks, stiffly starched and immaculate from the moment she arose until she went to bed, looked like she had been left in the washing machine too long, and wore dippy waves low on her forehead and plenty of "rooje" scrubbed into her cheeks.

Mr. Hicks, a large ruddy dullard, walked gingerly through life, being very careful not to get dirt on anything or in any way to irritate Mrs. Hicks, whom he regarded as a cross between Mary Magdalene and the County Agent.

Mrs. Hicks was good and she worked at it like a profession. Not only by going to church and helping the poor and lonely but by maintaining a careful check on the activities of the entire community. She knew who drank, who smoked and who "laid up" with whom and when and where, and she "reported" on people. She told husbands of erring wives and wives of erring husbands and parents of erring children. She collected and distributed her

Spring Comes, and So Do People 73

information on her way to and from Town, and apparently kept a huge espionage system going full tilt twenty-four hours a day. Having Mrs. Hicks living in the community was akin to having Sherlock Holmes living in the outhouse, and kept everyone watching his step.

The Maddocks had one of the most prosperous farms in that country. Six hundred acres of peat, drained and under cultivation; a herd of eighty-six Guernsey cows; a prize bull; pigs, rabbits, chickens, bees, ducks, turkeys, lambs, fruit, berries, nuts, a brick house, new modern barns and outbuildings; their own water and light systems, and a wonderful garden had the Maddocks. They had also five sons who had graduated from the State Agricultural College and Mrs. Maddock herself was said to be a college graduate. We drove past their beautiful ranch on our way to and from Town and one day there was a sign in the mailbox "Honey for sale," I persuaded Bob to stop. We drove through the gateway and up a long graveled drive which swept around the house and circled the barnyard. We stopped by the milkhouse and a large hearty man in clean blue-and-white-striped overalls came out, introduced himself as Mr. Maddock and invited us to go over the farm. The farm was everything we had heard. The epitome of self-sufficiency. The cows gave milk to the chickens, the chickens gave manure to the fruit trees, the fruit trees fed the bees, the bees pollenized the fruit trees, and on and on in a beautiful cycle of everything doing its share. The exact opposite of that awful cycle of the Kettles' where Peter robbed Paul to pay George who borrowed from Ed. The Maddock livestock was sleek and well cared for. The barns were like Carnation Milk advertisements—scrubbed and with the latest equipment for lighting, milking, cleaning and feeding; the bunkhouses were clean, comfortable and airy; the pigpens were cement and immaculate; the chicken houses were electric-lighted, many windowed, white and clean; the duck pens, beehives, bull pens, calf houses, turkey runs, rabbit hutches, and the milkhouse were new, clean and modern. Then we went to the house. The house had a brick façade and that was all. The rooms were dark—the windows small and few. The kitchen was small and cramped and had a sink the size of a pullman wash basin. In one corner on a plain sawhorse was a wooden washtub. Mrs. Maddock was as dark and dreary as her house, and small wonder. She told me that she hadn't been off the ranch for twenty-seven years; that she had never even been to "Town" or Docktown Bay. When we said good-bye Mr. Maddock shook hands vigorously. "Well," he asked proudly, "what do you think of my ranch?" At last I understood Mrs. Kettle. There was but one suitable answer to give Mr. Maddock and I was too much of a lady.

Mary MacGregor had fiery red, dyed hair, a large dairy ranch and a taste for liquor. Drunker than an owl, she would climb on to her mowing machine. "Tie me on tight, Bill!" she would yell at her hired man. So Bill would tie her on with clothes lines, baling wire and straps, give her the reins and away she'd go, singing at the top of her voice, cutting her oats in semi-circles and happy as a clam. She plowed, disked, harrowed, planted, cultivated and mowed, tied to the seat of the machine and hilariously drunk. A smashing witticism of the farmers was, "You should take a run down the valley and watch Mary sowin' her wild oats."

"She's a bad woman," said Mrs. Hicks, "and we never invite her to our basket socials." I asked Mrs. Kettle about her. She said, "She's kinda hard but she's real good-hearted. There ain't a man in this country but what has borrowed money from Mary and most of 'em has never paid it back. The women don't like her though and all because one time her old man was layin' up with the hired girl and she caught 'em and run a pitchfork into her old man's behind so deep they had to have the doctor come out and cut it out. She said that would teach him and it did because he got lockjaw and died from where the pitchfork stuck him. Mary felt real bad but she said she'd do it again if conditions was the same."

Our first spring on the ranch we didn't have any callers because no one knew we were up there and anyway at that time we didn't have anything to borrow or rather lend nor were we experienced enough to be sought out for advice. Those are the reasons for calling—the time for calling is between four in the morning and seven in the evening and the season is springtime. Summer is too hot, too busy, fall is for harvesting, winter is too wet and rainy. Spring is the time for building, planting, plowing, reproducing and the logical time for calling and borrowing. No one told me this; I learned by bitter experience.

I remember well how the night before I had been awakened by that taut stillness which presages mountain rain. I lay there in the thick dark, at once alert and unreasonably teetering on the edge of terror. No sound, no movement anywhere. Curtains poised in the middle of a sway, half in and half out the window. Shades gone limp. A trailer of my climbing rose clutching the window sill to keep from twitching. Breezes on tiptoe. Trees reaching. Trees bent listening. Everything in the mountains playing statue. Then the signal. Tap, tap. Tap, tap, tap. Tap, tap, tap, tap, tap, tap, tap. A great, soft sigh spread through the orchard, across the burn, over the mountains, everywhere. A frog croaked, the curtains bellied, a shade rattled, an owl hooted apologetically and the rain settled down to a steady hum.

I got up the next morning to a dreary world of bone-chilling air, wet kindling, sulky stove and a huddled miserable landscape. It was Spring's way of warning us not to take her for granted.

It took me from four o'clock until seven-thirty to care for my chicks, get Stove awake and breakfast cooking. Each time I went outdoors I was soaked to the skin by the rain, which was soft, feathery and scented but as penetrating as a fire hose. After using up three sets of outside garments, in chilly desperation I put on my flannel pajamas, woolly slippers and bathrobe until after breakfast. What luxury to be shuffling around in my nightclothes getting breakfast after all those months of being in full swing by 4:15 A.M. with breakfast a very much to the point interval at five or five-thirty. When Bob came in he acted a little as if he had surprised me buttering the toast stark naked. I patiently explained the reason for my attire and was defiantly pouring the coffee when a car drove into the yard. "Dear God, not callers at 7:30 and on this of all mornings!" I prayed. But it was.

A West-side dairy rancher and his sharp-eyed wife. Mr. and Mrs. Wiggins. Mr. Wiggins wanted some advice on fattening fryers and she wanted to look me over.

Who, Me?

I implored Bob, with every known signal, not to leave me alone with this one-man board of investigation, but Bob went native the minute he saw another rancher and became a big, spitting bossy *man* and I was jerked from my pleasant position of wife and equal and tossed down into that dull group known as *womenfolk*. So, of course, Mrs. Wiggins and I were left alone.

I tried to sidle into the bedroom and slip on a housedress and whisk everything to rights before the baby awoke, but the puppy chose that moment to be sick and instead of throwing up in one place he became hysterical and ran around and around the kitchen belching forth at intervals and mostly in the vicinity of sharp-eyed Mrs. Wiggins. She pulled her feet up to the top rung of her chair and said, "I've never liked dogs." I could see her point all right but it didn't improve the situation any, especially as Sport, our large Chesapeake retriever, managed to squeeze past me when I opened the back door to put the mop bucket out, and bounded in to lay first one and then the other large muddy paw on Mrs. Wiggins' starched lap. She screamed as though he had amputated her leg at the hip, which of course waked the baby. I retrieved Sport and wedged him firmly in behind the stove, we exchanged reproachful looks, I wiped up his many many dirty tracks, sponged off Mrs. Wiggins and picked up small Anne. As I bathed the baby, Mrs. Wiggins handed me flat knife-edged statements, as though she were dealing cards, on how by seven o'clock that morning she had fed and cared for her chickens, milked five cows, strained and separated the milk, cleaned out the milkhouse, cooked the breakfast, set the bread, folded down the ironing and baked a cake. It took all of the self-control I had to keep from screaming, "SO WHAT!"

Mrs. Wiggins, no doubt, had quite a juicy morsel for the next basket social, but I had learned my lesson and from that day forward I was ready for Eleanor Roosevelt at four-seven in the morning.

6

Game or Who Is

I WAS ALL RIGHT at flushing game, Bob decided, but at retrieving I was a washout. This was due to my nearsightedness and not to any lack of cooperation on my part, I might add. So Bob bought a dog and I uncovered another weak spot in my character.

"This dog," Bob dramatically informed me, as he gingerly untied a large, curly haired, mahogany-colored dog which he had roped in the back of the truck, "is a thoroughbred Chesapeake retriever, has a pedigree, is a wonderful hunting dog and is very, very vicious." Then, with what I considered an overdose of caution he secured the dog to the feed room door with a hawser large enough to anchor a man-o'-war. During all of this the vicious dog regarded us stonily with pale green eyes and didn't twitch a muscle.

Bob added, as he made a large safe detour around Dog to get his feed pails, "He has bitten almost everyone in Town, but I understand dogs and if I take all the care of him, keep him tied up and just use him for hunting, I think it will be safe enough." The dog trainer went importantly off to the chicken house and Dog and I looked at each other. He had on a handsome studded collar with a name tag but from a safe distance I couldn't make out the name and when I received only the cold pale green stare for my friendly overtures of "Here Boy" and "Old Fellah," I started on my evening chores, leaving Dog to brood.

During dinner that night Bob told me how, when I was in the hospital, he and the doctor had been discussing hunting and the doctor had told him about Dog. The doctor didn't finally make up his mind to part with the dog until it had bitten two postmen and three delivery boys. Bob talked about building a dogyard with eight-foot wire, the steady nerves it takes to train dogs, the heinous crime of treating dogs like pampered humans—here, I surreptitiously placed my napkin over the puppy who was lounging in my lap—and other firm manly things to do with discipline and hunting, and then he left for the Hicks' to see about borrowing the team for disking.

Later, remembering I had not fed my goslings and forgetting about Dog, I heedlessly rushed into the feed room and was scooping up chick feed when I felt a nudge at the back of my knees. I turned and there was Dog the vicious, Dog the terrible, offering me his large feathery paw. We solemnly shook hands and I learned from his nameplate that his name was Sport and from him that he never wagged his tail, was dignified and really very shy. Throwing caution to the winds I untied the rope and took him with me to feed the ducks. There I decided to test out the hunting theory to see if it was as ridiculous as the danger theory. I threw Sport a stick to retrieve and he lalloped after it, then tore down to the edge of the orchard and buried it under the plum tree. I confess that I hugged him for this because now there were two of us who seemed to have no vocational guidance.

When I heard Bob's car in the drive, I removed Sport from behind the stove and tied him in the feed room and that was the way things were. Sport knew that I knew that he was neither vicious nor a sport but we decided to let Bob dream on for a while.

When Bob was attacked by the she-bear, Sport just happened to be behind the stove—a little out of breath but trying to look as if he'd been there for hours.

When Bob and Crowbar and Geoduck Swensen and Crowbar's large bear dog were on the scent of the cougar, Sport came out of the woods like a streak of flame and plastered himself to me to shiver and whine. I attributed this to a ferocious attempt at his life on the part of the cougar. Bob said, "More likely a face-to-face encounter with a squirrel." Bob knew about Sport, then.

Our trouble with wild animals began in the summer. Of course, we had had many encounters with bats, weasels, owls, hawks, wood rats and field mice, but I'm talking now about the large wild animals like bears, cougars, wildcats, skunks, deer and coyotes.

Our summers came early—about May. The sun began to stretch and yawn a little after five and was up, fully dressed and ready to begin a day's work, before six. The days were hot and bright and the house was wrapped up like a Christmas package with roses and honeysuckle whose heavy scent flowed through the windows if the wind was right; and if the wind was wrong I comforted myself with the knowledge that manure was what made the roses and honeysuckle so vigorous and prolific.

In summer we made our trips to Town in the early morning and were home before the heat of the day. One morning we were fed and scrubbed and in the truck by seven, only to find, after coasting to the county road, that the truck had developed a consumptive cough overnight and had become so debilitated it couldn't even make the mild hill back to the house, let alone the vicious grades hemming us in on east and west. For an hour Bob tried to persuade it to go toward town; then in desperation attempted to guide it up the driveway to the garage. It would reel ahead a few steps then slide back, limp and gasping. Finally I was dispatched to retrieve one of the Kettle boys from under one of the Kettle cars to see if he could diagnose the trouble.

I put Anne in her carriage, told Bob to keep an eye on her, cantered down to the Kettles' and persuaded Elwin to come up and fix the car. Elwin ungraciously acquiesced and elected to drive up in the most sinister-looking of all of the jalopies, so I took the trail through the logging burn instead.

For a while the path ran beside the Kettles' stream and was well traveled and shaded by second growth. Then it became a perilous scramble through giant jackstraw piles of slashings and discarded logs. I threaded my way around brambles, through brush, stepping on logs which either swayed alarmingly over dark bottomless-looking pools or else gave way entirely and left me clinging to slender twigs and feeling for footholds over bramble-filled pits. There were still many great virgin trees left, for this logging had been done by a sloppy small outfit, and the woods were dark and cool and quiet. Occasional birds twittered, and chipmunks slithered over logs and then paused to stare at me glassy-eyed, but there was none of the twig-snapping, brush-rustling, chirping activity that had marked my walk along the road. At last the path miraculously reappeared and wound steeply upward along a ravine and through uncut virgin timber. Halfway up this home stretch I was aware of an uncomfortable feeling as though something were following me. I heard brush crackling across the ravine—even saw branches sway; but when I stopped the noise stopped and finally I convinced myself that I was imagining things. Then I leaped to the ground from a fallen log and there was a terrific crashing across the ravine. Certain that I had not made that much noise, I stopped again to listen, and this time the crashing continued and sounded as if, whatever it was, it was heading across the ravine to *me*. I broke into a lope and at last, panting and scared, I reached home and threw myself on Bob who patted me comfortingly and said that he didn't think that anything would follow me.

Before I could think of a suitable rejoinder Elwin appeared, and while he towed the truck into the yard and started taking it entirely apart, even to removing little tiny nuts and bolts, Bob took Sport and the Kettles' Airedale and went into the woods to look for a good cedar tree to cut into fence posts. He came back almost immediately to get his gun, saying that the dogs seemed uneasy and he thought he'd take a look around.

It seemed hours later when Elwin and I heard the shots. There were four or five close together—then silence. Dead silence. I hallooed. No answer. I began to be frightened and asked Elwin, who was sprawled under the truck, to go out and see what was happening, but he merely stuck his head out, shook his mane of hair out of his eyes, grinned his wide foolish grin, and said, "If he don't come back he's probably dead and there's no use of us both getting kilt, ha, ha, ha!" Then he went back to his tinkering under the truck. After another long wait Elwin came in for a drink of water and, after three dippers full, he wiped his mouth on his sleeve and said, "Well, looks like you're a widder-woman, ha, ha, ha!"

I'm sure I would have killed him if the truck had been fixed, but it definitely was not, so I had to content myself with withering looks and a scathing silence.

Bob at last came limping in, his shirt in ribbons, a great jagged bloody gash across his chest, and wearing a beaming smile. "Stepped into the root pit of a fallen tree and a she-bear jumped me. Fired five shots in her general direction and I guess one of 'em stuck because she's deader than a smelt."

"That gash!" I said weakly.

"Oh, that," he said looking offhandedly down at it. "Must have happened when Joe," he affectionately pulled the ear of the Airedale, "yanked the bear off me. Joe grabbed her hind leg just as she jumped and I guess you could say he saved my life." Then he and Elwin climbed into the jalopy and drove cross country to bring in the carcass.

I got out iodine, bandages, sleeping tablets and my self-control, because, though Bob was being brave and careless in front of Elwin, alone with me, he would act as if the bear had laid open both his lungs and his large intestine, and would spend many happy hours looking for the first signs of blood poisoning. It occurred to me then, that no mention had been made of our dog's part in the fray.

Bob and Elwin returned much later with a large black bear which reeked of iodoform (natural she-bear smell, Elwin said) over the hood of the car and a report of two cubs up a tree. I asked about Sport, but Bob said that he hadn't seen him; that he disappeared just as Joe, the Airedale, got the scent. I looked toward the stove and was relieved to see the dejected tip of a dark red tail. "That's all right, boy," I murmured, "I'll slip you a bone later on just to let you know that I feel the same way about bears."

Bob fixed a sumptuous meal for Joe who was so emaciated that we could follow the progress of each bite. I asked Elwin why Joe was so thin and he brilliantly replied, "I dunno—he should be OK. We been grainin' him!"

Oh, well, Elwin had fixed the truck, and it ran with purpose and vigor. With the five dollars Bob gave him he said that he was going to buy a fog light for his awful car, which at that time had no lights at all.

After Elwin had left, I hesitantly mentioned the fact that I may have been right in thinking something was following me earlier in the day. Bob said, "Didn't sound like a bear. Could have been, of course—the berries are coming on now—but it was more likely squirrels." With which odious remark he collapsed on his bed of pain and I was allowed to dress the wounds and listen to the stories of the attack.

I had about recovered from the bear, when the blackberries began to ripen. These were the low-growing small blackberries—not the Himalayans which were also plentiful and wild, but came later and did not compare in flavor—and we intended to gather enough for jelly, pies and wine. The summer before we had spent hours in the broiling sun in the old logging works down by the Kettles', getting scratched and stung and burned while we filled five-gallon cans with these elusive blackberries. The resultant jelly and wine were well worth the effort, we thought in the winter when the burns and scratches were healed and summer seemed far away; but here it was blackberry time again and it seemed that even the baby wasn't going to keep me from doing my share, for Bob had found a new picking ground—one where we could take the baby.

One evening after supper, armed with Bob's will power and impeded by two five-gallon cans, two lard buckets, the baby buggy, Sport and the puppy, we trekked a half mile or so through the woods in back of the ranch to a clearing where the blackberries were thick and ripe. Some twenty years before, this clearing had housed a small farm, but the farmer, an elderly bachelor, complained of hearing babies crying in the woods and spent most of his time in town pleading with the sheriff to organize searching parties to find "the little ones." Mrs. Kettle had told us about the bachelor when she heard we intended to pick blackberries back there. She said that the "little ones" crying in the woods were cougars which have a plaintive cry not unlike a lost child and that the woods were alive with them. Bob pooh-poohed this story and said that the old man had probably heard coyotes. Cougars or coyotes, the old man went completely insane and was put away, and no one in that country could be persuaded to move on to his farm. His debtors took his livestock, his neighbors stole his furniture and equipment, and the mountains took over the ranch.

The road which had once connected our farm with the old bachelor's was completely obliterated by fallen trees, vines, salal and huckleberry bushes, until Bob happened on it early in the spring when he was searching for an approach to a large fallen cedar. He cleared the road enough so that he could get the dragsaw in and haul the wood out, and even I could tell it was a road when he pointed it out to me, because it had two ruts and following it was a little less arduous than just lowering my head and charging through the brush. Pushing a baby buggy over its rooty, spongy, brushy surface was a maneuver which delighted the baby and made me seasick.

From the edge of our potato patch to the second growth, which marked the boundaries of the old farm, was dense virgin timber. The trees, some of them eight and ten feet in diameter, went soaring out of sight and it was dank and shadowy down by their feet. Thick feathery green moss covered the ground and coated the fallen timbers and stumps, which also sported great sword ferns, delicate maidenhair ferns, thick white unhealthy looking lichens and red huckleberry bushes beaded with fruit. The earth was springy, the air quiet except for our grunts and gasps as we extricated the buggy from the grasp of a root or lifted it over a sudden marsh. Bob pointed out the upturned toes of the tree where the bear had attacked him, and I suddenly remembered the cubs, which had disappeared during the night after the death of their mother. Bob stated reassuringly that they were probably still in the immediate vicinity and good-sized bears by that time. It was a distinct relief to reach the second growth of the old clearing and to have the familiar bird and insect noises begin again. Even the air had a different feeling, the pale green silky deep-forest air being replaced by the regular sharp evening-mountain variety. Sport and the puppy, who had been following in stately and unaccustomed dignity, began racing through the brush yapping and yipping at each other, and Bob and I forced the carriage through the waist-high grass to the whitened bones of the cabin and barn where the blackberries were.

When we were finally settled and the berries, as large as

thimbles, had begun to plink into the lard buckets, twilight was upon us and so were the mosquitoes, which spiraled out of the woods like smoke and made a direct line for the baby buggy. I slapped and fanned while Bob picked, but it was no use. The mosquitoes crawled into the crevices of the wicker buggy, up Bob's trouser legs, down our necks and inside our sleeves. I took the baby, Sport and the puppy and started home.

Going back through the dusky woods I found it difficult to guide the buggy and at the same time to search the underbrush fore and aft with nearsighted eyes, for cougars, coyotes and bears. It was also disquieting to know that my vision was so myopic that a wild beast would have had to lay its lip against mine and snarl before I could recognize it. In my haste to reach the farm I gave Sport and the puppy the impression that we were having a race and they went bounding out of sight leaving me alone in the gloom. Twigs broke with a loud snap to the left and right of me; overhead the deep quiet was broken by the loud sudden rush of wings. It was most irritating since I was intently trying to listen for a pursuing wild animal. Then just as I reached the point where I was going to scream "Shut up, so I can hear something, will you!" I saw our potato field and our lovely cozy farm buildings dead ahead.

I was putting the baby to bed when Bob came in on the run. "Have the dogs been barking? Have you heard anything?" he breathlessly demanded, as he threw open the closet door and began shuffling through his guns. I showed him Sport and the puppy playing tug-o'-war in the front yard with a piece of rope and asked what sound he had in mind? He snorted impatiently and said, "I was kneeling, picking berries under the leaves [where they hide long and black] and I had that prickly feeling you get when something you can't see is watching you. I looked up and the long grass between me and the woods was waving back together, closing the gap made by the passing of some animal. Some one of the cat family, I'll bet, because there wasn't even a rustle. Not a single sound. It gave me the creeps to think that something had passed so close to me I could have reached out and touched it and it hadn't made a whisper of noise." I thought of my recent trip through the woods with the baby, and the little blood I had left turned so cold my veins recoiled from it in horror.

"Do you think it followed you home?" I quavered, as I began a tour of the house, bolting and locking all of the windows and doors.

Bob disdained to answer such a ridiculous question and began whistling for Sport and pocketing shells. When Sport reluctantly slithered through the door, Bob took him by the collar and they left on an extensive inspection of the premises. I huddled by Stove, afraid to go to bed because I found that the only lock on the back door could have been wrenched off by an anæmic sparrow. I dragged the kitchen stool into the corner and, using it as a table, began a letter home:

"Dear Mother: I am enclosing my sterling salad forks. Please turn them in on some stout bear traps and a good skinning knife. Don't you think it is stretching this wifely duty business a bit too taut to ask me to spend the few minutes of the day when I'm not carrying water, baking, canning, gardening, scrubbing, and taking care of the chickens and pigs, in fending off wild beasts? It is beginning to look as if we are hemmed in by bears and cougars, yet we live in the day of the magnetic eye, automatic hot water heaters and television."

As I sealed the letter, Bob returned and reported small piles of feathers along the pullet runs, but no other tracks or signs. He said in his opinion the animal was a cougar, but it might be just a large wildcat. He also said, "Sport is without a doubt the dumbest animal alive and couldn't follow the scent of a roast duck at twenty paces." Sport hurriedly offered his paw, but Bob turned on his heel and slammed his gun into the rack. I wanted to lock the bedroom windows and have Sport, the puppy and the baby sleep with us, but Bob scoffed at such cowardice and insisted on night air and life as usual. The next morning Bob found prints as large as saucers in the dust of the road directly in front of the house. "It is a cougar and a whopper," he joyfully announced. Then with Sport and his gun he left for the valley to assemble a hunting party. "Am I supposed to handle this cougar with kindness or a hatpin?" I called after him resentfully.

"Would that I had it to do over again," I reflected bitterly as I put a chair under the knob on the kitchen door, "and I would choose the indoor type. Preferably a gambler in a green eyeshade, who sat all day and night indoors under electric lights wearing his delicious pallor which proved that he hadn't been out in the daylight or night air for years and years."

Things got worse. Bob returned from the valley and requested that I feed and water the chickens and gather the eggs while he drove up to some logging camp to get Crowbar and Geoduck Swensen, who were the best hunters in the country and the only ones he wished to trust with his precious cougar. I refused to do the chores on the grounds that I was not going to put my foot outside the house while the cougar was loose. It got very warm in the house with all of the doors and windows locked, but better to drown in a pool of my own sweat, I thought, than be torn limb from limb by a wild beast. Bob slammed through the chores and drove off again. He returned about four-thirty with Crowbar, Geoduck and Crowbar's large bear dog. While Bob finished his evening chores, Crowbar and Geoduck lay in the shade of the truck and gulped down a pint of moonshine each. Then Bob joined them in a third pint and, shouldering their guns, they disappeared into the woods directly back of the pullet runs. Almost immediately the dog began to bark and, guided by his excited yips, I was able to follow the progress of the hunt around the ranch.

The sun was beginning to yawn and edge toward his bed behind the far mountains, the livestock were making soft contented end-of-the-day sounds, the ducks were taking a last dip in the pond at the foot of the orchard and pre-evening coolness was in the air, when the barkings became wild and concentrated in the woods out by the old spring down past the potato patch. Then there were two shots. Then shouting, barking and at last the hunters appeared bearing the cougar in a stretcher made from their hunting coats and guns. The cougar measured eleven feet from head to tail tip and was the largest ever bagged in our community (according to Crowbar and Geoduck). He was an old-timer, quite grizzled about the head, but with the coldest yellow eyes and the largest sharpest teeth I had ever seen.

Toward the end of June when the cougar episode had cooled somewhat, Bob and I made several early morning pilgrimages to the abandoned farm and picked five gallons of wild blackberries —and the canning season was on. How I dreaded it! Jelly, jam, preserves, canned raspberries, blackcaps, peas, spinach, beans, beets, carrots, blackberries, loganberries, wild blackberries, wild raspberries, applesauce, tomatoes, peaches, pears, plums, chickens, venison, beef, clams, salmon, rhubarb, cherries, corn pickles and prunes. By fall the pantry shelves would groan and creak under nature's bounty and the bitter thing was that we wouldn't be able to eat one tenth of it. Canning is a mental quirk just like any form of hoarding. First you plant too much of everything in the garden; then you waste hours and hours in the boiling sun cultivating; then you buy a pressure cooker and can too much of everything so that it won't be wasted.

I crouched beneath the weight of an insupportable burden every time I went out to the garden. Never have I come face to face with such productivity. Pea vines pregnant with bulging pods; bean poles staggering under big beans, middle-sized beans, little beans and more blossoms; carrots with bare shoulders thrust above the ground to show me they were ready; succulent summer squash and zucchini where it seemed only a matter of an hour ago there were blossoms; and I picked a water bucket full of cherries from *one* lower branch of the old-fashioned late cherry tree that shaded the kitchen.

There was more of everything than we could ever use or preserve and no way to absorb the excess. I tried sending vegetables to our families, but the freight rates and ferry fares and time involved (plus the fact that Seattle has superb waterfront vegetable markets) made this seem rather senseless. I sent great baskets of produce to the Kettles, but with Paw on the road every day imploring the farmers to give him anything they couldn't use, even they had too much. I became so conscience stricken by the waste that of my own volition I canned seventy-five quarts of string beans and too late noticed that the new farm journal carried a hair-raising account of the deaths from botulism from eating home-canned string beans.

Birdie Hicks took all the blue ribbons at the county fair for canning. She evidently stayed up all night during the summer and early fall to can, for she would come to call on me at seven-fifteen, crisp and combed and tell me—as her sharp eyes noted that I still had the breakfast dishes and the housework to do, the baby to bathe and feed and my floor to scrub before I could get at my canning—that she had just finished canning thirty-six quarts of corn on the cob, twenty-five quarts of tomatoes, eighty-two quarts of string beans and a five-gallon crock of dill pickles.

By the end of the summer the pullets were laying and Bob was culling the flocks. With no encouragement from me, he decided that, as chicken prices were way down, I should can the culled hens. It appeared to my warped mind that Bob went miles and miles out of his way to figure out things for me to put in jars; that he actively resented a single moment of my time which was not spent eye to pressure gauge, ear to steam cock; that he was forever coming staggering into the kitchen under a bushel basket of something for me to can. My first reaction was homicide, then suicide, and at last tearful resignation.

When he brought in the first three culled hens, I acidly remarked that it wasn't only the cooker which operated under pressure. No answer.

Later, because of my remark, he said that I did it on purpose. I didn't, I swear, but I did feel that God had at last taken pity on me—for the pressure cooker blew up. It was the happiest day of my life, though I might have been killed. A bolt was blown clear through the kitchen door, the walls were dotted with bits of wing and giblet, the floor was swimming in gravy, and the thick cast aluminum lid broke in two and hit the ceiling with such force it left two half moon marks above Stove. I was lyrical with joy. I didn't know how it happened and I cared less. I was free! *Free F-R-E-E!* After supper as I went humming about the house picking pieces of chicken off the picture frames and from the mirror in the bedroom, Bob eyed me speculatively. Then he picked up the Sears, Roebuck catalog and began looking for a bigger, quicker and sturdier variety of pressure cooker.

7

And Not a Drop to Drink

THE WELL at the back of the place dried up during the spring; the spring at the foot of the orchard disappeared during the summer; and we carried August's and September's water from a spring in a valley eighteen hundred feet from the house if we cut across the burn, a mile and a half by road. I was really glad when the spring dried up, for it meant that Bob hauled the water in the truck in ten gallon cans and I didn't have to feel guilty if he caught me washing my face more than twice a day. Bob was so parsimonious with the water when he was carrying it, that one would have thought we had pitched camp in a dry coulee instead of being permanently settled in the wettest country in the world outside of the Canadian muskeg. "I have to have more water!" was my perpetual cry. "More water?" Bob would shout. "More water? I just carried up two buckets." "I know you did," I would explain patiently. "Two buckets equal twenty quarts. Twenty quarts equal five gallons and the stove reservoir holds five gallons. In addition to filling the reservoir I made coffee and boiled you two eggs, made cereal for the baby and wet my parched lips twice. The water is gone."

With set mouth Bob would go down through the orchard and dip out two more buckets. These would see me through the first tub of baby's washing. There were still the rinsings, the baby's bath, the luncheon tea, the luncheon dishes, the floor scrubbing, the canning, the dinner and the dinner dishes—not to mention occasional hair washings, baths and face washing. For these I carried the water from the spring myself—it was so much easier than explaining.

I estimated that I carried a minimum of sixteen buckets of water a day—sixteen ten-quart buckets or one hundred and sixty quarts a day for about three hundred and sixty days. Is it surprising that my hands were almost dragging on the ground and my shoulders sagged at the sight of anything wet? That I was tortured by mirages of gushing faucets and flushing toilets? I could not believe it when Bob announced casually one fall morning, "I'm going to start laying the pipe for the water system tomorrow." He had been plotting the course, tiling the spring and ordering equipment for a long time now, but none of it had been definite enough to bring running water out of the mirage department. But pipe laying was different. Each day I could actually watch the water being brought nearer and nearer the house—foot by foot.

Then the six hundred gallon water tank arrived, knocked down and looking disappointingly like a bundle of faggots. Bob spent a day out in the woods locating four poles, straight, clear and approximately eighteen inches at the butt end to support the platform for the tank. I scanned the bathroom fixture section of the catalogs, and Bob decided that the bathroom would have to go where my rhododendrons *sans* taproots were thriving. Did I care? Not a whit. I jerked them up and put them by the woodshed.

Fall was a wonderful time in the mountains. The sun got up at six, but languorously, without any of her summer fire, and stayed shrouded with sleep until about nine. She shone warmly and brightly then, but I knew it wasn't summer because, though the earth was still warm and the squashes were still blossoming, when I looked heavenward I saw the tops of the trees swimming filmily in mists and the big burn smoked and smoldered with rising fog until noon.

Fall and school were still closely linked in my mind, and I could almost feel the pinch of new school shoes when I saw the first red leaf, heard the first hoarse shouts of foghorns. I remembered last fall when we had driven along a valley road one morning early and had seen the children scrubbed and clutching their lunch boxes, waiting at each gate for the school bus. I wondered if we would still be on the ranch when Anne started to school. I thought what a long day eight o'clock to four-thirty must be for six-year-old first graders. While I was absorbed in such reverie one morning, Bob shouted that the water tower was finished—except for the water. To the casual outside eye it was just a very sturdy, well-constructed platform on which rested a round wooden water tank. To me it was lovelier than the Taj Mahal.

Bob shouted down from the high platform, "I feel like running up an American flag."

I was so excited that I decided to go down and tell Mrs. Kettle about it. In the baby buggy I put Anne, a bucket of extra eggs and half a chocolate cake and, with Sport and the puppy racing fore and aft, we started down. It was a delightful walk and our cheeks were rosy and our spirits high as we trundled up the last lap to the Kettles' porch. I was startled out of my intent maneuvering of the buggy wheels around axles, stray fenders, car parts and tools, by a terrified roar from Paw Kettle in the barnyard. I turned just in time to see him streak out of the milkhouse into the barn and to see the water tower, which was on a platform about thirty feet high and supported by four straddled spindly legs, give a great groan and collapse with a splintering crash on the milkhouse roof.

A geyser of water flooded the barnyard and frightened an old Chester White sow and her pigs so that they went right through the discarded bed spring which was part of the barnyard fence and disappeared into the oat field.

After a time things quieted down and Paw came sidling cautiously out of the barn and Elwin called from under his car, "Hey, Paw, you dropped something! Haw, haw, haw!" Maw shuffled down from the back porch and for a while they stood and looked. Then Paw whispered, "The bugger almotht got me! It almotht got me!" Maw said, "For Krissake, what happened?" Mr. Kettle looked belligerently at the hole in the milkhouse roof and at the shattered tank. "All I wanted wath a little piethe of two by four. How would I know the bugger'd collapthe." Mrs. Kettle said, "Paw, what *was* you doing?" Mr. Kettle said, "I needed a little piethe of two by four for the apple bin and I thought the other leg could hold her all right. I only took a piethe about a foot long from that leg by the milkhouthe." Maw said, "Well, I'll be goddamned. It was only a little piece you took out of the water tank support? What in hell did you think would hold it up—air?"

At last the pipe was all buried, the engine was started and one bright fall morning I heard the musical splash and gulp of water being pumped into the tank. The tank was then scrubbed and drained and at last filled, and I stood underneath it and said a little prayer, then went into the kitchen to find that the faucet in the sink had been turned on and water was an inch deep all over the floor. I didn't care—it was in the house.

Even with the continual rain, July, August, September and even October were bad fire months in the mountains. If you were unfortunate enough to live on a ranch near the Kettles, any month was dangerous. It was said that the Kettles set the original peat fires in the valleys and that one summer, Paw, to save himself the effort of mowing the lawn, set fire to the grass and burned off the front porch. The Kettles burned brush any old time of year and if the brush fire got away from them and burned five or ten acres of someone's timber, that was too bad.

It was late October of the second year when Elwin Kettle drove excitedly into our yard one morning to tell us that their barn was on fire. He said, "Paw filled the hay mow with wet hay and the darned stuff's combusted spontaneous. The barn's burnin' and it's set the brush in the ravine on fire, too. Maw said to warn you that it'll probably come up this way because the wind's from the south." I was frightened and ran out to the chicken house to fetch Bob. Bob said, "Oh, I don't think it will amount to anything," but he took the truck and followed Elwin back to the ranch. Bob did not return until noon. When he did come home he was black from head to foot and very angry. He said that he was quite sure Paw had set the barn on fire to solve the manure situation; that the

And Not a Drop to Drink 93

barn had burned, but the fire had left the Kettle ranch and was sweeping up the draw with terrible velocity.

He said that if the fire crossed the road, our ranch would go. I asked if the Kettles were helping fight the fire and Bob said, "They helped only as long as the fire was on their land. The minute it crossed their boundary fence they went back to the house on the pretext of protecting the house and outbuildings. When I went to get the truck I saw them all on the back porch, drinking home brew and laughing and talking."

Bob told me to spend the afternoon hosing off our roof and soaking the dry orchard grass and preparing to feed the fire fighters. He left to get help.

All afternoon cars chugged up our road and then scooted down toward the Kettles'. Bob had spread the alarm and the farmers were answering the call for help. I learned later that Bob had gone even farther—he had asked Maxwell Ford Jefferson, the moonshiner, to help and Jeff passed the word on to all his good customers. I made gallons of coffee and hundreds of sandwiches and at about four the fighters began filing wearily in, black faced and dirty. They ate sandwiches, drank coffee, and cursed the Kettles. The smoke rolled up the draw and obscured the sun and stung my eyes while I put out the lanterns and fed the chickens. Each batch of fighters brought more frightening news. "The fire was almost to the road in several places." "The wind was getting stronger." "Once the fire hit the timber on our place we would have to run for our lives."

About seven o'clock Max Jefferson knocked at the back door. He was all alone. He said in his soft liquidy voice, "Just thought I'd drop up and tell you not to worry, honey. I've got the biggest bunch of drunkards in the United States out fightin' that fire 'cause they think my still's up this away." Jeff was a tall, tobacco-colored, lithe man with old world courtesy of manner, a southern drawl and light yellow eyes which saw in the dark and spotted every exit in a room before he crossed the threshold. He drank his coffee and ate his sandwiches, tilted back in a kitchen chair, occasionally fingering the gun in his coat pocket and flashing his big white teeth. After he had finished his coffee he said he had something for me in his car and went out and brought in a ten-gallon keg of whiskey. He set it down carefully in the middle of the kitchen. "That theah is fine whiskey," he said. "It's been hangin' in a tree and should be smooth as oil now." Before I could thank him he had slipped out the door and was gone.

I put the baby to bed, then went out to the front porch to watch the fire. It was only about two city blocks from the house and the snapping and crackling were fearful sounds. The fire fighters reported that they had kept it out of the heavy timber down by the water pump and that the wind was dying down. I wandered aimlessly around after each batch of fighters had eaten and left, trying to choose what I would take in case we had to run for it. It narrowed down finally to the baby, the keg of whiskey and the animals. I put my sorority pin and my high school graduation ring in my purse, my silver in the didy bag and we were ready.

About eight o'clock Mrs. Hicks arrived with two chocolate cakes, two pounds of butter and two quarts of cream. The smoke had grown heavier with the lessening of the wind, but by closing all of the doors and windows I was able to keep most of it out of the house. A group of fighters arrived simultaneously with Mrs. Hicks and we had first to feed them before we could talk. Then we poured out cups of coffee and sank down to discuss the fire. I noticed with pleasure that in the excitement Mrs. Hicks had pulled the keg of whiskey over by the stove, had placed a pillow on it and was sitting there primly drinking her coffee.

Bob came excitedly in, grimy beyond recognition, and demanded help in soaking and loading in the truck the hundreds of feed sacks we had stored in the loft of the tool house. As we worked he told me that Jeff had the Kettles working at the point of his gun. He said that poor Maw Kettle was so humiliated about the whole thing that she had come to him in tears to ask if there wasn't something she could do. She had made coffee and fried bread and had fed many of the fire fighters.

After Bob had driven away with the wet sacks and ten milk cans of water, I went out to see how the heifer was reacting. She was in her stall, standing quietly but not eating. She had a nice new little barn beyond the pig houses, the farthest from the house of any of the buildings, so I led her back to the house and tied her to the cherry tree. Sport and the puppy trailed me everywhere, whining and begging me to explain the smoke and excitement. Sport's method of eliciting understanding and comfort from me was to shake hands. Every time I hesitated during the whole of that long, dreadful day, I would look down and there would be Sport, pale green eyes spilling over with love, offering me his large soft paw. By ten o'clock his paw and my hand were calloused and I was tired and scared so I yelled at him, "Oh, Sport, don't be such a bore!" Whereupon he gave me a look which said, "Here I am willing to die for you, trying to comfort you in your hour of need, and you speak to me like that." I gave him six chocolate creams and put him behind the stove where he remained for the rest of the night, shivering occasionally and whining steadily. Birdie Hicks left about ten-thirty with my promise that if anything happened I would stay with her indefinitely.

After she had gone I sat down by the stove with a magazine and I must have dozed for I was awakened by loud shouting down by the road. "This is it," I thought. "Let me see, should I wake the baby now, or wait until Bob comes." I was shivering and so I put some more wood on Stove thinking what a useless gesture that was when the whole house would soon be in flames. I put the diaper bag on the whiskey keg, laid my purse on the diaper bag, glanced out the window to see if the heifer was still tied to the cherry tree, and we were ready. I could hear voices coming up the lane and my heart beat wildly. "Where was Bob? Had the truck been burned?" The back door opened and Jeff came in looking like something from a minstrel show. He said, "It's all OK, honey, the fire's in the burn and it's fixin' to rain in about ten minutes. Better start slicin' ham and fryin' eggs and boilin' coffee—there's an awful hungry mob on the way up."

I rushed and untied the heifer and led her back to her stall. The smoke was so thick it was like a heavy fog but there was a cool wet feeling in the air.

I fried eggs and ham and bacon and made toast and coffee until five the next morning. I also listened to the details of that and every other fire on the coast, since the days of the first settlers. Paw Kettle and the boys were very much in evidence, behaving like heroes instead of the guilty perpetrators of the disaster, and with the camaraderie produced by success and my keg of whiskey every one else adopted the same attitude, getting Paw to tell over and over when he first smelled smoke, what he did, if he lost any livestock, and so forth. I was very grateful when Paw at last brought the gathering to an abrupt close by pointing out that in the early days when a farmer needed a new barn all of his friends and neighbors got together and helped him build it. Being Paw, he couldn't let it go at that—he had to add, "And I heard tell that eath NEIGHBOR WOULD BRING thomething—thay, one would bring nailth—another the two by fourth, another THINGLE BOLTH . . ." Before he could finish this big lie, everyone but Bob and Jeff had eased out the door.

The next day it rained hard and all that remained of the fire was a hillside of glistening black stumps, occasional sharp cracks, wispy smoke and an acrid smell. Bob slept until noon, then arose groggily, gulped a cup of coffee and drove to Town to see about the lumber and millwork for an addition to the chicken house. He planned to brook twenty-five hundred baby chicks in the spring, which would give us, even with heavy culling of the old flock, two thousand laying hens the following fall. He also planned to buy a cow, scheduled to come fresh in March, one hundred baby turkeys and five young pigs. He was also going to see a farmer in the West Valley who had a light plant for sale.

Our future prospects were very good but my enthusiasm was at a low ebb. I was overtired by the fire and insufficient sleep and even the magic words "electric lights" couldn't dispel the gloom in my outlook. My life on the ranch had reached some sort of climax and it was the aftermath which worried me. We were just about to go into another long, dreary winter and I felt harried and uncertain as though I were boarding a steamer with no passport and no luggage. I was leaning on the drainboard of the sink, staring moodily out of the window at the driving rain and drooling eave troughs when a figure in a long billowing white dress and without a coat or hat came loping into the yard. My reactions were delayed that day, for I pensively watched while this odd person galloped through the rustic gate, her long dress flapping wetly at her legs, dashed over to the cherry tree, picked up a wooden duck of Anne's, cuddled it to her bosom and began dancing around and around the cherry tree. Suddenly I came to. Something was not right. The woman had a shorn head and was obviously crazy. This is all I need, I remember thinking frantically. This finishes it. I knew that there was not a lock on the house which would keep this woman out if she made up her mind she wanted to come in. I was so frightened that I was probably right on a mental plane with my visitor. All the blood had drained from my body with a rush, leaving me perfectly flaccid. I thought, I must lock the doors. That will give me time. I got to the kitchen door somehow and locked it. The kitchen door had one of those ridiculous locks which is a small black box with a tiny lever on the top; an angleworm could have forced it. My fumblings at the back door attracted the woman's attention and she came running across the yard crab fashion and peered in the kitchen window. Her eyes rolled in her head like marbles and she laughed wildly as she hurried from window to window playing peek-a-boo with me. I was leaning on the stove whimpering, "What *will* I do? What will I do?" when I remembered the open screenless window in the baby's room where she was taking a nap. I grabbed the stove lifter and started for the baby's room which was across the living room on the other side of the house. I couldn't hurry. I felt as if I were wading in water up to my waist. It took every ounce of strength I could muster to push one foot ahead of the other. When I finally reached the baby's room the woman was there already, her head and shoulders in the open window. I brandished the lifter, feebly croaking, "Get out of here. Go away!" She stopped rolling her eyes and laughing and looked at me. Her face crumpled; she looked as if she were going to cry. Then, slowly she retreated from the window, turned and went loping off down through the orchard toward the Kettles.

I watched until she had rounded the first bend in the road, then I sank weakly down on the bed and thought, Now I'm going to have hysterics. I'm going to explode just like a skyrocket. But the baby awoke then and, in the adorable way of babies, was overjoyed at seeing me and jabbered and held out her arms and that was that.

Bob came home an hour or so later and he had new magazines and cigarettes and candy and a truckload of lumber. He was bubbling over with ideas and plans for the ranch and so I waited until after supper to tell him about the crazy woman. I didn't even try to convey my terror because I knew by then that Bob and I were poles apart as far as emotions were concerned. I knew before I had finished the story what he would say and he said it. "Why didn't you get out a gun? Always remember that with a loaded gun in your hands you have the upper hand of anything." That was true for Bob but not for me. With a loaded gun in my hands the gun had the upper hand and besides, if you are the kind of person who grabs a stove lifter instead of a gun when danger is at hand, you are that kind of person and you have to face it.

After supper Bob and Anne and I drove to the Kettles' to find out if they had seen the crazy woman. Mrs. Kettle was not at all perturbed. She said, "Oh, she was in here this afternoon. She's the loony sister of a woman down in the West Valley. Mostly she is shut up in a institute but whenever they can save the money, they have her over for a visit. She won't hurt nobody—she's just loony."

"Where is she now?" Bob asked.

"Why, she's down at the Larsens' farm," Mrs. Kettle said. "They phoned for the sheriff and he'll probably send her back to the institute."

I thought, That valley woman must be even more isolated than I, if she's that desperate for companionship.

The next morning the storm had increased in tempo and there were pools on the floor beneath the open windows and the rain had oozed under the doors during the night. The baby's washing festooned the kitchen once more and Stove had his back up and refused to digest the fuel and became constipated with ashes. Swathed in oilskins Bob began work on the new chicken house. After I had finished the lunch dishes and put the baby down for her nap, I donned my rain clothes and went out to help him. I peeled stringers and measured two by fours. I ran and got the hammer, the saw, the level, the rule. I was more skilled than last year but I had lost all of my drive. Bob said, "Would you like to start splitting the shakes for the roof?" I loved to split shakes and ordinarily I would have been enthusiastic but all I could manage then, was a weary, "All right."

At dinner Bob shattered all precedent by suggesting that we drive to Town to a movie. He said he had asked Max Jefferson to stay with the baby, so we hurried with the dinner dishes and the chores, dressed, stoked the fire and then sat down to wait. When fifteen minutes had elapsed, we realized that we would have to see the second feature anyway, so took off our coats and Bob lit us each a cigarette. We sat and smoked and were self-conscious with each other. Bob studied the burnt end of the match he had used for our cigarettes, turning it around slowly in his lean brown fingers. I watched him and the clock ticked off the minutes. "Do you think he's coming?" I asked at last. "Oh, he'll be along," Bob said, not looking at me. I thought, Heavens, we act like neighbors who suddenly find themselves in a hotel bedroom together. The clock ticked on. Bob said, "Did you order those hinges?" I said, "Oh, I forgot," and jumped up guiltily and started for the cupboard where we kept the catalogs. Bob said, "Don't bother now," and got up and put his cigarette in the stove. I came back and sat down. Bob was poking aimlessly at the fire, his back still toward me. I lit another cigarette and reflected, Husband and wife teamwork is just fine except when it reaches a point where the husband is more conscious of the weight his wife's shoulder carries than of the shoulder itself. I said, "I don't think that Jeff is coming."

Bob said, "I guess not," and sat down and lit another cigarette. The clock ticked on and after a while we went to bed.

PART II

8

"Going Home, Going Home"

WHEN I MARRIED and went to live in the mountains on a chicken ranch, my sister Mary plunged headfirst into a business career, which eventually resulted in her being fired from every firm of any size in the city of Seattle.

Mary's being fired was never a reflection on her efficiency, which was overwhelming, but was always a matter of principle, usually involving the morale of the entire firm.

"Labor Day is a National Holiday and I'm an American citizen and won't work if you call in the Militia," Mary announced to the front office of a legal firm whose senior partner was anti-labor and got even with the A.F. of L. by making all his employees work on Labor Day.

"Go pinch somebody who can't type," she told a surprised and amorous lumber exporter.

"If you want to say 'he don't' and 'we was,' that's your affair," Mary told a pompous manufacturer, "but I won't put it in your letters because it reflects on me."

Even though Mary's jobs didn't last long, she never had any trouble getting new ones. All the employment agency people loved her and she enjoyed applying for new jobs.

"There are only two ways to apply for a job," she said. "Either you are a Kick-Me-Charlie and go crawling in anxious for long hours and low pay, or you march into your prospective employer with a Look-Who's-Hit-the-Jackpot attitude and for a while, at least, you have both the job and your self-respect." Anyone could see that all Kick-Me-Charlies kept their jobs the longest but they didn't have as much self-respect or meet as many people as Mary.

While Mary changed jobs and met people, I raised chickens, had two children and didn't meet anybody. Finally in March, 1931, after four years of this, I wrote to my family and told them that I hated chickens, I was lonely and I seemed to have married the wrong man.

It was the beginning of the depression and I didn't really expect anything but sympathy, but Mary, who was supporting the entire family, replied in typically dependable and dramatic fashion by special delivery registered letter that she had a wonderful job for me and that I was to come home at once. I wrote back that I didn't know how to do office work and it was five miles to the bus line. Mary wired back, "Anybody can do office work and remember the White Russians walked across Siberia. Your job starts Monday."

It was late on a rainy Friday afternoon when a neighbor brought the telegram but I checked the bus schedule, dressed the children and myself in our "town clothes," stuffed my silver fish fork, my graduation ring and a few other things into a suitcase, wrote a note to my husband, and leading three-year-old Anne by the hand and carrying year-and-a-half-old Joan and the suitcase, set off across the burn toward the six o'clock bus to Seattle.

It was not an easy walk. The road, following the course of an ancient river bed, meandered around through the sopping brush, coiled itself around huge puddles and never ever took the shortest distance between two points. When we made sorties into the brush to avoid the puddles, the salal and Oregon grape drenched our feet and clawed vindictively at my one pair of silk stockings. Every couple of hundred feet I had to stop and unclamp my purple hands from the suitcase handle and shift the baby to the other hip. Every half mile or so we all sat down on a soaking stump or log to rest. The rain was persistent and penetrating, and after the third rest all of our clothes had the uniform dampness of an ironing folded down the night before.

The children were cheerful and didn't seem to mind the discomforts—I was as one possessed. I was leaving the dreary monotony of the rain and the all-encompassing loneliness of the farm to go home to the warmth and laughter of my family and now that I was started I would have carried both children and the suitcase, forded raging torrents and run that last never-ending mile with a White Russian on each shoulder.

Just before we got to the highway, the road had been taken over by some stray cows and a big Jersey bull. Under ordinary circumstances this would have meant climbing a fence and going half a mile or so out of our way, because I am scared to death of bulls, especially Jersey bulls. Not that day. "Get out of my way!" I shouted at the surprised bull and small Anne, brandishing a twig, echoed me. The bull, sulkily grumbling and shaking his head, moved to one side. If he hadn't I think I would have punched him in the nose.

When we finally reached the highway, I sat the children on the suitcase and listened anxiously for the first rumble of the bus. I knew that I would have to depend on hearing it because the highways had been braided through the thick green tresses of the Olympic Peninsula by some lethargic engineer who apparently thought that everyone enjoyed bounding in and out of forests, dipping down into farmyards and skirting small rocks and hillocks with blind hairpin turns, and at the intersection where I hoped to catch the bus, and catch was certainly the right word, the bus would be visible only for that brief moment when, having leaped out of Mr. Hansen's farmyard by means of a short steep rise, it skirted his oat field before disappearing around a big rock just beyond his south fence.

I knew that I had to be ready to signal the driver just as he appeared over the brow of the Hansens' barnyard and in my eagerness, I flagged down two empty homeward-bound logging trucks and the feed man before I heard the bus. When its gray snubbed nose peered over the hill, I rushed out into the road and waved my purse but the driver saw me too late and for one terrible sickening instant I thought he was going on and leave us to walk back up the mountains in the rain. But he screeched to a stop and waited at the big rock and I grabbed the suitcase and the children and ran down the road, and then we were aboard, in a front seat where I could urge the bus along and be ready for the city when it burst upon me with its glory of people and life.

The bus driver was not at all friendly, due no doubt to a large angry-looking boil on the back of his neck, the bus smelled of wet dogs and wet rubber, there were two drunken Indians in the seat across from us and a disgusting old man in back of us who cleared his throat and spat on the floor, but everything was bathed in the glow of my anticipation and I smiled happily at everyone.

Down the mountains, through valleys, up into the mountains again we sped. We were going very fast and the bus lurched and swayed and belched Diesel fumes but we were heading toward home. I was going to live again.

"Going home, going home," I hummed to myself as the bus nosed its way along in the thin early evening traffic, its tires saying shhhhh, shhh to the nervous wet highway, its lights making deep hollows and sudden mounds out of shadows on the smooth pavement. We went slowly and carefully through the little town by the ferry landing, then for miles and miles the road was dark with only an occasional lonely little house peering out of the night, and we sailed swiftly along.

Both children were now asleep, their bodies warm and soft like dough against me, and I must have dozed too, for suddenly we were in downtown Seattle and lights were exploding around me like skyrockets on the Fourth of July. Red lights, blue lights, yellow lights, green, purple, white, orange, punctured the night in a million places and tore the black satin pavement to shreds. I hadn't seen neon lights before. They had been invented, or at least put in common use, while I was up in the mountains and in that short time the whole aspect of the world had changed. In place of dumpy little bulbs sputteringly spelling out Café or Theater, there were long swooping spirals of pure brilliant color. A waiter outlined in bright red with a blazing white napkin over his arm flashed on and off over a large café. Puget Sound Power and Light Company cut through the rain and darkness, bright blue and cheery. Cafés, theaters, cigar stores, stationery stores, real estate offices with their names spelled out in molten color, welcomed me to the city. The bus terminal was ringed in light. Portland, New

York, San Francisco, Bellingham, Walla Walla, it boasted in bright red. How gay and cheerful and prosperous and alive everything looked. What a wonderful contrast to the bleak, snag-ridden, dark, rainy, lonely vista framed for four long years by the farm windows.

The children had awakened and their glazed, sleepy eyes reflected the lights as they flashed by. Then the faces of Mary and Dede appeared right outside our windows and that was the brightest rocket of all, the *pièce de résistance* of the entire show.

According to real estate standards Mother's eight-room brown-shingled house in the University district was just a modest dwelling in a respectable neighborhood, near good schools and adequate for an ordinary family. To me that night, and always, that shabby house with its broad welcoming porch, dark woodwork, cluttered dining-room plate rail, large fragrant kitchen, easy book-filled firelit living room, four elastic bedrooms—one of them always ice cold—roomy old-fashioned bathrooms and huge cluttered basement, represents the ultimate in charm, warmth and luxury. It's something about Mother, who with one folding chair and a plumber's candle, could make the North Pole homey, and it's something about the warmth and loyalty and laughter of a big family.

It's a wonderful thing to know that you can come home anytime from anywhere and just open the door and belong. That everybody will shift until you fit and that from that day on it's a matter of sharing everything. When you share your money, your clothes and your food with a mother, a brother and three sisters, your portion may be meager but by the same token when you share unhappiness, loneliness and anxiety about the future with a mother, a brother and three sisters, there isn't much left for you.

Two things I noticed immediately. Mother still smelled like violets and Mary still believed that accomplishment was merely a matter of will power.

"I hear that we are sliding into a depression and that jobs are very hard to find," I told Mary about three o'clock the next morning as she and Mother and I sat in the breakfast nook eating hot cinnamon toast and drinking coffee.

Mary said, "There are plenty of jobs but the trouble with most people, and I know because I'm always getting jobs for my friends, is that they stay home with the covers pulled up over their heads waiting for some employer to come creeping in looking for them. Anyway, what are you worrying about, you've got a job as private secretary to a mining engineer."

I said, "But, Mary, I don't know shorthand and I can only type about twenty words a minute." Mary clunked her coffee cup into her saucer and looked directly at me with flashing amber eyes. "Leave the ninety words on the typewriter and the one hundred fifty words a minute in shorthand to the grubs who like that kind of work," she said. "You're lucky. You have a brain. Use it! Act like an executive and you get treated like an executive!" (And usually fired, she neglected to add.)

It was very reassuring, in spite of a sneaking suspicion I had that if put to a test I would always prove to be the grub type, not the executive, and that only by becoming so proficient in shorthand that I could take down thoughts, would I be able to hold down even a very ordinary job.

"I have been planning to go to night school," I told Mary.

"Not necessary at all," she said. "Experience and self-confidence are what you need and you'll never find them at night school. Have you ever taken a look at what goes to night school? No? Well, they aren't executives, I'll tell you that. Now go to bed and forget about shorthand. I'll always be able to find us jobs doing something and whatever it is I'll show you how to do it." That was Mary's slogan at home. Downtown it was, "Just show me the job and I'll produce a sister to do it." And for some years, until Dede and Alison were old enough to work and she had figured how to fit Mother into her program, I was it.

From two o'clock Saturday afternoon until two o'clock Monday morning, the house was filled with people. Mary, who was very popular, was being intellectual so her friends were mostly musicians, composers, writers, painters, readers of hard dull books, and pansies. They took the front off the piano and played on the strings, they sat on the floor and read aloud the poems of Baudelaire, John Donne and Rupert Brooke, they put loud symphonies on the record player and talked over them, they discussed politics and the state of the world, they all called Mother "Sydney" and tried in vain to convince her that she was prostituting her mind by reading the *Saturday Evening Post*. Mother said, "Yes?" and ignored them.

One of Mary's favorite friends, a beautiful brilliant Jewish boy, played "With a Song in My Heart," on the strings of the piano and told me I had a face like a cameo and I grew giddy with excitement. Anne and Joan loved the laughter and the people too, and Saturday night when I was putting them to bed, Anne said, "Oh, Betty, I just love this fambly!"

Sunday afternoon, Mary's new boss, a Mr. Chalmers, who was coming to Seattle to instill some new methods into the lumber industry, called from New Orleans and talked to Mary for almost an hour. The conversation left her overflowing with enthusiasm.

"At last I've found the perfect job," she said. "Mr. Chalmers is much more of an executive thinker than I am. 'Don't bother me with details and hire all the help you need,' he said. He also asked me to find him a bootlegger, one who handles Canadian liquor, put his daughters in school, send for his wife, introduce him to the right people, have his name put up at the best clubs, get him an appointment with a dentist to make him a new bridge, open charge accounts with the Yellow Cab Company, a florist, a stationery store, office furniture company and a catering service, and I'm to rent him a suite of offices in a building in the financial district."

We all listened to Mary with admiration and I asked her if in this new wonderful well-paid secretarial job, typing and shorthand had been requirements.

Before answering, Mary lit a cigarette, pulling her mouth down at one corner in true executive fashion, a new gesture, then said, "Betty, for God's sake stop brooding about shorthand. There were hundreds of applicants for this job, among them many little white-faced creeps who could take shorthand two hundred words a minute and could type so fast the carriage smoked, but who cares? Do they know a good bootlegger?" "Do you?" someone asked, and Mary said, "No, but I will by the time Chalmers gets here. To get back to shorthand, the world is crawling with people who can take down and transcribe somebody else's good ideas. We're lucky, we've got ideas of our own." It was certainly nice of her to say we.

Monday morning my hands trembled like Jello as I adjusted the neat white collar on the sage-green woolen office dress Mary had lent me. I was very thin, pale with fright, and with my long red hair parted in the middle and pulled tightly back into a knot on the nape of my neck, I thought I looked just like one of the white-faced creeps Mary had derisively described. Mary said I looked very efficient and very sophisticated. Mother, as always, said that we both looked beautiful and not to worry about a thing. I kissed the children, who didn't cling to me as I had expected, and started out the front door to catch a streetcar.

I had been anticipating just this moment over and over and over ever since I had gotten Mary's wire. I knew exactly how I would feel waiting on the corner with the other people who were going to work. Breathing the cool, wet spring air and listening to the busy morning sounds of cars starting with tight straining noises, of children calling to each other as they left for school, dogs barking and being called home, a nickel clickety-clacking into the paper box, footsteps hurrying grittily on cement. I was going to swing on a strap, sway with the streetcar and think about my wonderful new job. Life was as neatly folded and full of promise as the morning newspaper.

My reverie was interrupted by Mary, who called out, "Where are you going?" "To catch a streetcar," I said. "Come back," she said. "From now on we ride to work in taxis. Mr. Chalmers wants us to." "Not me," I said. "Only you." Mary said, "Betty, Mr. Chalmers couldn't have me for his private secretary if it weren't for you. Don't you forget that and I'll see that he doesn't. Now sit down and relax, I've called the cab." And that is the way we set off to inject our personalities and a few of our good ideas into the business world.

The mining engineer's office, where I was to work, was on the top floor of a building in the financial district. The other occupants of the building were successful lawyers, real estate men, brokers and lumbermen, most of whom Mary seemed to know quite well.

In the lobby she introduced me to about fifteen assorted men and women and explained that she had just brought me down out of the mountains to take her place as private secretary to Mr. Webster. In her enthusiasm she made it sound a little as though she had had to wing me to get me down out of the trees and I felt that I should have taken a few nuts and berries out of my pocket and nibbled on them just to keep in character.

When we got out of the elevator, I took Mary to task for this. "Listen, Mary," I said. "I have little enough self-confidence, and your introducing me to all those people in the lobby as the little Mowgli of the Pacific Coast didn't help any." Mary said, "You're just lucky I didn't ask you to show them some of your old arrow wounds. Anyway, what difference does it make? Most of those people have such dull lives I feel it my duty to tell them a few lies every morning just to cheer them up."

Mr. Webster's offices were luxuriously furnished in mahogany and oriental rugs and had a magnificent view of the docks, Puget Sound, some islands and the Olympic Mountains. My little office was also the reception room and after Mary had showed me where to put my hat and coat and how to get the typewriter to spring up out of the desk, I wanted to sit right down and begin to practice my typing.

Mary would have none of it. Sitting herself down at Mr. Webster's desk and lighting a cigarette, she said, "Stop being so nervous and watch me. Learn how to act in an office." I said, "I wouldn't be so nervous if I knew what time Mr. Webster gets here." Mary said, "Oh, he's out of town and won't be back for two weeks." My sigh of relief almost blew some rocks off his desk. "Does he know about me?" I asked. "Nope," said Mary, opening the mail, glancing at it and throwing most of it in the wastebasket. "You're going to be a surprise."

The phone rang. Mary answered it in a low well-modulated voice and Standard English. "Mr. Websteh's office, Miss Bahd speaking," she said. Somebody on the other end of the wire said something and Mary said, "Well, you big stinker, what do you expect when you don't call until eight-thirty Saturday night?"

While she talked to the big stinker, who she later said could take her to lunch, I roamed around the office, examining the files, looking into drawers, opening cupboards, unrolling maps, reading the titles of some of the books in the enormous mining library and looking at the view.

When someone came into the reception room, Mary, still on the phone, waved to me imperiously to see who it was. It was a large fat man who held up a little canvas bag and shouted, "Where's Webster?" I said, "Mr. Webster is out of town, may I help you?" The fat man said, "Sister, I got the richest placer property the world has ever seen!" He went on and on and on about available water, smelter reports, equipment needs, etc., and finally handing me the little bag and a business card said, "Just give this sample of ore to Webster and tell him to call me the minute he gets in town," and left.

I waited until Mary had finished three more telephone calls, one to the manager of a building across the street, demanding a suite of offices with a good view, one to a florist giving a standing order for daily fresh flowers for the new office, the other to an office supply firm for *two* executive's desks, largest size, and then I gave her the business card and the ore sample.

"The man said that this is the greatest placer property the world has ever seen," I said excitedly. "Do you suppose we should telegraph Mr. Webster?" Mary glanced at the card and with a bored look dropped both it and the sample of ore into the wastebasket.

"Mary Bard," I said, "what are you doing?" She said, "I'm doing just what Mr. Webster would have done. In other words I'm saving him trouble, which is the first duty of a good private secretary. Now I'm going to pound a few facts into that humble little head of yours. In the first place you have *two* of the *greatest assets* a mining engineer's secretary could possibly have. A, your father was a mining engineer; B, you have seen a mine and when Webster talks about an assay you don't think he's referring to a literary composition. The rest is all a matter of common sense and practice. Here's the telephone number of the smelter, here's Webster's address. Open and read all the mail and keep a record of all telephone calls."

"What about visitors like the fat man?" I asked. Mary said, "For a while you can keep all that trash and show it to Webster, after you get more used to things you'll be able to tell the crackpots from the real mining men. Or at least you can pretend you can," she added honestly.

"What about the home office," I said. "They're one of the richest corporations in the world. How will they feel about me?" "They'll never know about you," said Mary. "We're both Miss Bard and to the richest corporation in the world, a Miss Bard more or less at one hundred dollars a month in the Seattle office isn't that much." She snapped her fingers and we went out for coffee.

In spite of Mary's vehement and reiterated assurance that I possessed the *two greatest assets* the secretary of a mining engineer could possibly have, I had an uneasy feeling that Webster's reaction to a secretary who could neither type nor take shorthand, might be that of a hungry man who day after day opens his lunchbox and finds it empty.

So, with feverish intensity, I tried to remedy the situation. I practiced my typing, I studied shorthand, I memorized the number of spaces to indent on a letter, I tried to remember which was the right side of the carbon paper and I prayed that Mr. Webster would begin every letter with weareinreceiptofyoursofthe, the way all John Robert Gregg's business friends did.

Mary said it was all a waste of time. She told me to read some of the geology books, to study the maps, to thumb through the files and to try and get the feeling of mining. I suggested that I might buy a miner's lamp and wear it in the office and she said it would go further with Mr. Webster than that scared look I put on every time I opened the office door.

I couldn't help the scared look, I felt like an impostor, and as the days succeeded each other and the return of Mr. Webster grew more and more imminent, every morning when I took out my key and inserted it in the lock of the door marked menacingly

CHARLES WEBSTER, MINING ENGINEER, I drew a deep quivering breath and prayed that Mr. Webster's office would be empty.

Then one morning when I opened the office door there in Mr. Webster's office, sitting at Mr. Webster's big mahogany desk was Mr. Webster. I almost fainted. Mr. Webster had very brown skin and nice bright blue eyes and he called out, "Who are you?" So scared I had tears in my eyes, I said, "Well, ah, well, ah, I'm Mary's sister Betty and I'm your new secretary." He said, "Where's Mary?" "Oh, she's in an office right across the street," I said, adding hurriedly, "She said that if you wanted to dictate to call her and she'd come right over." He said, "This all sounds very much like Mary. Well, as long as she's deserted me she doesn't deserve the present I've brought her. Here," and he handed me a huge green barley sugar Scottie dog.

I took the dog and because I was nervous and felt guilty, I was too effusive in my thanks and kept saying over and over and over, "Oh, Mr. Webster, you shouldn't have done it!" as though he were trying to force a diamond anklet on me. Then, God knows why, but in an effort to offer further proof of my gratitude, I bit into the candy dog and one whole enormous green leg came off in my mouth just as Mr. Webster, who by this time was sick to death of me and obviously trying to think of some kind way to get rid of me, looked up to ask if there had been any mail or calls. I couldn't answer, I just stood there in my hat and coat, trying desperately to maneuver the huge leg around in my mouth, my eyes full of tears and green drool running down my chin. It was not a sight to inspire confidence in my efficiency. In fact, if I had been Mr. Webster I wouldn't have kept me if I'd been able to produce degrees in shorthand, typing, mining, geology and map drawing, but Mr. Webster was very kind and had been a good friend of Daddy's so he went over and looked out the windows at the mountains while I pulled myself together.

As I look back on it now, it would have been cheaper and less of a strain for Mr. Webster to have dispensed with me and hired a cleaning woman, because, eager though I was to help, all I could do well was to dust the furniture and his ore samples and clean out cupboards. I typed a few letters but I was so nervous that I made terrible mistakes, used reams of paper and the finished product usually had little holes in it where my eraser had bitten too deeply.

Mr. Webster, upset by the holes in his letters but not wanting to hurt my feelings, said I was much too thin and ordered a quart of milk to be delivered to the office every morning and at ten and three came out and stood over me while I drank a glass. This embarrassed me so I gulped the milk down in huge glurping swallows, which brought on terrible gas pains and several times made me belch loudly into the telephone when I was following Mary's instructions and trying to use Standard English.

The first day Mr. Webster was back he took Mary and me to lunch at a small French restaurant in an alley. While we ate goslings en casserole and drank Chablis, Mary told him that he had nothing to worry about because she had figured out everything. Whenever he wanted to dictate he was to tell me and I would call her on the phone and while she took his dictation I would go over and answer her phone. To my intense relief Mr. Webster laughed and said that he thought it was a wonderful scheme, and it did work out very well until Mary's very demanding boss arrived in town and it became harder and harder for her to get away.

Then Mr. Webster suggested that I take his easier dictation and I did and one morning when I had written "dead sir" and "Kinkly yours" on a letter, he offered to send me to night school to learn shorthand and typing. I told him that I would like to go but I didn't think that Mary would approve and he said, "Betty, my dear girl, you and Mary are entirely different personalities and anyway she is a whizz in both shorthand and typing."

So, I went to night school, which Mr. Webster paid for at the rate of fifteen dollars a month, and studied shorthand and typing. My shorthand teacher, a small sandy man with a nasal voice and thin yellow lips, seemed to be an excellent shorthand teacher because at the end of three months everyone in the class but me could take down and transcribe business letters and little stories.

I couldn't learn shorthand. I got *p*'s and *b*'s mixed up, I couldn't tell *m* from *n* and even when I could write it I couldn't read it back. I didn't have too much trouble with Mr. Webster's letters because he dictated very slowly and I knew what he was talking about but I was such a miserable failure at night school that the only thing that kept me from shooting myself was the amazing fact that, although everyone in the class, and there were forty-two of them, was an expert typist and shorthand dynamo, I was the only one with a job. When I told Mary, she said, "Naturally. I told you you wouldn't find any executives at night school."

I never did get to feel like an executive and I never did conquer my obsession that there was a mysterious key to office work which, like holding a letter written in lemon juice over a candle, would one day be revealed to me all at once; but by the end of June I had stopped getting tears in my eyes when Mr. Webster called me for dictation; the letters I typed had fewer, smaller holes in them, I occasionally got the right side of the carbon paper so the copy was on onion skin instead of inside out on the back of the original letter; I could sometimes find things in the files and I had almost finished the maps.

The maps and the files were the worst things I did to dear, kind Mr. Webster. I never was able to figure out the filing system; why letters were sometimes filed by the name of the man who wrote them, sometimes by the name of a mine, sometimes in a little black folder marked *Urgent* and sometimes in a drawer marked *Hold*.

Of course, if I'd stopped batting around the office like a moth around a nightlight, had read the correspondence and asked a few intelligent questions, I might have learned the secret of the filing system, but I didn't. I operated on the theory that always hurrying wildly, never asking questions and shutting up Mr. Webster with "I know, I know," any time he tried to volunteer any information, were proof of great efficiency on my part. Because of this unfortunate state of affairs, Mr. Webster is still looking for things.

I'd pick up a letter, notice that the letterhead was Fulton Mining Company, or that it was signed by a man named Thompson, so eeny, meeny, miney, mo—it would go either in *F* or *T*. Then Mr. Webster would ask for that letter on the Beede Mine and I would look under *B*, under *Urgent*, under *Hold*, under *M*, under my desk, under his, and finally days later, quite by accident, would find it under T or F because the Fulton Mining letter, written by Thompson, was *about* the Beede Mine.

It is hard now for me to believe that I was that stupid, but I was, and it was easy for me. Take the matter of the maps.

One rainy, dull morning, when Mr. Webster was away on a short trip and I was flitting around the office, I happened to bump into the map case. Now there was a messy thing. Thousands of maps all rolled sloppily and stuffed in the case every which way.

"How does poor dear Mr. Webster ever find anything?" I said, opening the glass door and settling myself for a good thorough cleaning job. Now, a mining engineer's maps, like an architect's drawings or a surgeon's living patients, are the visual proof that he did graduate from college, has examined the property and does know what he is doing.

"Here is the ore deposit," Mr. Webster would say, spreading out his maps and indicating little specks. "By tunneling through this mountain, changing the course of this river, bringing a railroad in here and putting a smelter here . . ."

So, I unrolled all the maps, cleaned the smudges off them with an artgum eraser, and rolled them all up again, each one separately and each one with an elastic band around it. Then I sorted them according to size, the littlest ones on the top shelf, the medium-sized ones on the next shelf, the biggest one on the bottom. I was very tired and dirty when I finished but I glowed with accomplishment.

That night at dinner I told Mary about my wonderful progress at Mr. Webster's; how I took dictation, found things in the files and had even sorted his maps. Mary said, "I told you mining was easy."

Then Mr. Webster returned from his trip, accompanied by an important man from Johannesburg, South Africa, and for the first time since I had been working there, asked me to find him some maps. "Get me those maps on the Connor mine," he said and I jogged happily over to the map case but when I got there I realized that with my new filing system, it wasn't the name of the map that counted but the size.

I called to Mr. Webster, "What size is the Connor map?"

He answered rather testily, "What do you mean, 'what size'? It's that big bundle near the front on the bottom shelf."

My spirits fell with a thud that rattled the glass doors of the map case as I suddenly realized that the big bundle near the front on the bottom shelf was now about twenty-five bundles on all the shelves. So Mr. Webster, who had heretofore always filed the maps and knew exactly where each one had been, the man from Johannesburg and I spent the rest of the day on the floor by the map case unrolling maps. We had found most of the Conner mine by eight-thirty and I was released.

The next morning there was a note on my desk. "Betty: Have gone to Denver, will be back Monday—please return maps to their original confusion—Webster." Before I finished, however, the home office closed the Seattle office and mining was over.

"You thought you couldn't learn mining," Mary told me when she installed me as her assistant in the office across the street. "There's nothing to lumber, it's just a matter of being able to divide everything by twelve."

"What about Mr. Chalmers?" I asked. "Does he know you've hired me?"

"He knows that I've hired an extremely intelligent young lady who has spent the last four years practically living in logging camps in the greatest stand of timber in the United States and anyway what's it to him? You're my assistant. Go sharpen this pencil."

I was worried. I hadn't yet met Mr. Chalmers and, though I knew that he didn't want to be bothered with details, I had no assurance that he would consider Mary's new assistant at $125 a month, a detail; especially when he learned that in Seattle most female office workers were paid from seven to twenty dollars a week and $125 a month was considered a *man's* salary, except in a few rare instances where a woman with years of experience showed terrific and unusual efficiency.

I was quite sure that as soon as Mr. Chalmers found out about me he would fire me, but what worried me more was a fear that he would also fire Mary for having hired me. Of course, I was reck-

"*Going Home, Going Home*" 119

oning without Mary or Mr. Chalmers. Mr. Chalmers was not a figment of Mary's imagination, but was a real, unique individual whose sole aim actually was to be the biggest-time executive that had ever hit Seattle, no matter what it cost the lumbermen, and in Mary he had certainly chosen the right person to help him.

About ten-thirty Mr. Chalmers made his entrance into, or rather descent upon, the office. The door to the outer office crashed open and banged shut; the door to the conference room crashed open and banged shut; the door to his private office crashed open and banged shut; then the buzzer on Mary's desk began to buzz with short angry bursts like a bee in a tin can. I flinched nervously at each slamming door and jumped to my feet at the first ring of the buzzer.

Mary, who was checking some lumber reports, didn't even look up. The angry buzzing continued. Finally, anxiously I asked, "Do you want me to see what he wants?" Mary said, "I already know what the old stinker wants. He wants somebody to yell at because he is nasty in the morning. Come on, let's get a cup of coffee. He'll be pleasanter when we get back."

She picked up the phone, pressed a bell at the side of the desk and said, "Mr. Chalmers, I'm going out for coffee, will you please take any calls?" There was a roar from the inner office and the phone sputtered like water on a hot stove, but Mary put it back on the hook, beckoned to me and we skittered out of the office and down the stairs to the next floor to wait for the elevator. While we waited we could hear via the elevator shaft and the stairwell, Mr. Chalmers charging around on the floor above, slamming doors and bellowing, "Miss Bard! Miss BARD!"

I certainly did not look forward to meeting him and couldn't understand how Mary could laugh and talk and eat a butterhorn in the coffee shop while that monster waited for her upstairs. She said not to worry, he would be cooled off by the time we got back, and he was.

Mary dragged me, quivering, in to introduce me, and Mr. Chalmers, looking like a hair seal with a cigar in its mouth, smiled at me kindly and said, "Humph!" For the next two or three days he buzzed for me (my signal was two short) to get him drinks of water, to open and close the windows, to pick up scraps of paper off the floor, to lower the Venetian blinds four inches and to unlock the safe and get him his whiskey. Once he asked me some questions about logging on the Olympic Peninsula and when I was able to answer he seemed terribly pleased and retaliated with stories of logging in the cypress swamps.

I still don't know exactly what Mr. Chalmers was doing or what the office was for but it was a very pleasant place to work. When I wasn't answering the buzzer and ministering to the many little personal needs of Mr. Chalmers, I was in the outer office typing reports for Mary, learning to cut stencils, running the mimeograph or working on a story we were writing, called "Sandra Surrenders."

Then one day Mr. Chalmers buzzed for me and when I came eagerly in, dustcloth in hand, instead of ordering me to kill a fly or empty the ash trays, he announced that starting the next morning, I was to spend all my time in the Seattle Public Library reading everything that had been written on the Sherman Anti-Trust Act.

He didn't tell me what he had in mind and I was too timid to ask him, so I asked Mary. She wrinkled her forehead in a puzzled way and said, "It sounds as if I might have told him that you had studied law. Oh, well, don't worry about it, you've got as good a brain as he has, which isn't saying much for you. Go on up and read everything you can find, take notes and write a report. He'll never look at it but he'll be very pleased at your industry."

So, for the next week or two, feeling as though I were still in college trying for straight A's, I dutifully spent my days in the library reading and taking notes and when I handed Mr. Chalmers an original and two copies of the voluminous report, he, obviously having forgotten who I was or what I was doing, glanced at it and put it in the bottom drawer of his desk then gave me a long lecture on Pitman shorthand, which he wrote and I didn't.

A week after the Sherman Anti-Trust laws had been disposed of, Mr. Chalmers announced one morning that from then on I was to read the *Wall Street Journal*, *The Banker's Digest* and a couple of other financial papers, pick out all items of importance and interest and relay them weekly, by means of an *interesting*, he

"Going Home, Going Home" 121

stressed this word vehemently, bulletin to all the lumbermen in the State of Washington. Friday I was to assemble my material, write it up and leave it on his desk for him to peruse and digest (and confuse and insert "point of fact" every other word); Saturday morning I was to cut the stencils, run them off on the mimeograph and assemble and mail the bulletin.

In actual fact, I read all the boring financial magazines, but I shook everything I had read up in a big bag and issued in my own words and well-seasoned with my own personal prejudices, a bulletin as to the state of the world's finances. I remember one bulletin that I headed, "War with Japan Inevitable!" I don't know where this dope got that dope.

Mr. Chalmers, who never took the trouble to read any of the magazines or to check my facts, used to make huge blue-pencil marks around single words and then quote Matthew Arnold and Emerson at me to prove that other words would more accurately convey the exact shade of meaning I had in mind. I was reasonably sure that none of the lumbermen read my dull bulletin and I was also reasonably sure that no one of them would come storming into the office and demand a showdown because I had said money instead of pelf, or Mammon or lucre, but I didn't dare argue with Mr. Chalmers, who was at his worst on Saturday morning.

In the meantime, or interim or interregnum, Mary took Mr. Chalmers' dictation, arranged bouquets of lovely out-of-season flowers for his desk and hers, ordered his whiskey from Joe the bootlegger and left me alone with him in the office more and more.

He would buzz for her and I would answer and he would roar, "Where's Mary?" and I would tell him that she was out paving the way for him to meet the right people and he would say, "Humph, well as long as you're here, lower that Venetian blind three and five-eighths inches, empty this ash tray and fill my pen." When I had finished, he would say, "Betty, did I ever tell you about the time I organized the lumber industry in Louisiana?" and I would say no and he would say, "Sit down," and I would and hours later when Mary returned, he would be pouring little drinks of bourbon and tap water and I would be listening to Volume XVII, Chapter

32 of *Mr. Chalmers Is Smarter Than Anyone in the World, Living or Dead*. Lumber was a lot of fun.

Occasionally Mr. Chalmers became mildly irritated at Mary and me and threatened to tear us apart, tendon by tendon. One such outburst was precipitated by his being unusually unreasonable and hateful all week long, then leaving for Chicago by plane without his teeth, which he had carelessly left at his club. "Go to Athletic Club and airmail me bridge," he wired Mary. "You can starve to death, you disagreeable old bastard," said Mary, throwing the telegram in the wastebasket. "Mary, send bridge or you are fired!" was the next wire. Mary crumpled it up and threw it out the window. "Am calling tonight," was the next wire so Mary airmailed his teeth that afternoon and when he called that evening she was like honey and told him that she had mailed his teeth the minute she had gotten his first wire and she did hope he was chewing and having a good time.

The very closest we came to being fired was on the occasion of Mr. Chalmers' visit to New Orleans and arrival back at the office a week ahead of schedule. It was a very hot summer afternoon and Mary and I, who had received a rather unexpected invitation to dine on board a battleship, were in Mr. Chalmers' private office freshening up. We had removed and washed out our underwear and stockings and pinned them to the Venetian blinds to dry. We had steamed out the wrinkles in our silk print office dresses by holding them over Mr. Chalmers' basin while we ran the hot water full force, and had hung them on hangers on the Venetian blinds.

We had washed and pinned up our hair and finally in bare feet and petticoats were taking refreshing sponge baths in Mr. Chalmers' basin, when there were knocks on the outer door, which we had locked. Mary called through the transom, "Mr. Chalmers is in conference—who is it?" It was a telegram so she told the boy to put it through the mail slot. A little later, Mr. Chalmers' lawyer knocked and she told him that she had torn her dress and was in her petticoat mending it and he laughed and said that he had some papers for Chalmers but she could get them in the morning.

"Everything is just working out perfectly," we exulted as we felt our underwear and stockings, which were almost dry, and I ran the water for my bath. Suddenly there was a loud pounding at the outer door. "Shall I call through the transom?" I asked, taking my right foot out of the basin full of warm suds. "No," Mary said, "it's almost five. We'll pretend we've gone home." But the knocking continued, getting louder and louder and even sounding, to my sensitive ears, as if it might be accompanied by hoarse shouts. "Maybe I'd better put on my coat and see who it is," I said nervously. "I wouldn't if I were you," Mary said, "it might be some out-of-town lumberman who has read your financial bulletin." We both laughed gaily but I was very relieved when the knocking finally stopped.

Mary was patting eau de Cologne on her neck and shoulders and I was drying my left thigh on the last of Mr. Chalmers' hand towels, when I thought I heard the outer-office door open and voices. "Did you hear the door open?" I asked Mary. "No," she said.

I heard voices again and this time they sounded as if they were coming from the conference room. "Mary," I said, "do you hear anything?" Spreading her makeup out on Mr. Chalmers' desk, she said, "Stop being so nervous! You know we're going to a lot of trouble considering the fact that all the Navy men I've ever met were liars, short and married." We both laughed.

Just then the door of Mr. Chalmers' office opened and in charged Mr. Chalmers like a bull from a chute at the rodeo. His face was pomegranate-colored, his cigar hung from his lips like brown fringe, and his voice was a hoarse croak as he roared, "Who locked the door? What in hell's going on here?"

Behind him stood the building office manager, swinging some keys and looking embarrassed. Mary, sitting at Mr. Chalmers' desk in petticoat and pin curls with all her makeup spread out on his blotter and her pocket mirror propped against his inkstand, said quite calmly, "You're not supposed to be here."

Mr. Chalmers dropped his briefcase and his suitcase and yelled hoarsely, "I'm not supposed to be here? What in hell's going on?"

Mary said, "You said you weren't coming back until next week."

Chalmers said, "I wired you this morning."

Mary said, "I didn't get it."

He said, "Of course you didn't. I found it unopened under the door. Here," and he threw the telegram at her. "Now clean up this Goddamn Chinese laundry and get out! You're fired!" He tripped over his briefcase, kicked it and slammed through the door.

Mary and I finished dressing, wiped up the spilled bathwater and eau de Cologne, lowered the Venetian blinds, put Mr. Chalmers' mail on his desk and prepared to leave. Perhaps because Mr. Chalmers was hot and tired and we looked so clean and fresh, he rescinded the order about firing and in gratitude we took him to dinner with us on board the battleship, where he had some excellent Scotch and sat next to the Executive Officer, who turned out to be a bigger "and then I said to Andrew Mellon" and "Otto Kahn said to me" than Mr. Chalmers.

By the end of six months, Mr. Chalmers' office force had been increased to include, besides Mary and me, a certified public accountant and a liaison man between Mr. Chalmers and the lumbermen. I was still killing Mr. Chalmers' flies and filling his fountain pen but I had to take dictation for the liaison man and so Mr. Chalmers was sending me to night school for fifteen dollars a month.

For reasons of pride I did not go back to the school Mr. Webster had sent me to, but chose one further uptown, nearer to my streetcar. My teacher, a nice motherly woman, grew exasperated with my inability to read my notes and made me read them back aloud in front of the whole class, night after dreary night.

I grew to dread night school and probably would have quit if it hadn't been for the woman who sat across from me. She worked for an insurance company, dressed in black crepe, musky perfumes and big hats and told me that every single good job in the city of Seattle required that the girl also sleep with her boss. "And they won't get me to do that for eighty dollars a month," she told me as she furiously practiced her shorthand. "But they might get me for a lot less!" I told myself, as I tried desperately to figure out whether I had written pupil, purple, purposeless, billious, blurb or babble.

The CPA and the liaison man were very nice but they kept Mary and me so busy we never did get to finish "Sandra Surrenders" and they insisted on taking sides in our fights so that they were seldom on speaking terms with each other and one or the other was always not on speaking terms with one or the other of us.

Mary and I had many violent fights, sometimes even slapping each other, but we made up instantly and it was most disconcerting to come back from lunch and find the fight of the morning still hovering around the office like stale smoke and the accountant and the liaison man wanting to take sides and talk about us, one to the other.

They thought I really meant it when I screamed at Mary, "It's no wonder you're an old maid, for twenty-five years you've always gotten your own way and you think you can boss everybody!" and Mary screamed back, "It's better to be twenty-five years old and unmarried than to shuffle through your old marriage licenses like a deck of cards," or "You haven't done a stroke of work in this office since I came—all you do is smoke and order me around like a slave," and "I will continue to order you around like a slave as long as you act like a slave, think like a slave and smell like a slave."

By the fall of 1932, the depression was very bad and we were sure that the lumbermen weren't going to put up with Mr. Chalmers much longer. Now I grew more and more conscious of the aimlessness and sadness of the people on the streets, of the Space for Rent signs, marking the sudden death of businesses, that had sprung up over the city like white crosses on a battlefield, and I lifted up myself each day timidly and with dread expecting to find the dark despairing mask of unemployment staring at me.

Mary was so unworried about it all that she took two hours for lunch, another hour or two for coffee, and when Mr. Chalmers finally took her to task, she told him that the interesting part of his job was over and she guessed she'd leave and sell advertising.

Then for a few terrible weeks, until one of the lumbermen sent over his girl, I had to stop dusting and filling pens and take Mr. Chalmers' volumes of dictation. He mumbled so and used so many enormous and obscure words that I could never read my notes and had to bring them home at night for Mary to transcribe. She was always able to read my shorthand but finally doing both our jobs must have palled for she told me that I should quit Chalmers and sell advertising. With great tact she said that red-haired people were not meant for dull office work and instead of bawling because I couldn't learn shorthand, why didn't I use some of my many other talents?

I said that considering that Mr. Chalmers had put up with me this long and had paid my way to night school, I thought I should stay until the end. And I did, in spite of Mr. Chalmers' telling me many times that the depression was all my fault, the direct result of inferior people like me wearing silk stockings and thinking they were as good as people like him.

One day my brother Cleve came in to take me to lunch and caught the tail end of one of these little talks. "The only way to get rid of the poor is to line them up against a wall and shoot them," said kind old Mr. Chalmers, chewing his cigar. "I feel the same way about sons of bitches like you," said my tall, handsome, red-haired brother smiling in the doorway. Chalmers went into his office and slammed the door shut. Cleve and I went to lunch.

Two days later, the office closed and its closing, like the death of an invalid who has hovered for long wearisome months at the brink of death, brought relief rather than sorrow. I cleaned out my desk, throwing away the accumulation of half-filled bottles of hand lotion, packages of personal belongings and went home. I never saw Mr. Chalmers again. I called his club and left word for him to call me but he didn't and when I called again I learned he had checked out and left no forwarding address.

Lumber was over.

9

Anybody Can Do Anything

FEBRUARY, 1933, was a terrible time to be out of a job.

The HELP WANTED—FEMALE section of the papers offered "Egg Candler—Piecework basis" and "Solicit Magazine Subscriptions at home." The employment agencies had very few jobs but were packed to overflowing with applicants—the overflow often sagging wearily against the walls clear around corners and down to the elevators.

Every day found a little better class of people selling apples on street corners and even tips about jobs from friends were embarrassingly unreliable, I learned when I applied for a supposedly excellent secretarial job and was coldly informed, to my horror, that they weren't quite ready to interview new applicants as the former secretary had only just jumped out the window.

Business colleges persisted in the attitude that getting a job was merely a matter of dressing neatly (which according to their posters meant wearing a small knot, a short lumpy blue suit and medium-heeled black oxfords), being able to write shorthand, even words like "onomatopoeia" and "psychotherapeutic," 150 words a minute, typewriting without errors or erasures, and not putting "he don't" or "I seen" in business letters.

Either they didn't know or were ashamed to mention to their students that in those days when any kind of labor was a glut on the market, an inexperienced girl, even one with a nice fresh diploma in switchboard, comptometer, mimeograph, dictaphone, calculator, adding machine, multigraph, business law, business English, business spelling, shorthand, typewriting and arm movement handwriting, could seldom get an interview, especially in those low-heeled black oxfords.

I never did learn to enjoy applying for jobs like Mary did, and I never conquered my fear of employment managers, whose intent glances and prodding questions could crush my ego like an eggshell and expose a quivering and most unemployable me—I even hated the smell of employment offices—the hot, varnishy, old-lunch-baggy, desperate smell—"but at least," I told myself after Mr. Chalmers' office closed, "now I've got experience." I was a private secretary of almost two years' duration and could lower a blind or kill a fly with the best of them.

So I made the rounds of the employment agencies. Mary said, "Remember, tell them you can do anything, and in any language and check *all* the machines."

At the first employment agency I heard the woman at the desk turn down about twenty applicants because of lack of experience. "Sorry, kids," she said, "but these days you gotta have experience."

Instinctively I brightened. But when it came to my turn to be interviewed, the woman glanced at my card, on which I had checked typewriting, shorthand, filing, stencil cutting, legal forms, dictaphone, calculator, switchboard, addressograph, adding machine, multigraph and bookkeeping, in spite of never having seen most of the machines, and said sadly, "Too old."

"Too old!" I said in amazement. "I'm only twenty-four."

"Sorry," she said. "For general office work, most firms want girls around eighteen."

At the next place I didn't check quite so many machines and the woman offered me a job as cost accountant for a lumber broker. I got as far as the elevator with the little white card and then I began to think about all that dividing everything by twelve to say nothing of trial balances, linear feet and trying to remember whether it was #2 or #3 that had the knotholes, so I tore up the card and went to the next place.

The next place was crowded but there was a brisk steady movement in and out like cans on a belt going through a labeling machine. "Must be some big plant opening," I heard the woman in front of me say to the woman in front of her. "Everybody's being sent out on a job," I heard another one say jubilantly to her friend.

I filled out my card, lying about my experience and claiming proficiency in even more things like power machine operation, pattern draughting, advertising layouts and lettering, but when my turn came I saw immediately why everyone was getting a job. The woman at the desk was taking cards out of a file box at her elbow and without looking at either the applicant or the card was sending them out. Little old ladies were handed jobs as usherettes: requirements—age 25 or under, bust 34, waist 25, hips 34; stenographers were sent out as waitresses and factory workers were sent to work in beauty parlors. As she handed out the cards, the woman rolled her eyes and mumbled, "Sure, there's a job for everybody. Sure, I'm just keeping them for my friends. I like to see people out of work, sure I do." The card she handed me said, "Chuck's Speedy Service—tire repair—boy to park cars at night— salary $12.00 a week." The card was dated July 2, 1928.

The next employment agency was across the street and was run by a woman Mary loved, who had gotten her hundreds of jobs. I showed her the card for Chuck's Speedy Service and she said, "That poor old woman's really slipped her trolley—she's always been queer but this depression has finally gotten her. Now let's see, what's come in this morning. Nursemaid, practical nurse, experienced furrier, medical secretary, waitress and car hop. Things are tough, Betty, they really are. What's Mary doing?"

"Selling advertising," I told her. She said, "Well tell her to scout around for you. You'll stand a lot better chance of getting a good salary."

I said, "Are things really so bad?"

She said, "Things are terrible. A little girl I knew committed suicide and before the papers had been on the street ten minutes the company had had about fifty calls for her job."

I said, "I was one of the calls. A friend of mine told me about the job but neglected to mention why it was open."

"Well, if it's any comfort, the job required bookkeeping experience and I know that's not one of your or Mary's strong points. Well, keep in touch with me and you know I'll call you if anything good comes up."

Even Mary's unofficial employment agency went through a slump that year but we, her steady customers, stayed close to her anyway because just being around her was so invigorating and gave us so many new slants on the employment situation.

"More girls have lost their jobs because of red fingernail polish than for any other reason," Mary told Dede one day, pounding on the table in a tearoom so emphatically to prove her point that a muffin bounced into the cream pitcher.

"Absolutely the only way to get a job," she announced another time, "is to pick out the firm you want to work for, then march right in and announce that you are going to work there because they need you."

I said, "What if they say they do not?"

Dede said, "Show them your colorless nail polish. They'll hire you."

Another time when she wanted me to take a job as a practical nurse, Mary said that there was no point in even trying to get an office job any more—that girls in offices were past history—that from now on everything was to be machines.

Somewhere in between red fingernail polish and the machine age, Mary got me several different jobs. The first she heard about from a friend of an office boy who used to work for a shipping firm she sold advertising to. The job was described as being private secretary to a mining engineer, which at the time seemed too good to be true.

The mining engineer was staying at a small but elegant hotel and we were to meet him at two o'clock on the mezzanine. We repaired to Mary's advertising agency to wash our faces and put on fresh makeup and for a briefing on my *two greatest assets*.

At exactly two o'clock we appeared in the mezzanine lounge, rainsoaked but clean and ready to lie and say I could do anything.

The mining engineer, a Mr. Plumber, who was not only very prompt, but had aristocratic silvery hair and a firm handshake, got right down to business.

"Do you like to dance?" he asked me.

"Yes, I do," I said.

"Do you have some girl friends who also like to dance?" he asked.

I looked over at Mary and she was shaking her head and spelling something out with her lips. I said, "I thought this was a secretarial job."

Mr. Plumber reached over and patted my knee and said, "It is, haha, but, haha, you girls will work at the placer mine, haha, and the boys down there like to dance in the evenings and would a little girl like you be afraid to stay up at a beautiful mountain camp in California with a lot of handsome young engineers sitting around the campfire in the evening strumming guitars and singing?"

I was just going to say, "Haha, I should say a little girl like me wouldn't. When do we start and can I bring the children?" when Mary grabbed my arm, stood us both up and said, "Come on, Betty, we'll be late for that appointment. Mr. Plumber, the job sounds fascinating but we'll have to talk it over with the family."

He said, "Fine, fine and what about your girl friends?"

Mary said, "We'll send them down to see you."

Mary kept a firm grip on my arm but didn't say anything until we got to the lobby. Then she rushed into a phone booth and began dialing furiously. "What are you doing?" I asked. She said, "Calling the Better Business Bureau. That man's a white slaver. Secretaries, indeed. He's shipping prostitutes to California."

"How come California?" I asked. "I thought they had a lot of their own."

"The Orient," Mary hissed only now that she was on the trail of the biggest white slave ring in America she said, "Odient."

But the Better Business Bureau didn't get the point at all. They kept talking about interstate commerce and they wanted Mary to come down and get a lot of forms for Mr. Plumber to fill out. Finally in exasperation Mary said, "Oh, my God!" hung up and went up to see a friend of ours who was a lawyer.

He said, "Probably just some lonely old buzzard who wants to meet some girls."

Mary said, "Don't be ridiculous, Andy. This man's a white slaver. Why he didn't even ask Betty if she could type. All he was interested in was whether or not she could dance."

Andy said, "Maybe he's a front man for Arthur Murray."

"No wonder this country's rotten to the core!" Mary said. "You businessmen are such ostriches you refuse to recognize the fact that eighty per cent of our high school graduates are being shipped to the Orient as prostitutes."

"Do they require a diploma before shipment?" Andy asked, and Mary said, "You wouldn't do anything about a white slave ring if it was operating in your desk drawer," and slammed out of the office. She was very pleased the next day to be able to call Andy and report that the Better Business Bureau had called her and told her that Mr. Plumber had checked out of the hotel, minus his brace of secretaries who could dance, and had left no forwarding address.

"What do you do when you sell direct mail advertising?" I asked Mary.

"It's the simplest thing in the world," she said. "You get an idea, then you convince somebody who has never had one that he thought of it and it is so outstandingly brilliant, so unusual, the product of such a scintillating mentality that it should be mimeographed and sent to some long list of people. Say the Boy Scouts of America or the Teamsters' Union, whichever list has the most names on it."

"Sounds simple," I said. "But how do you know what kind of an idea they want?"

"Well, in the first place, any idea is better than none, which is most people's problem," said Mary. "In the second place, the only thing people are interested in these days is sales promotion. Ideas that will sell more butter, shoes, davenports, permanent waves, gasoline, ferry rides, or popcorn to the public. Now take Standard Oil . . ."

Which was one of my few criticisms of Mary, she was always

taking Standard Oil or Sears, Roebuck or some other great big important firm whose name scared me to death, to use as testing grounds for either my ability or her ideas. I didn't want to sell advertising at all. I wanted some sort of very steady job with a salary, and duties mediocre enough to be congruent with my mediocre ability. I had in mind sort of a combination janitress, slow typist and file clerk. Not for a moment did Mary entertain any such humble idea. She had in mind for me any job up to and including the President of the United States.

The thing about selling is that you're either a salesman or you're not. If you are the type of person who remembers your second grade teacher's pinching you on the neck because you exhibited a doll dress your mother had made as your own handiwork at the school carnival; who buys brown print dresses that are too short in the waist and are unbecoming anyway, because you are afraid of the saleswoman; who could never ask the butcher for half a turkey; and can still exhibit all the symptoms of pure animal terror at the sight of any dance program; then the chances are you would be the next to the worst salesman in the world. I was the worst.

I followed Mary up and down town and in and out of offices for three days and all I learned was a lot of basic differences between Mary and me and the location of fourteen coffee shops where a butterhorn and coffee were only ten cents. Mary, who seemed to get an order with every call, used the same approach on steamship offices, bakeries, garages, oil companies, candy stores, department stores, shoe repair shops or lending libraries.

The approach was that she was vitally interested in every single person in the organization, knew the location and condition of every tumor, sacroiliac, heart condition, bunion and crippled relative, knew who was mistreated, how much and by whom, knew who had gone where on their vacations and who had been gypped out of theirs, who was in love and who was lonely.

It was fun making calls with Mary but I dreaded the day when I'd have to go alone. I didn't dread it half enough.

On Wednesday morning, Mary gave me a little stack of cards, some briefing and sent me off. My first call was on a Mr. Hemp in an automobile agency. Mary had said, "Sell him that list of

Doctors and Dentists—they're about the only people who can afford cars now. Sell him on the idea of a clever but dignified letter stressing price and mileage per gallon of gas."

I left the office. It was a soft spring morning. The sky was a pale bluing blue and the breeze from the Sound smelled salty and fresh. The automobile company was about fifteen blocks uptown but I decided to walk both to save carfare and because I wanted to delay as long as possible the moment for seeing Mr. Hemp and selling him the clever idea I didn't have.

The automobile company's wide front door was propped open with a wooden wedge and four salesmen with their hats pushed to the back of their heads lounged in the sunshine on tilted-back chairs, smoking and looking sad. Timidly I asked one of them for Mr. Hemp. The man gestured toward some offices at the back. All the salesmen watched my progress across the huge showroom, which made me so self-conscious I walked stifflegged and cut a zigzag path across the shiny linoleum floor.

The offices were guarded by a long counter, behind which several girls were talking and laughing. I asked one of them for Mr. Hemp and she said she wasn't sure he'd have time to see me but she'd ask him. She went into a glass-enclosed cell and spoke to a man who was lying back in his swivel chair, his feet on his desk, talking on the phone. He turned around and looked at me and shook his head. The girl came back and said, "Did you want to see him about a job?"

I said, "No, I don't want to see him about a job."

She waited for me to reveal what I wanted to see him about but for some silly reason I was ashamed to tell her and acted evasive and sneaky and as though I were trying to sell something either dirty or "hot."

The girl went in and whispered to Mr. Hemp and I watched him peer at me and then shake his head. When she came back she said, "Mr. Hemp's terribly busy this morning and can't see anybody."

I said, "Oh, that's all right, I'm busy myself, I've got another appointment," and I hurried out leaving my purse on the counter.

I missed it after walking a block or two, and when I came back to get it the girl looked at me with such a puzzled look I didn't leave my Advertising Bureau card, which by now was quite bent and sweaty anyway.

My next call was on a school for beauty operators. I entered the La Charma Beauty School with the same degree of enthusiasm Daniel must have evinced when entering the lion's den. A woman with magenta hair, little black globules on the end of each eyelash, eyebrows two hairs wide, big wet scarlet lips and a stiff white uniform, was sitting at a little appointment desk. The minute she saw me she shoved a paper at me and told me to sign it. So I did and she said, "Black or brown?" I picked up the paper and it seemed to be a waiver of some sort having to do with La Charma not being responsible if I went blind.

I said, "I don't understand. I'm from the Advertising Bureau." She laughed and said, "Gosh, I thought you was my ten o'clock appointment. An eyelash dye job. Say, hon, Mrs. Johnson wants to see you. She wants a letter to all the girls who will graduate from high school in June." I almost fainted. Somebody *wanted* to see me. I was going to sell something.

Mrs. Johnson, who looked exactly like the woman at the appointment desk except that she had gold hair, was very friendly, offered me a cigarette and thought my ideas for a letter were "swell and had a lotta bounce." I left with a big order and my whole body electrified with hope. Maybe selling advertising was easier than prostitution after all.

My next call was on a shoe repair shop. I went in smiling but the little dark man said, "Business is rotten. No use throwin' good money after bad. I don't believe in advertisin'. Good work advertises itself. Go wan now I'm busy." So I slunk out and went back to the bureau.

Mary, who was in giving the artist some instructions, was so very enthusiastic about the beauty shop and my first order that I didn't tell her about the other calls. We took our sandwiches, which we brought from home, unless we were invited out for lunch, and walked to the Public Market where for five cents we could get an unlimited number of cups of wonderful fresh-roasted coffee and the use of one of the tables in a large dining room in the market loft, owned by the coffee company.

The Public Market, about three blocks long, crowded and smelling deliciously of baking bread, roasting peanuts, coffee, fresh fish and bananas, blazed with the orange, reds, yellows and greens of fresh succulent fruits and vegetables. From the hundreds of farmers' stalls that lined both sides of the street and extended clear through the block on the east side, Italians, Greeks, Norwegians, Finns, Danes, Japanese and Germans offered their wares. The Italians were the most voluble but the Japanese had the most beautiful vegetables.

The market, offering everything from Turkish coffee and rare books to squid and bear meat, was the shopping mecca for Seattle, and a wonderful place to eat for those who liked good food and hadn't much money. It had Turkish, Italian, Greek, Norwegian and German restaurants in addition to many excellent delicatessens and coffee stalls.

The nicest thing about it to me was its friendliness and the fact that they were all trying to sell *me* something. Everybody spoke to us as we went by and in spite of the depression, which was certainly as bad down there as anywhere, everyone was smiling and glad to see everybody. A small dark fruit-dealer named Louis, who was a great admirer of red hair, gave us a large bunch of Malaga grapes and two bananas. "Go good with your sandwiches," he said.

The dining room was three flights up in the market loft, so we climbed the stairs, got our coffee, climbed more stairs and sat down at the large table by the windows always saved by our friends and always commanding a magnificent view of the Seattle waterfront, the islands and Puget Sound. Our friends, mostly artists, advertising people, newspapermen and women, writers, musicians, and bookstore people, carried their sandwiches boldly and unashamedly in paper bags. Others who ate up there were not so bold.

Bank clerks, insurance salesmen and lawyers were lucky because they had briefcases and could carry bottles of milk, little puddings and potato salad in fruit jars, as well as sandwiches, without losing their dignity. But accountants and stenographers usually put down their coffee, looked sneakily around to see if they knew someone, then slipped their sandwiches out of an inside coat pocket, purse or department store bag, as furtively as though they were smuggling morphine.

I must admit that I had false pride about taking my lunch and hated the days when it was Mary's turn to fix the sandwiches and she would slap them together and stuff them into any old thing that came to hand—a huge greasy brown paper bag, an old printed bread wrapping, or even newspaper tied with a string.

Mary, one of those few fortunate people who are born without any false pride, laughed when I went to a Chinese store and bought a straw envelope to carry my sandwiches in. The straw envelope made everything taste like mothballs and incense and squashed the sandwiches flat but it looked kind of like a purse. Mary said, "So we have to take our lunch. So what?" and went into I. Magnin's swinging her big brown, greasy, paper bag.

I forced myself to make calls the rest of that week but I diluted the agony with visits to secondhand book stores. I rationed myself, one call—one secondhand book store. Saturday morning I told Mary that we might as well face the fact that I couldn't sell anybody anything.

"I'll never be a salesman," I told her as she checked her accounts and figured her commission. "I'm scared to death all the time and I don't have the faintest idea what I'm supposed to be selling. Friday, when I called on that piston ring company, the girl asked me what I wanted and I said I didn't know. She thought I was crazy." Mary argued with me a little but finally had to admit that she would never get me in a frame of mind where I thought my ideas were better than Standard Oil's.

"I guess you should take an office job," she said. "Only don't try to find one for yourself or you'll end up paying them and working twenty-four hours a day. Leave it to me."

So I did and when the next five or six months were over I had certainly had all kinds of experience or experiences, to say nothing of the several new trades I had learned and could now proudly X on employment agency cards without lying.

The first job Mary got me she told me about by saying, "It's certainly fortunate you're so thin." I was so anxious to go to work I already had one arm in my coat but I stopped right there and came back to face her.

"Is this job stenography?" I asked.

"Well, in a way," she said. "It's a combination bookkeeper and fur coat modeler. That's why it's so lucky you're tall and thin."

"It would also be lucky if I could keep books," I said. Mary ignored me.

She said, "Remember, Betsy, we are in a depression. Nowadays anybody can do anything and does."

"Where is it and when am I supposed to be there?" I said.

"I told Mr. Handel you'd be down this afternoon," Mary said, writing the address on a scrap of paper. So I put my other arm in the other sleeve of my tweed coat and headed toward the manufacturing district.

The farther downtown I went the more congested the streets were with aimless, unemployed people. It had been raining all morning, it seemed to me it always rained when I was out of work, and the sky between the buildings was heavy and gray, the sidewalks were wet and everything and everybody looked cold and miserable.

The address Mary had given me was down past the Skid Road, Seattle's flophouse district and the hangout of the unemployed loggers and millworkers, as well as the gathering place for all radicals, bums and religious crackpots.

This will be a good place to study the unemployed and test Mary's theory that only the inefficient are out of work, I thought, but as I worked my way farther and farther downtown, my progress along the streets was hailed with so many catcalls and whistles that I had to abandon testing and keep my eyes straight ahead.

There seemed to be a pawnshop on every corner, huge screaming banners announcing FIRE SALES, CLOSE OUT SALE, FORCED OUT OF BUSINESS SALE, every other doorway.

The musty choky smells of unwashed clothes, rancid grease, fish, doughnuts and stale coffee mingled with and overpowered the delicious seaweedy salty smell of the Sound that was carried up every cross street by the wind.

I asked a policeman where Handel's was and he kindly escorted me the rest of the way to the dark, gloomy, pleasantly deserted manufacturing district, and pointed out Handel's sign in the second-floor window of a very old red brick building. The elevator, an old-fashioned open cage, had an operator with no teeth and crusty eyes, who was too feeble to close the door and asked me to help him. I did and he said, "Shanks, lady," and wiped one of his crusty eyes on his dirty black sleeve. The marble floors of the building had a decided list to the right and I felt as if I were on board an old sailing ship as I walked down the long gloomy corridor.

Mr. Handel had apparently been crouched behind the door waiting for me, for when I timidly opened the door I almost fell over him. I apologized but he, not at all non-plused, grabbed me and shook my hand clear to my shoulder.

"Come in, come in," he said. "Glad to see you. Take off your coat and let's see what kind of shape you got." I disentangled my hand and arm and took off my coat and Mr. Handel looked me over very, very carefully, then said, "Kid, you got elegant lines and real class. Now let's see you walk." The office was only about six feet square but I walked back and forth and around the desk, weaving sinuously to avoid Mr. Handel's groping, stroking, clutching, fat little hands.

He said, "That's fine but don't be in such a hurry, Baby. Now I'll get a coat and we'll see how you look." He slipped through a door in the back and returned with a silver muskrat coat, a fur I had never cared for, even before it came equipped with Mr. Handel's arms as an extra dividend.

I shrugged away from him, dodged behind the desk and asked about the bookkeeping. "Oh, that," he said. "We usually do that at night." Just then a man with a tapemeasure around his neck and a white fox fur in his hands came to the back door of the office and beckoned to Handel, who said, "Wait for me, Baby, I'll be back in a minute." I didn't. I ripped off the muskrat, grabbed my tweed and ran all the way to the elevator.

"Mary Bard," I yelled ten minutes later when I burst into her office, "I'll go back to the farm before I work for that Mr. Handel. He pinched and prodded me like a leg of lamb and he said we'd do the bookkeeping at night."

Mary said, "You know he used to be such an old raper I had to sell him his advertising from across the street but I thought he'd changed."

"What made you think so?" I said.

"Oh, I saw him up at the Olympic Hotel at a fur show I'd done the invitations for and he seemed very quiet and dignified. Of course, we were in the main dining room," she added reflectively.

The next job she got me was tinting photographs. She said, "This darling little woman has a photographic studio just a few doors from here and she needs somebody to tint photographs and she's swamped with work."

"Does the fact that I've never tinted photographs interest you?" I asked.

"No it doesn't," said Mary, "because I know somebody who knows how and she's going to teach you this afternoon. Her name's Charmion and she works across the street in that sporting goods store. She's waiting for you now."

Charmion had green eyes, and long black hair on her legs and arms and while she was teaching me to dip dabs of cotton in paint and rub it on photographs she also sold basketballs, golf clubs and duck decoys and went through three husbands, four lovers and four bottles of ergot, which she said worked like a charm on her. At five-thirty, Charmion had a date to have her palm read and I was pretty good at the photographs, so Mary and I went home.

The next morning, which was of course rainy, armed with my new accomplishment and the knowledge that we needed a ton of coal, I reported for work at Marilee's Photo Studio. The studio, which was narrow and two-storied and gave the impression of a tall thin person squeezed into a dark doorway out of the rain, was in the middle of the block on a hill so steep it had cleats on the sidewalk and all the little shops located along it seemed to be either bracing their backs against their upper neighbors or leaning heavily on the one below. There was a shoe repair shop on one side and a print shop on the other, all a little below the street level and sharing the one trash-littered entryway.

The studio had a small show window with a skimpy, rather soiled tan half-curtain across the back and a bunched-up ratty piece of green velvet on the floor. Arranged on this were tinted photographs of bold, feverish-looking girls, brides wearing glasses, and sailors and girls leaning on each other. The subjects of all the photographs bore a remarkable resemblance to each other due, no doubt, to the wholesale application of purple on cheeks and lips, red jabs in the corners of the eyes, red to the lining of the nostrils and large, white dots in the pupils of the eyes.

I tried the door but it was locked so I flattened myself against the doorway, out of the rain, and waited. I knew I was early and so was not resentful of the ten or fifteen minutes I spent watching female office workers come toiling up the hill, their chins stuck out, their behinds lagging, their faces red with exertion, or go finicking down, their black licoricy galoshes feeling for the cleats, their knees stiff so they bounced from cleat to cleat like pogo sticks.

At last the shiniest, blackest, pointiest-toed pair of galoshes turned into our entryway and I recognized Marilee instantly because she looked exactly like all her photographs, even to the rimless octagon brides' spectacles, except that she had ash-blond hair instead of the black or bright brassy yellow that adorned most of her clientèle.

Marilee smiled at me, winked, said, "Wet enough for you?" and unlocked the door. The studio, square room with walls covered with a dark brown material like burlap, and a floor of a completely patterned mustard-colored, terribly shiny linoleum, had a green-curtained doorway at one end behind which Marilee disappeared, an appointment desk in one corner, a table with a screen around it just behind the show window and hundreds and hundreds of pictures of the bespectacled brides, bold girls and sailors and brides or sailors and bold girls. There was not one picture of a plain man, a child or somebody's mother. Either Marilee didn't take men, children or older women or she didn't consider their pictures glamorous enough to adorn her walls.

When Marilee appeared again, she had removed her black satin belted raincoat and black felt policeman's cap and was wearing a black pin-striped suit, a high-necked white blouse, black patent leather pumps, big pearl earrings and orange silk stockings. She snapped on a light over her desk, checked her appointment book, winked at me and said, "Good weather for ducks. Let's see. Nothing doing till nine-thirty. That'll give us time to get you started."

She ushered me behind the screen, showed me a hook where I could hang my hat and coat, gave me a very dirty Kelly-green smock, handed me a huge stack of pictures and said, "Your sis says you was experienced so I'm going to start you right in on some orders. I take all my own photos but I send them out for developing, retouching and printing. Now up here in the corner I've wrote the color of hair, eyes and so forth and so on. When you get done with a photo put it over here on this rack to dry. Here's the cotton, here's the paints, here's the reducer but don't use much. I like the color strong. Now I gotta get set up for my first appointment. If you want to know anything, just holler."

I picked up the first pictures. A brunette with pale eyes, a heavy nose and a straight thin mouth stared boldly right at me. I looked at the slip of paper clipped to one corner. "Eyes—blue . . . hair —black . . . light complected," it read. I gave the girl turquoise-blue eyes, luminous white skin, a bright pink mouth, a shadow on her bulbous nose, and blue highlights on her black hair. It took me quite a while but the girl looked pretty and not nearly so hard when I had finished.

I was doing the mouth when I heard the studio door open and close and then voices. The appointment said, "I vant yust the head. Not the body. Yust the head." Marilee said, "Four dollars, payable in advance, entitles you to four poses and one five-by-seven without the folder. A tinted photo is two dollars extra. Now do you want to fix up any before I take you?"

"No," said the appointment. "Yust the head. My modder vants to see how I look before she die."

At noon Marilee came in to examine my work. I had all my finished pictures on the rack and was frankly proud of them. Marilee squinted her eyes, clicked her tongue with her teeth and said, "God, honey, you're not gettin' the idea at all. Not enough color. When people pay for tinting they want color. Now here watch me."

At first I was resentful, then I thought, How ridiculous—it's Marilee's studio and if she wants purple lips and flaming red nostrils it's her privilege. So I tinted the photographs the way she wanted them and the work went much faster.

By Saturday noon I had caught up with all the orders and Marilee and I were "real girl chums." I knew all about Mama, who was a Rosicrucian, a diabetic and raised lovebirds. I knew all about sister Alma who was married to a sailor and followed him to "Frisco, Dago, L.A. and Long Beach." I knew about Marilee's boy-friend, Ernie, who was a chiropractor and would love to give me a treatment any night after work.

She said, "Honest to God, some nights Mama is all tied up in knots and Ernie works her over and you can hear her bones crack a block away—it's just like pistol shots. Mama says she don't think she could carry on if it wasn't for Ernie."

I didn't want any bones cracking like pistol shots and I didn't relish being worked over by Ernie but I didn't want to hurt Marilee's feelings so I said I'd call her and set a date.

She said, "Gosh, honey, it's been like a shot in the arm havin' you here. I'm real sorry the work's all caught up but I'll call you the minute I pile up some more orders."

Marilee gave me $28.45 in crumpled bills and a little package. "Open it," she said, winking and smiling. "It's a surprise. Go wan." I did and there in a little leather frame was a tinted photograph of me. I could tell it was me because the hair was orange. "Oh, it's beautiful! Thank you, Marilee," I squealed, looking with horror at the turquoise-blue, hard, sexy eyes, flaring red-lined nostrils and purple lips.

Marilee said, "You remember that day I asked you to pose for me so I could adjust the camera?" I remembered. "I tinted it last night," she said.

I kissed her good-bye and promised to have her out to dinner but I never did, because when I went to look for her, after working for a rabbit grower, a lawyer, a credit bureau, a purse seiner, a florist, a public stenographer, a dentist, a laboratory of clinical medicine and a gangster, I found her little shop closed, the bespectacled brides and sailors and girls gone from her show window.

Mr. Webber, the rabbit grower, who was tall and thin and had a high-domed forehead like pictures of the Disciples, was raising Chinchilla rabbits and trying to organize the other growers. For two weeks he laboriously wrote out reports and letters in longhand and I copied them. In the afternoons he made tea over an alcohol stove and as we drank it he told me how much he admired Mary. He said that she was a flame in this burned-out world.

Mr. Webber was as gentle and soft as his rabbits and never ever pointed out my mistakes but secretly, behind his arms, wrote over them in ink. At the end of the two weeks he gave me a check for seventy-five dollars, which was twenty-five dollars more than I expected. The extra money, I knew, was a tribute to Mary rather than an appreciation of my efficiency.

After Mr. Webber, I was out of work for three days but I wasn't as sad as I might have been because of that extra money, so I painted the kitchen, using a very remarkable yellow paint which never dried. It looked very nice but it grew more and more irritating as weeks and weeks went by and we still had to pry dishes off the drainboards and peel the children out of the breakfast nook.

On Wednesday night Mary told me she had found me a job with a darling old lawyer. I protested that I didn't know anything about legal forms but Mary said they were easy. All you had to do was go through the files and copy. She also explained that the old lawyer used a dictaphone and gave me a demonstration on the coffee table of how to use one, which wasn't too helpful as I'd never even seen one.

However, the next morning I reported for work at Mr. O'Reilly's law office, which was in an old but very respectable building in the financial district. Mr. O'Reilly had thick gray hair, an oily manner and a most disconcerting habit of appearing behind me suddenly and soundlessly.

By the trial and error method I got the dictaphone to work, learned about legal forms and phraseology, but I needn't have bothered. Mr. O'Reilly had very little work and the little he did have he didn't attend to. All he really wanted me there for was to talk about sex. He edged into it gracefully and gradually and by constantly referring to cases tried to make it seem as if he were merely discussing business. When I left he promised to mail me my salary but he never did.

Mary finally admitted that she had never seen Mr. O'Reilly but had been told about the job by an elevator starter in another building.

Then I went to work in a credit bureau typing very dull reports implying that everybody in Seattle but the President of the First National Bank had rotten credit. One day when my boss was out of his office I sneaked over and looked up our family's credit. We took up almost a whole drawer and from what I read it sounded as if the credit bureau not only wouldn't recommend us for credit, they wouldn't even let us pay cash. This, however, didn't make me feel too badly because I knew they didn't like anybody.

The next job Mary got for me was taking dictation on a dock for a purse seiner, who was trying to settle an estate involving hundreds of relatives all named Escvotrizwitz and Trckvotisztz and Krje and living in places called Brk, Pec, Plav and Klujk. My shorthand, feeble enough in English, collapsed completely under Mr. Ljubovija's barrage of Serbo-Croat mixed with a few By Gollies and Okays, which he fondly thought was English. Finally, I told him that if he'd give me a general idea of what he wanted to say and would spell out all the names, I would write the letters.

I could not understand why he wanted the letters in English when there was a good chance that, as none of the family, including him, spoke it, not one would be able to read it, but he was insistent. To him, writing in English was synonymous with success. He was a very nice man and I loved sitting in the sun on the dock listening to the raspy-throated gulls, smelling the nice boaty smells of creosote and tar and watching the purse seiners work on their nets.

My next job was working for a public stenographer, a large woman who wore wide patent leather belts around her big waist and had a most disconcerting habit of sniffing her armpits, reaching in her bottom drawer for her deodorant and applying it via the neck of her dress, when she was talking to clients.

The first time I saw Mrs. Pundril go through this little routine was when she was talking to a lumberman from Minnesota. He was in the midst of explaining a report, when suddenly she sniffed her right armpit, grabbed out her Mum, took off the lid, gouged some out with her right forefinger and with a great deal of maneuvering managed to apply it even though her blouse had a very high neck. As he watched, the lumberman's face turned a dull red. I laughed so hard I had to stuff my handkerchief in my mouth and Mrs. Pundril was as unconcerned as though she were filling her pen.

After one week, Mrs. Pundril fired me. She said I wasn't fast enough for public stenography and I made too many errors. She pronounced them "eeroars." I didn't blame her for firing me, but it didn't do my self-confidence any good. Then for a few weeks I typed bills for a florist, a dentist and a laboratory and then Mary got me the job with the gangster.

His name was Murray Adams, he had an office in a funny old building that housed beaded-bag menders, dream interpreters, corn removers and such, and I still don't know what he intended to do. He was big and dark and handsome and wore an oyster-white fedora and a tan camel's-hair overcoat even in the office, which was hot.

Mary met him in some oil promoter's office and he asked her if she knew of a girl to sit in his office and answer his phone. Mary naturally said of course she did, her sister Betty, and so there I was.

Murray—he told me to call him that—told me that he'd been a member of a mob in Chicago and a rum runner on the Atlantic Coast and had "a bucket of ice in hock in Washington, D.C."

He was very sweet to me and used to take me out for coffee and tell me about different "dirty deals" he had gotten from different "babes," but he used to make me nervous when he sat by the office window, которое was on the second floor, pretending that he was holding a Tommy gun and mowing down the people in the street.

"Look at that bunch of slobs," he'd say. "Not one of 'em got anything on the ball. Jeeze I'd like to have a machine gun and ah,ah,ah,ah,ah,ah [he'd make motions of moving a machine gun back and forth], I'd let them all have it. Especially the dames."

I don't know why Murray had me and I certainly don't know why he had a telephone because whenever he left the office he told me to tell whoever called that he wasn't in and whenever he was in the office he said to tell whoever called that he was out. I had a typewriter but nothing to type so I wrote letters to everyone I had ever known. Murray paid me in crisp new bills, twenty dollars a week, for three weeks and then left town owing his rent, telephone bill, and for his furniture. I never heard of him again.

"This is the best job I've ever gotten you," Mary said. "You get twenty-five dollars a week for being Mr. Wilson's private secretary and you have a chance to make thousands more on the dime cards."

So I went to work for Mr. Wilson and his dime card scheme, which was the depression version of Pyramid Clubs.

Mr. Wilson, an advertising man, thought up the dime card scheme and if Seattle hadn't been such a stuffy city he might have made a million dollars and I might have made about ten thousand.

The idea, as I remember it, was that you bought a printed share in Prosperity for two dollars—you turned your share and a dollar more into the Prosperity office, where I worked, and got an envelope containing a dime card (cards with round slots for ten dimes each and ten places for signatures)—and two more printed shares in Prosperity. You sold your two shares for two dollars each, kept three of the four dollars to pay yourself back for the two dollars you spent on your original share, plus the one dollar turned into the office, had the other dollar changed into dimes, inserted them in the dime card and passed it to the person you bought your share from. That person took one dime from the card, signed his name and passed it back to the person he bought from. That person did the same, etc., etc., etc.

Because I was the originator of several chains I got ninety cents from the first four, eighty cents from the next eight, seventy cents from the next sixteen and so forth. As each share was turned into the office I entered the name on a chart so that I knew who had bought from whom and where the dimes were or weren't.

After the first week the office was a madhouse, and I had to hire four girls to help me and every night at home all the family sat around and picked dimes out of Mary's and my dime cards. One night we counted seventy-two dollars' worth of dimes. All day long people stormed into the office demanding a share in Prosperity and then rushed out again to sell their shares and start their chains. I knew that there had to be an end to this delightful game some time because Seattle only had about 300,000 citizens, but I didn't anticipate how or when it would come.

One day after the office had been running for about six weeks, a fat man came in and asked me to explain the dime card game to him. I did, slowly and succinctly and he said, "That's it, sister. I'm closing up this joint!" Whereupon he called in a huge task force of policemen, who came loping in swinging their billy clubs. All the girls who were working for me began to bawl, and I tried vainly to locate Mr. Wilson, who had gone to the bank.

"I'm from the D.A.'s office and I'm going to take you all to the station house," the fat man said. I said, "You are not. We only work here and anyway what's the matter?"

"Plenty's the matter," said the fat man.

Then a photographer took a lot of pictures of the policemen seizing the files, which was pretty ridiculous as nobody was holding on to them. Finally in an hour or so a small pleasant gray-haired man appeared, dismissed the fat man, sent all of us home, and that was that.

"Crime is too nerve-racking," I told Mary. "Just get me a plain job." So she did. Typing estimates for an engineer. The work was dull and so was the engineer but it was a job.

10

Finance Can Be Fun, or Can It?

IT SEEMS TO ME, as I look back, that when we were the poorest we had the most fun. Our ability to enjoy ourselves in the face of complete adversity was astounding to the people who believed that you had to have money to have fun; appalling to those others who believed that it is an effrontery for the poor to laugh. I am not sure that individually we would have been so "happy in spite of it all," but together we felt we could survive anything and did.

The world was a very sad place, in those days. The people who had jobs were so obsessed with the fear of losing them that they balanced precariously on each day of employment like a hummock in a quicksand bog, and the people who didn't have jobs had their eyes so dimmed by the fear of hunger, sickness and cold that they walked right over golden opportunities without seeing them. I belonged to the latter group—Mother and Mary to neither.

Mary, one of those fortunate people who are able to bring forth great reserves of strength and fortitude during times of stress, accepted the depression as a personal challenge. She always had a job, she tried to find jobs for her family and hundreds of friends and, while she was looking, propped up everyone's limp spirits by defying big corporations.

When the telephone company threatened to disconnect our telephone because the bill hadn't been paid, Mary marched right down to see the president and told him that if he cut off our phone and left us with no communication with the outside world, she was going to sue him personally. Her exact words, which she recounted to our amusement at the dinner table, were, "I told him a telephone and telegraph company is a public service operating under a special grant from the state. If you cut off my telephone you will not be performing a public service and I will sue you. In fact from this day on I'm going to be known as the biggest suer in the city of Seattle." It did keep the telephone from being disconnected and it certainly bolstered our morale. She tried the same thing with the power and light company, but they turned off the lights anyway and for a week or so left us to burn old Christmas candles and not iron.

During this interlude, Mary, who was inclined to keep up with our friends of private school days, brought home to dinner a terribly snobbish young man who remarked, as we sat down to our candle-lit vegetable soup, "You Bards absolutely delight me. You have a simple meal of vegetable soup and toast and then you make it elegant by serving it by candlelight." He was so elegant, of course, that he didn't go out into the kitchen to note that we were also washing the dishes by candlelight. When he left he amused us greatly by standing by the front door for a full ten minutes flipping the switches and trying to make the porch light go on. Finally he called to Mother, "Sydney darling, I hate to mention it but your porch light's burned out. Have one of the great beasts who come to court your daughters put a new one in." When we all laughed he thought he'd been witty and repeated his asinine remark.

When we ran out of fireplace wood, Mary unearthed a bucksaw and marched us all down to a city park two blocks away, where we took turns sawing up fallen logs. We were just splitting up the first cut on our first log when two park gardeners came up and asked us what the hell we thought we were doing. Mary told them exactly what we were doing and why we were doing it. and to our surprise and relief they helped us saw and carry the wood up to the house, and after that saved logs and bark for us.

During the depression we all came home right after work and Mary brought home to dinner, to stay all night, or to live with us, everyone she met whom she felt sorry for. Some of these people were brilliant, talented and amusing. Some were just ordinary people. Some unconscionable bores. Mary didn't care. They were alive, or at least pretended to be.

Every night for dinner we had from two to ten extra people to tax Mother's ingenuity in stretching the meatloaf, macaroni and cheese, spaghetti, chili, tuna fish and noodles, vegetable soup, park wood and beds. After dinner we played bridge or charades or Chinese checkers or the piano, rolled old cigarette butts into new cigarettes on our little cigarette-rolling machine, drank gallons of coffee which was seventeen cents a pound, ate cinnamon toast, read aloud Mark Twain, made fun of each other and all our friends, sang songs, played records, followed the dance marathons on the radio, and complained because our bosses tried to stifle our individuality by making us work.

We were in love most of the time, but being in love in those days didn't seem to be such a crystallized state as it is today. Nobody had enough money to get off by themselves, let alone get married, so grand passions flamed and were spent in front of the fireplace reading Rupert Brooke, listening to "Body and Soul" on the radio, or walking up by the reservoir to watch, across its flat black surface, the lights of the city made teary by the rain.

Every Saturday in the fall, Mother made a huge kettle of chili and we all sat around and listened to the football games. Mother, an ardent fan, kept a chart, groaned in agony over the stupidity of the announcers who commented on the crowd and didn't tell where the ball was and invariably told us that there was no football spirit in the West, we should go to a Yale-Harvard game. When our side made a touchdown we all shouted at the top of our voices, which made the dogs bark, the children wake up from their naps and bawl and our neighbors pull aside their curtains and peer over at us.

I always looked forward to Saturday. I loved the tight expectant feeling I had as I opened the front door and wondered who would be there. I loved Saturday's dusk with the street lights as soft as breath in the fog or rain, the voices of the children, filtering home from the matinee, clear and high with joy and silliness; the firm thudding comforting sound of front doors closing and shutting the families in, the world out; the thick exciting sound of a car door slamming in front of the house; the exuberance of the telephone bell. Everybody came over Saturday night, brought friends and stayed until three or four Sunday morning.

Sundays were always marked by a strong smell of gasoline and meatloaf and tremendous activity. First we got the children ready for Sunday School, which always meant a wild hunt for matching socks, misplaced mite boxes and Sunday School lessons, then we all pitched in and cleaned the house, Mother made an enormous meatloaf (hamburger was only twelve cents a pound), then Mother and Dede left for church, while Mary and I repaired to a small covered areaway by the basement door, filled a little washtub with cleaning fluid and sloshed our office dresses, our skirts, even our coats in it then hung them slightly less spotty and dripping gasoline, on a line under the porch. The cleaning fluid was twenty-five cents a gallon and could be strained through flannel and used over and over again and doing our own cleaning, besides being an economic necessity, burned our hands and made us feel so virtuous that we often cleaned things that didn't need it.

By dinnertime the house had been scrubbed and the smells of shampoo and scorch from the iron were mingled with the gasoline and meatloaf. Sunday evenings, which usually drew the biggest crowds of all, ended earlier than Saturday but not as early as they should have considering that Monday was a workday and on Monday night we usually went to the movies because Monday was family night at our neighborhood theatre and an unlimited group arriving together and appearing reasonably compatible could all get in for twenty-five cents.

Tuesday nights we went to bed early unless someone was giving a party. Parties were indistinguishable one from another. They were always given in someone's apartment; the food was always spaghetti, garlic bread and green salad; the drinks were either bathtub gin and lemon soda or Dago red; the entertainment sitting on the floor and listening to Bach or sitting on a studio couch and listening to Bach. I didn't care much for Bach, even when partially anesthetized by bathtub gin, but redhot nails in my eyeballs wouldn't have made me admit it, because Mary had made it very clear to me that everybody who was not down on all fours liked Bach, Baudelaire, Dostoevski, Aldous Huxley,

Spengler, almond paste on filet of sole, Melochrino cigarettes and the foreign movies.

I liked Baudelaire, Huxley and Dostoevski, I loathed Spengler, felt that almond paste on filet of sole had a lot in common with chocolate-dipped oysters, Melochrino cigarettes tasted like camel dung and the foreign movies would have been dandy if only they hadn't been foreign.

The foreign movies were on Wednesday nights at eleven-thirty at a University district theatre. The reason I kept going, aside from a false pride that made me say I thought they were "magnificent," "a new approach," "delicately directed," etc., when I really thought most of them were boring and dull, was the fact that after each one the theatre management served little cups of black coffee and free cigarettes.

We saw a French film of Joan of Arc which showed only the heads and shoulders of the actors. "Terribly new approach," I said, grabbing at the cigarettes and trying to shake off the stiff-necked feeling of having spent the evening peering over a high board fence.

One winter Saturday afternoon, quite by accident, as we were walking through the University district, my sister Dede and I discovered what was to become one of our chief and most enjoyable forms of free entertainment.

"I wonder why all those people are going into the basement of that church?" I asked Dede, as we strolled along the street. "Let's go in and find out," Dede, always one to face things, said. So we did and found that Miss Irma Grondahl was presenting her pupils and herself in a piano recital. Having nothing else to do we decided to stay and seated ourselves on folding chairs in the front row. Immediately Miss Grondahl, in a long gold velvet cape, appeared and assuming that we were relatives of some performer, solicited our help in moving the upright piano over to the left side of the stage and arranging large bouquets of dusty laurel leaves along the footlights.

The recital began and was more or less routine, except that all the performers made mistakes, swayed back and forth like pendulums as they played and even a baby only about four years old, who played "Baby Bye See the Fly, Let Us Watch Him You and I," standing up, used the loud pedal.

Then Miss Grondahl announced that she would play "Rustle of Spring" and "Hark, Hark the Lark." She had shed her gold cape and was simply clad in a sleeveless black satin dress and some crystal beads. She settled herself on the piano bench, folded her hands in her lap and began to sway. Back and forth, back and forth, back and forth and then suddenly, like running in backdoor in jumping rope, she lit into the first runs of "Rustle." Miss Grondahl was a vigorous very loud player but what made her performance irresistible to Dede and me were the large tufts of black hair which sprang quivering out of the armholes of her dress each time she lifted her hands at the end of a run or raised her arms for a crashing chord.

After that we rarely missed a recital. We watched the neighborhood papers and clipped out the notices and attended every single singing, dancing, elocution or piano recital that didn't conflict with working hours and was within walking distance. We grew very partial to modern dance recitals whose uninhibited antics, often resembling the pangs of childbirth or someone who had just been stung by a bee, so delighted us that we were sometimes asked to leave.

Our attendance at recitals so stimulated our appetite for simple pleasures that we began clipping out and attending other little functions. The Annual Tea of the Northwest Driftwood Society was remembered for its few guests and enormous platters of openfaced sandwiches which we wolfed down as we exchanged opinions on patina, good beaches and time of year to look.

Most groups of Penwomen had very little food but lots of cigarettes; we were too young and regarded suspiciously by most garden clubs; but North American Indian Relic Collectors, the Society for the Protection of the Douglas Fir and the Northwest Association of Agate Polishers, etc., were glad to see anybody.

Another simple pleasure we enjoyed in those poverty-ridden days was looking at real estate. My brother Cleve through a long involved series of trades, beginning, I believe, when he was ten years old with a saddle Mother had had made in Mexico, had acquired a long low cream-colored Cord convertible with dark blue fenders and top. On spring Saturday afternoons we would all climb in the Cord and go househunting.

I suppose in a way it was taking an unfair advantage of the real estate dealers, who invariably, when they saw our gorgeous car drive up, often primed with Mary's and my cleaning fluid, came careening out of their offices brandishing keys and carrying fountain pens and a contract. But on the other hand they tried awfully hard to take advantage of us.

"This magnificent structure," they would say, as they tried to force open the sagging door of some termite-infested old mansion, "was the home of one of Seattle's finest old families and is being sold for taxes. Just given away, really." In we would all troop, the children racing up the stairs or down to the cellar, the rest of us walking slowly, examining everything and noting with amusement the empty whiskey bottles, lipstick-smeared walls, and other irrefutable evidence that this fine old family must have been supplementing their income by making whiskey or dabbling in white slavery.

Sometimes we found wonderful bargains. One was a huge brick inn, north of the city, about an $85,000 structure, on sale for $5,500. There were thirteen bedrooms, a living room eighty feet long, a dining room, breakfast room, library, music room and billiard room, every room with a fireplace, magnificent barns, a stream and ten acres of land, and we had many violent fights over who would have which room and how we would furnish it. The real estate dealer finally got so sick of taking us out there that he gave us the keys and we used to take picnics and make plans while we ate our peanut butter and pickle sandwiches. The real estate dealer was more than anxious to make an even trade for our very salable house in the University district and we were all ready to move in when Mary, distressingly practical, pointed out that the nearest bus line was five miles away, the nearest school about eighteen miles and the former owner had, upon questioning, admitted that it cost from $200 a month up to even take the chill off the lower floor.

We were all so disappointed that Cleve went right out and rustled up an enormous yacht which was on sale for almost nothing and would really be a much more economical home for us because it would eliminate real estate taxes, light, gas and telephone bills, we could catch fish from it and we could pull up the gangplank when bores or bill collectors approached. The yacht unfortunately was in Alaska and Cleve never did get around to sailing it down.

A bill is a thing that comes in a windowed envelope and causes men to pull in their lips and turn the oil burner down to sixty degrees and women to look shifty-eyed and say, "Someone must have been charging on my account."

A bill collector is a man with a loud voice who hates everybody. A collection agency is a collection of bill collectors with loud voices who hate everybody and always know where she works.

I could no more have a complete feeling of kinship with someone who has never had bills than I could with someone who doesn't like dogs. Owing money is not pleasant and undoubtedly stems from weakness, but those of us who have known the burden of debt; have spent our long wakeful night hours peering into that black sinkhole labeled "the future"; have grown wild with frustration trying to yank and pull one dollar into the shape and size of five; have flinched at the sight of any windowed envelope; have cringed with embarrassment at the stentorian voices of bill collectors; have been wilted by money lenders' searing questions; and have often resorted to desperate dreams (in my case usually involving scenes where a beautifully dressed, charming, red-haired lady says to a lot of different people, "Your pleading just bores me—close my account!"), emerge finally, if we are able, kicked and beaten into a reasonable facsimile of a human being and/or dogliker.

Which is why, I guess, I've never felt very close to bankers. Bankers remind me of a little girl I used to play with in Butte, Montana—a little girl named Emily, who always had a large supply of jelly beans which she carried in a little striped paper bag, the top of which she kept closed and tightly twisted. When Emily wanted a jelly bean she untwisted her bag, reached in, took one, put it in her mouth, retwisted the bag and told us, her loyal playmates drooling on the sidelines, "Gee, kids, I'd like to give you some jelly beans, I really would, but my mother won't let me."

Experience has convinced me that all bankers are little Emilys. The only time they untwist their little striped bags and take out a jelly bean or two is after you have proved conclusively that you already have plenty of jelly beans of your own and aren't hungry anyway. When you don't have any jelly beans and are starving they say, "Gee, kids, I'd like to give you some jelly beans, I really would, but my Board won't let me."

The best pal I'd like to have least after a banker, is a credit manager. Credit managers are people who, by birth or training or both, live entirely in the past, have no faith in the future, are not interested in the present, hold grudges indefinitely or at least for six years, never forget old slights and are always ready and eager to rehash old quarrels. Credit managers collect, the way other people collect recipes, all the nasty things anybody has ever said about anybody else.

The only person ever able, to my knowledge, to completely confuse credit managers is my mother. Mother has no more financial sense than a hummingbird, arguing with her about money is like trying to catch minnows in your fingers, and what is worse she adopts a reasonable attitude toward bill paying.

When a credit manager would call Mother and shout accusingly, "You promised to be down here on Monday and you didn't show up," Mother wouldn't cringe or get tears in her eyes, but would say pleasantly, "I know but I was busy with something else."

When the credit manager said, "Why didn't you come down on Tuesday, then?" Mother would say, "Would you mind holding the phone a minute, the cat seems to have a fur ball in her throat?"

Sometime later, having disposed of the cat, Mother would pick up the phone and resume, "Hello, Mr. Crandall, I'm sorry to have kept you waiting. Let's see, Tuesday, oh, yes, there was a program at school."

"What about Wednesday?" Mr. Crandall would ask.

"Wednesday is a very bad day to get someone to take care of the children," Mother would say.

"What about Thursday?" Mr. Crandall would ask irritably. "Couldn't you have come down Thursday?"

"No," said Mother, "I couldn't. I was having the chimney cleaned and I had to get Mrs. Murphy's lunch." Mrs. Murphy was the cleaning woman but the credit manager, whose head was beginning to buzz, thought she cleaned the chimneys.

"Then will you be down today?" he would finally ask wearily.

"Oh, not today," Mother would say. "I'm making Alison's dogwood costume."

"Next Monday then?" he'd say, still with hope.

"All right, next Monday," Mother would say, adding after he had hung up, "If my primrose woman doesn't show up."

Mother employed the same infuriatingly reasonable tactics with Mary and me.

"Mother," I'd shout in exasperation, "I gave you twenty-five dollars Thursday to pay the gas bill and they called me today and said it hadn't been paid."

Mother, intent on frosting an applesauce cake, would say, "Which man did you talk to?"

"A Mr. Ellsworth," I'd say.

Mother would say, "Is Mr. Ellsworth the one with that lump behind his ear?"

"I don't know about the lump," I'd say, "but he has a Southern accent."

"Oh, then the one with the lump must be Mr. Hastings," Mother would say. "Mr. Ellsworth is the one whose daughter failed her college board examinations and he is awfully upset about it."

"Which college was she going to?" Dede would ask.

"Wellesley," Mother would say, "and I told him that I had a very dear friend who teaches at Wellesley and promised to write to her and see if anything can be done."

"Who do you know at Wellesley?" Alison would ask.

"Charles Horton's sister, Mabel," Mother would say.

"Is she old 'there is rhythm and grace in every pore of the human body' who used to sit on the couch with her skirts clear up around her thighs?" Dede would ask.

Finance Can Be Fun, or Can It?

Mother would say, "She wore tweeds she wove herself and she is very nice."

"Oh, that old bore," Mary would say. "She's not coming out here is she?"

Dede would say, "She's probably packing her loom right now."

Mother would say, "I think Mabel is very charming."

Mary would say, "You do not. You think she's a great big bore but you won't admit it because she's from Boston."

I would yell, "WHAT ABOUT THE TWENTY-FIVE DOLLARS FOR THE GAS COMPANY?"

Mother would say, "Lower your voice. I gave it to the egg man."

"But I promised it to the gas company and the egg man isn't due until next week," I'd wail. "Why did you give it to him?"

"Because," Mother would say, gently and with great reasonableness, "his wife has arthritis. Now let's eat this applesauce cake while it is hot."

Mother's approach to any direct unpleasant question is to pick out the least important word in the question and make an issue of it. I can best illustrate this by an incident depicting a similar type of mind. When Anne and Joan were nine and ten, we overheard the following conversation one day as they sat on the back steps discussing school.

Anne said most dramatically, "Do you know that Janice Price is only ten and she *smokes!*"

Joan said, "What brand?"

My first experiences with debt were mild and vicarious but they fostered in me a strong and lasting belief that bills were shameful things and should always be kept secret.

When my brother Cleve was about twelve he decided one desperate day that his only hope in a world which seemed to be peopled entirely with females (Mother, Grandmother, sisters, cats, dog, cows, horses, even the turtle and canary were she's) was to answer an advertisement in a magazine and become, with nothing down and plenty of time to pay, a "high-paid executive" and show a few people!

To his chagrin, immediately upon receipt of his evasively filled out coupon, he received from the advertiser, not a magic formula, not explicit instructions for brain control, not one darn thing that overnight would enable him to emerge suddenly from his messy, cough-drop-boxy, gun-littered room, a suave, smooth, high-paid executive in a blue, pin-striped suit, but a great big, thick arithmetic book labeled *First Steps in Accounting* and filled, he discovered to his disgust, after he had thumbed through a few pages, with nothing but "thought problems"—that most detested of all types of arithmetic problems. Cleve immediately abandoned all idea of becoming an executive, tossed the accounting book under his bed and returned to his job as unofficial assistant to the Laurelhurst bus driver.

Unfortunately, the Executive Builders didn't give up so easily. They had started to mold a high-paid executive and by God, man, they were going to finish. Every week or two for months they deluged Cleve with courses, ledgers, notebooks, examinations, books of receipts and mimeographed letters on character-building, cooperation, don't be a quitter and forging ahead. Surreptitiously Cleve garnered them from the mailman and shoved them under the bed.

Then one day the courses stopped and the letters began.

"Mr. Bard," said the President of the Executive Molders, his long admonishing finger appearing across the entire face of the letter, "have you no honor? Don't you know that buying things and not paying for them is STEALING?"

"Mr. Bard: Cheat is a terrible word. Honesty and GOOD CREDIT are a high-paid executive's most *important* assets."

"Mr. Bard: If there is some reason why you cannot pay, tell us what it is. We want to be FAIR WITH YOU! We want to give you every CHANCE!"

"Mr. Bard: PLEASE REMIT!"

"Mr. Bard: Unless full payment is made AT ONCE, this long-overdue account will be turned over to our attorneys."

Mr. Bard, who by this time was scared to death, appealed to Gammy, who kept all her money in her Bible and could always be counted on to bail us out of any monetary difficulties. Gammy heard the story, read the advertisement, saw the accounting book and said, "Only robbers take things they can't pay for. Never buy anything unless you have the money in your pocket. Now go gather everything up and we'll send it back to these people. Imagine enrolling a boy your age. The big grafters."

So Cleve and I started hunting up the stuff but somehow or other most of the paper had been marked on with crayons or used for scratch paper, the books and notebooks all bore traces of apple core or puppy's teeth and somebody had spilled a cup of cocoa on one of the biggest ledgers. So Gammy wrote and told the Big Grafters that she would pay for the books and supplies but not one cent for the instructions. She wrote, "In the future, I think you had better check on the qualifications of your high-paid executives-to-be, the one in question is only in the seventh grade and has never to my knowledge shown the slightest aptitude nor liking for numbers" (Gammy's name for arithmetic in any form).

Years passed and then I came winging in from a farm, where budgeting had been simply a matter of subtracting the feed from the eggs, adding the sacks, subtracting the gasoline, adding the potatoes, subtracting the buttermilk and adding the pig, and tried to cope with a system where I was paid every two weeks, the main bills came once a month, Mother's little businessmen came every week or every day or by the seasons, insurance payments were quarterly, taxes were yearly, and no matter how many times we had macaroni and cheese there was always somebody left over. Somebody who came at dinnertime and announced in ringing tones, "Collect for the *Times!* . . . Collect for the sewing machine! . . . Collect for the slab wood! . . . Collect for the sheep guana! . . . Collect for the *Saturday Evening Post!* . . . Collect for the Belgian hares!"

We all pooled our money and Mary and Mother and I distributed it to the best of our ability and Mother's reasons, but it was a losing game. Like climbing up a rock slide. We'd just get to the top and the front porch would sag, or the toilet would overflow or the downspouts would leak or Christmas would come and down we'd go to the bottom again.

Then of course there were things like the five green party dresses I charged in the course of one winter.

My darkest memories are of that spring after my first winter of charge accounts. For months, as I rode to and from work on the streetcar, I had been confronted at exactly eye level with advertisements that pleaded "Use your credit! Don't go without! Buy from US—take a year to pay! NEVER SAY HOW MUCH—SAY CHARGE IT!"

So one day I did. I opened a charge account at a large department store and bought a handwoven tweed coat on sale for fifteen dollars. "A charge account," I told the family, "really saves you money. This coat was a marvelous bargain and I never could have gotten it if I hadn't had a charge account. After this we'll charge whatever we need and pay at the end of the month."

"Good idea!" "Sound reasoning!" "Oh boy," said the family.

At first we were very careful and limited our charges to pots and pans, stockings, water glasses and bathmats. The small bills came in, I paid and said, "You see, a charge account makes life much simpler." So I opened a few more, and a few more and a few more and then came Christmas. "Charge it, charge it, charge it," I said all over town and if I hesitated the least little bit the clerks said, "Don't worry, honey, things bought in December aren't billed until February." In December February seems as far away as July and so I staggered through the Christmas crowds, my arms loaded with rich gifts, the smells of fog and pine tingling my nostrils, certain disaster dogging my heels.

Then Christmas was over and so was Lumber and bearing down upon me as surely and relentlessly as death was February tenth. Mother said, "Go down and talk to them. Explain that you have lost your job and won't be able to pay until you find something permanent." I said, "Yeah, something permanent that pays about five thousand dollars a month. Somebody *must* have been charging on my accounts."

Mary said, "Pay each one a little bit. That's what I do. Even fifty cents lets them know that you owe the bill and intend to pay."

How could I give Mr. Beltz of the fishy eye, reluctant credit and five green party dresses, fifty cents? I said I'd handle it my way.

My way was to lie awake all night in the bed I shared with Mary, flinching as occasional raindrops bounced from the sill of the

Finance Can Be Fun, or Can It?

open window to my face, and watching the street light through the window make prison bars on the wall. My way was to toss and turn and beat my brains and wail, "Why did I do it? What was I thinking of? What will I do now?"

The raindrops hitting the ground at the bottom of the narrow black crevass between our house and a neighbor's with a heavy spull-lit! spull-lat! plup, plup, plup, like ripe fruit falling from the trees, seemed to my tortured brain to be saying, "Charge-it, charge-it, charge-it—payup, payup, payup."

The drops that went splink, splink, as they bounced off the window sill, and ploop, ploop, ploop, as they searched for and found the empty flower pots Mother kept underneath the cut-leaf maple at the corner of the house, seemed to be saying, "The clink, the clink, the clink, you Fool! Fool! Fool!"

I turned my pillow over and over trying to find a cool side and was resentful of the rest of the family blissfully suspended above reality in their hammocks of sleep. The house was as quiet and depressing as a vault, but outside the rain, apparently to make up for the fact that it couldn't be heard on the roof, splashed noisily on the sills, splatted down between the houses, hissed on the pavements, slurped into the drainpipes, raced in the gutters and finally went gulping into the sewer. How harsh and unmusical were its noises compared to those of country rain. Country rain thrummed like a woodpecker, pit-a-patted across the roofs with quick light strokes like bird's feet, swished moaning through the orchards, slid like quicksilver from leaf to leaf, thudded hopefully against windows like June bugs and plopped in the dusty roads like small toads. City rain sounded businesslike and as though it were metered and I hated it—I hated everything about the city. Why had I ever left the farm? What would I do?

Mary had said, "You are a victim of circumstance and you are not alone. There are millions of Americans who have suddenly lost their jobs and owe bills. I imagine the people we owe money to, owe money themselves to someone else. Think of that."

I did and it wasn't comforting because I reasoned that if Mr. Beltz, for instance, was as worried about the bills he owed as I was, then he'd get the money out of me for those party dresses if he had to chisel it out of my bones. Five green party dresses.

What had I been thinking of? I must have been crazy. I hardly ever went to formal parties and even if I did was there any reason I always had to be in a charged green?

I finally got through February, which was a short month, but I lost twelve pounds, was as jumpy as a cricket and had such circles under my eyes I looked like a marmoset. I had to do something immediately.

Then one day I was walking along the street and right up ahead of me on a huge signboard was an awfully nice-looking man. His outstretched hands were filled with ten and twenty dollar bills and in a big white bubble to the right of his head he was begging me to come on down to the Friendly Loan Company. "We want to help you," he said. "We want to make life easy for you. Stop worrying. Come down and let us share our money with you." There it was. The answer.

I hurried right up to the small, dark office housing the Friendly Loan Company.

"Whaya want?" said the friendly little lady at the desk, whose mouth should have been set out in the woods to catch raccoons.

"I want to borrow some money," I said, adding with a gay little laugh, "a lot of money."

Miss Friendly Loan looked at me coldly, threw her lips over to the left and yelled, "Chawrlie! Customer!"

Chawrlie, who had close-set pale green eyes and a small head, took me into his office and shot questions at me for about an hour. I had intended to lie about my job, my salary, my bank account, my bills, everything, but I found that I couldn't lie to Chawrlie. He caught me up every time, picked the lie up in two fingers, handed it back to me still wriggling and told me to keep it.

When I had finally told all, Chawrlie had me sign a note for a hundred dollars and then handed me only sixty-two. The other thirty-eight, he said, went for carrying charges, upkeep, risk insurance and probably that great big advertisement. The interest was twelve per cent and I was to pay five dollars every two weeks. I thanked Chawrlie profusely and skipped out to distribute the sixty-two dollars among my charge accounts and to make rash promises about future payments.

Finance Can Be Fun, or Can It? 165

When I got home, I bragged to the family about my great financial acumen, told them about darling old generous Chawrlie and that night slept soundly for the first time in weeks.

It was fortunate I did, because from then on my life became the living hell. My jobs were all temporary—a week here, a week or two there, and though I was almost always paid, there was something about that temporary money, usually in cash, that made it seem as if I'd won it on a punchboard. I'd use my salary to buy little presents for the family, a string of gold beads, take us all to a show, buy candy, and pay Mother's "at the doors" and tell myself, "When I get a permanent job I'll start in on the big bills."

It was the other way around, of course, the big bills started on me. Each of my charge accounts had a collector, equipped apparently with second sight. They knew about my jobs before Mary had found them for me and would often be milling around the door before I'd been properly hired.

"Who in hell are all those people?" one of my short-term bosses asked me.

"Bill collectors," I told him humbly.

"All of them?" he asked in amazement.

"Yep," I said, "and I've more that haven't found me yet."

"And I thought I had troubles," he said and was very kind about my shorthand.

I might have been able to duck a few of my bill collectors if it hadn't been for Mother. When they called at the house, she invited them in for coffee and they told her about their wives and children and sicknesses and ambitions and Mother retaliated with where I was working, had worked, hoped to work and could no longer work.

"Don't tell them *anything*," I used to scream at her.

She'd say, "Now, Betsy, you're taking the wrong attitude entirely. Mr. Hossenpfiester knows all about Mr. Chalmers' office closing and what a hard time we've had this winter and about having to buy a new gas heater and taking Sandy [our collie] to the veterinary and all he wants is for you to talk to him and explain when you can pay and how much."

"He's very nice when he's drinking your coffee," I said, "but when he comes to my office he yells and calls me 'sister.' Don't you dare tell him about this job."

But Mother did and pleaded with me to go down and talk to all my creditors. I wouldn't. Only too well I remembered what Gammy had said about only robbers buying things they couldn't pay for. I was ashamed of owing money, I was scared to death of all credit managers and I hated my bill collectors. I sneaked around town, jumping six feet if anyone touched me on the arm, getting tears in my eyes every time I was called to the phone and dashing for the restroom if a stranger came into my office.

Then I got behind on the payments to the Friendly Loan Company and I learned what trouble really was. The Friendly Loan collectors were everywhere. They yelled at me in the lobby of movie theatres when I had dates, shouted at me on the streetcar, and the woman with the coontrap mouth called me on the telephone three or four times a day no matter where I was working.

One time I lied to old Coontrap and told her that she had called me so much I'd been fired. I went up to her office after work and cried real tears and she said she was sorry, but the next day at work she called and when I answered the phone she said, "Well, hello, you dirty little snake. You better come up here tonight after work or else."

Then I went to work for the Government and the first week so many bill collectors came roaring into the office or called me on the phone that I expected to be fired but instead my boss took me down to the Federal Employees Union and they not only loaned me the money to pay all my bills, but paid them for me.

They paid the Friendly Loan exactly twenty-seven dollars—the difference between the thirty-five I had paid them, which they had apparently credited to cleaning the rugs, new draperies, etc., instead of the principal, and the sixty-two dollars I had actually received, and told them that if they didn't like it they could come into court and fight charges of usury.

In all my life I will never forget the deliriously free, terribly honest feeling I had the day the Federal Union notified me that all my bills had been paid and that from that day forward, except for a little matter of several hundred dollars I owed them and was to pay back so much out of each pay check, I was solvent.

Is it any wonder that I love the Government and don't mind paying my income tax?

11

I Love the Government

ONE OF THE first things I learned and loved about the Government was that I wasn't the only bonehead working for it. There were thousands of us who didn't know what we were doing but were all doing it in ten copies.

I got my first Government job by falling down a flight of stairs. Mary and I had gone to a dinner party at the apartment of friends of ours. I can remember that I didn't want to go. "I should be going to night school," I told Mary. She said, "Betty, you only live once. There will be some very charming people at this dinner party and we're going to a concert afterwards. Now for God's sake let's forget night school."

So we went to the party and the people were so charming that I didn't look where I was going and fell down my host's small winding stair and ripped the knee out of my stocking.

"Oh," I moaned as they all hurried to help me. "No job and my only pair of stockings."

"Don't you have a job?" said a very shy man with a French wife.

"No," I said. "Not since yesterday."

"I'd like you to work for me," he said. "The Government. National Recovery Administration. It'll only be temporary for a while but then there should be some good permanent jobs."

"You see," said Mary later. "People like Mr. Sheffield

don't hang around night schools. He's terribly brilliant, an Oxford graduate and speaks French."

"Not in the office, I hope," I said, remembering my struggles with the Serbo-Croat.

"For heaven's sake, Betty," said Mary. "You haven't even started to work and you don't even know what the job is but you're already worrying about not being able to do it. This is your chance! You're in on the ground floor and you can get to be an executive."

I'll always remember my first day with the Government. At eight-forty-five Monday morning Cleve and his Cord convertible deposited me in front of the Federal Office Building. It was a cool bright July morning but the irritable croaking of foghorns from the Sound two blocks away, indicated low, heavy morning mists and gave promise of a hot afternoon.

The Federal Office Building, occupying a whole block on the west side of the street, bathed placidly in the summer morning's warmth and brightness and radiated respectability and solid worth from every one of its neat red bricks.

I looked across at the occupants of the other side of the street, a burlesque theater, pawnshop, cigar store, pool hall and old hotel, huddled in the shadows in a pitiful attempt to protect their aging faces from the searching rays of the sun, and thought, How unfair—it is like putting some poor, old, unshaven, shabby Alaskan prospectors in competition with a fat, pink, smooth-shaven, pompous young businessman.

Then I flicked a speck of dust from my skirt, straightened my seams, adjusted my clean white gloves and went skipping up the marble steps. I was on the right side of the tracks, at last. The Government. Working for the Government! What a firm ring it had. How pleasantly it would slide off my tongue when I applied for credit. I waved to Cleve, who, in spite of a gas tank that had registered empty all the way to town, was easing sleekly away from the curb accompanied by many envious glances, and pushed open the swinging door.

The inside of the building was as cool as a springhouse. The tiled foyer, crowded with people going to work and waiting for elevators, had a nice, gay, relaxed atmosphere and afforded a complete contrast to mornings in other office buildings where I had worked. Mornings marred by worried grumpy businessmen, shuffling their feet, glancing irritably at their watches, hunching their shoulders, twitching, blinking, rattling things in their pockets, and jerking at their collars as they awaited their chance to push into the elevator and be whisked up to where they could hurry and get started doing something obviously distasteful to them.

Government people had a delightful "It'll keep until I get there" attitude. "What a day!" they said to each other. "Look at those mountains rising out of the fog! This is beautiful country." "When are you taking your leave, Joe? Looks like vacation weather." They exchanged morning pleasantries with the elevator starter and the operators and laughed and kidded a small colored man called Bill who loaded his car as though it were a train —"All aboahd for Evrett!" he shouted. "This cah's goin' to Evrett! Shake a leg, Colonel, youh julep's gettin' wahm waitin' foh you."

Several people looked at me, recognized me as a stranger and smiled. I smiled back and felt welcome.

I asked Bill where Mr. Sheffield's office was and he grinned and said, "Eighth flooh. You startin' to work theah?" I said I thought so and he said, "Well, now, I'm real glad. We don't have any red haih in this building at all. It look mighty nice on cold mornings."

I said, "Maybe I won't last until winter."

He said, "You'll last all right. Don't worry about that. Evybody last with the Govment." As I got in, he winked and whispered for me to look behind me. A woman in a coonskin cap and sheepskin coat was leaning on the window sill eating doughnuts out of a greasy bag. "She lasted," Bill said. "She left over from Daniel Boone's time, he, he, he!"

Mr. Sheffield's office, on the top floor, was labeled Bureau of Foreign and Domestic Commerce but taped below the black lettering was a white cardboard bearing a large blue eagle and the letters NRA. I opened the door and walked into what might have been a receiving room at a terminal post office. Everywhere were bulging gray canvas mail bags and new confused employees.

I waited uncertainly by the door. The room was large and light with huge windows that framed a magnificent view of mountains and islands, all up to their knees in mist which made them appear detached and like mirages. Some of the windows were open and let in the croaking foghorns, the shouts of warehousemen and truckers on produce row just below us and a pungent odor of burning coffee and vanilla beans.

At the far end of the room, against the windows, seated facing each other at mahogany desks, were two young women. They were opening mail, exchanging occasional remarks and exuding an air of stability and leisure that seemed to cut them off from the hurrying and confusion of the rest of the room as completely as though they were glass-enclosed. I knew instinctively that they were Civil Service—and had nothing to do with the new regime.

I was watching them enviously when a tall, dark girl, who introduced herself as Miss Mellor, told me to hang my hat up and follow her. She led me into what had been Mr. Sheffield's private office, and to a chair by his desk which had been pushed against the wall.

Mr. Sheffield, a slender, nervous man, was talking on the phone, running his hands through his hair and staring wildly at a stack of telegrams, airmail, and airmail special delivery letters that the office boy added to continually, in spite of its already overflowing the desk and spilling onto the floor.

This room was also very attractive. The large windows along its west wall had the same wonderful view of mountains, islands and mist; against the other walls were bookcases and files; the mahogany furniture was large, simple and comfortable and there was a thick rug on the floor. It had obviously been a quiet, delightful place in which to write leisurely letters and reports and to contemplate the price of grain in Algeria. Now it was like a subway station. At long mahogany tables in the center of the room were seated about fifteen assorted people, old, young, male and female, all armed with letter openers and canvas bags of mail. As they grabbed out letters, slit them open and unfolded the contents, they laughed and talked.

I asked Miss Mellor what was in the mail sacks. She said, "PRA's

—President's Re-employment Agreements. Everybody in business is supposed to sign one and promise that he'll pay his office employees at least fourteen dollars a week and cut their hours to forty a week and pay his factory workers at least forty cents an hour and cut their hours to thirty-five a week. When he signs he gets a sticker like this to put in his window." She pulled from under the confusion on Mr. Sheffield's desk a sticker about five by eight inches with the letters NRA in bright red across the top, then small letters in blue stating MEMBER, then a fierce-looking blue eagle with one foot on some sort of gear, the words WE DO OUR PART across the bottom. Miss Mellor said, "According to the National Industrial Recovery Act that was passed June thirteenth, you can't have Government contracts unless you have a blue eagle in your window. This is the district office for four states."

Just then Mr. Sheffield hung up the phone, jumped to his feet, and looked at me dazedly for a minute without the slightest sign of recognition.

I said, "Remember me, I fell down the stairs Friday night and you offered me a job."

He said, "Oh, yes. Betty Bard." The telephone rang again. He picked up the receiver and began talking.

Miss Mellor, who drawled and appeared to be as unrufflable as slate, laughed and said, "That's enough. He recognized you. Come on, I'll put you to work."

She led me to the table, introduced me, gave me a paper knife and a stack of mail and I set to work at the first job I had ever had that really fitted my capabilities. Lift, slit, take out, unfold, lift, slit, take out, unfold, lift, slit . . . By eleven o'clock my shoulders ached and my slitting hand was cramped, so I got up and went down the hall to the restroom for a cigarette.

The restroom, clean and light, with large windows facing the Sound, was deserted except for a slender girl with tinselly blond hair and gray eyes, who was smoking and staring pensively at the jagged pale blue mountains in the fog. We looked shyly at each other and then she said, "Are you working for Mr. Sheffield?" I said I was and she said so was she, she typed.

I said, "I thought I would like a monotonous job but I'm already bored and tired."

She said, "This is my third day and by five o'clock I'm so tired I could die but I keep saying, 'Four dollars a day.' 'Four dollars a day,' and going out for a cigarette whenever I can."

I said, "Is four dollars a day all we get?"

She said, "All? I think that's dandy. My last job paid eight dollars a week and I ran the whole company. Anyway, as soon as we're put on a permanent basis, we'll get either a hundred and five or a hundred and twenty dollars a month. Can you type?"

"Sure," I said, adding bravely, "shorthand too."

"Better tell the office boy," she said. "He assigns the work and he needs typists. Are you going to eat lunch with anybody?"

"No," I said.

She said, "I brought my sandwiches but we can eat at a grocery store in the next block. They have little tables upstairs and if you buy coffee and dessert they let you take your sandwiches up there. My name's Anne Marie Offenbach and my mother's a friend of the Sheffields."

I said, "My name's Betty Bard and my sister Mary is a friend of the Sheffields."

We walked back to the office together and on the office boy's next trip I told him that I could type and take shorthand, so he moved me to another room, sat me at a wiggly little table back of Anne Marie and started me typing alphabetical lists of the PRA signers.

At twelve o'clock, Anne Marie and I went over to the grocery store which catered to charge customers and carried things like cherimoyas, canned tangerines and rattlesnake meat and had a wonderful over-all smell of cinnamon, roasting coffee and ripe cheese.

The restaurant, a small balcony around the store, had the regulation faded parsley-colored tearoom tables and chairs, very inexpensive, very delicious food and terrible service, owing no doubt to the crowds and a dumbwaiter that never seemed to work except when a harassed waitress leaned down the shaft and yelled to someone below.

For twenty cents I had shrimp salad, fresh brown bread and butter and coffee. Anne Marie had a Mocha éclair with her coffee and as we ate she told me that she hated being poor, hated bringing her lunch, and already hated most of the people working with us. She said, "A woman came over to me yesterday, gripped my arm and hissed, 'Don't work so fast. Make it last.'"

I said, "That's the trouble with big offices, if you're slow you get fired, and if you're fast everybody hates you."

She said, "Already there's a strained feeling in the office—everybody listening and watching to see who you know. Don't tell anybody you know Mr. Sheffield."

I said, "How can I? Nobody speaks to me."

She said, "That's because you came to work in that big cream-colored car. Somebody saw you and the word has already gone around the office that you're rich and don't need to work."

I laughed, told her that we were on our sixty-third straight Sunday of meatloaf and I didn't see how we could be any poorer. Anne Marie said, "Well, if I were you, I'd have your brother let you off a block from the office, a lot of those people seem kind of desperate."

When we got back to work at one o'clock, I asked the office boy if he'd heard I was rich and he said, "Sure, that's why I like you," and winked. A woman sitting across the room nudged her neighbor, whispered something to her and they both glared at me. I typed my lists and tried to ignore them but I could feel their hostility smoldering across the room, its acrid smoke growing thicker and more noticeable as the hours passed.

The afternoon was very hot, the minutes crept by and there sprang into being that oldest and most bitterly fought of all office feuds. No air versus fresh air. Anne Marie and I both sat by windows which we had opened wide. When we came back from lunch we found them shut and locked, the office thick with heat and acrid with the smell of perspiration. We opened our windows wide again and immediately remarks, like little darts, went flitting through the air. "Brrr, it's so cold I can hardly type," or "Pardon me a minute while I get my sweater. Some people seem to have been raised in the North Pole." "Would you mind if I put your coat around my knees. It's so draughty."

At three o'clock, Anne Marie signaled to me and we went over to the grocery store for coffee. When we got back the windows were shut and locked again and there was a note on my typewriter: "Listen, you, type slower—you're working us out of a job."

I crumpled the note up and threw it in the wastebasket and opened the window again. There wasn't any air either inside or outside now, and my fingers splashed on the typewriter keys. As soon as I would get to the last of a large stack of the PRA's another appeared in its place. I had to stop and think whether C came after or before E and there were sharp shooting pains between my shoulderblades.

Noticing that several of the typists were hunt-and-peckers, I tried to tell myself, "Look, that's their problem. They should have gone to night school." But I knew that these people were desperate for work and there wasn't going to be enough to go around. One of the hunt-and-peck typists was as old as my mother and had a gentle, most unbusinesslike face. I smiled at her and she smiled back and just before we went home she gave me a recipe for a one-egg cake. On the streetcar I prayed that there would be some sort of a permanent filing job for her.

That night we had supper with our neighbors in their back yard. Everyone was eager to hear about my new job and I was eager to tell everything. When I reached the part about the woman gripping Anne Marie's arm and the note on my desk, Mary said, "Communists undoubtedly. They are everywhere. We're tottering right on the edge of a revolution."

Rhodsie, our dear little neighbor, said, "I thought that revolution was averted when Roosevelt closed the banks." Mary said, "Just held up temporarily. Frankly, I think we should put cots in the basement and lay in groceries."

"Why should we lay in groceries when we've got cots?" Dede asked and Mary gave her a cold look.

Mother said, "I think everything is going to be all right from now on."

I said, "Well, there's certainly room for improvement. Why Anne Marie Offenbach, a girl who sits in front of me, ran a whole office for a year for only eight dollars a week."

I Love the Government

Mary said, "And I hate her because she did. It's the Anne Maries of this world who cause depressions. People are just so constituted that if they can get some little Kick-Me-Charlie to run their whole offices for them for eight dollars a week they are not going to hire you or me and pay us twenty-five dollars a week."

"Now they are," I said. "They've all signed pledges saying they will. Anyway, Anne Marie isn't a Kick-Me-Charlie. She's smart, pretty and very independent. She just couldn't get another job."

Mary said, "Nonsense. Anybody can find a job."

I said, "They can not. You know very well if it hadn't been for you we would have stayed home and starved to death."

"Which," said Dede, "would have been a welcome change from some of the jobs Mary got *me*."

Alison said, "Lorene, a girl in my room at school, says her mother and father are Communists. She says they go to meetings all the time and they say that the bricks on the Federal Office Building where you work, Betty, are only stuck together with chalk and the whole building's going to crumble any day and the relief shoes are made of cardboard and the commissaries give people horsemeat."

Mary said, "You tell Lorene that if she really wants to taste awful food she should go to Russia and if her mother and father are so sure about the chalk instead of mortar in the Federal Office Building they must have put it there."

Dede said, "Let's not get an X put on our gate or whatever Communists do to mark their enemies. Alison, you tell Lorene that every cloud has a silver lining and hard work never hurt anybody."

Alison said, "Lorene says her father doesn't ever work. He just makes beer and hits her mother."

Cleve said, "Sounds like a natural executive to me. Surely you could fit him into your program somewhere, Mary."

Alison said, "Lorene says that when the Communists take over everything she is going to have an ice skating costume with white fur on the skirt and white figure skates that cost twenty-three dollars."

Mary said, "You tell Lorene that when the Communists take

over all she'll get will be a job in a factory, cabbage soup and a book on birth control."

Mother said, "Do you really think the NRA can do any good?"

I said, "Well, of course I've only worked there seven hours."

Cleve said, "Plenty long enough for a Bard to become an expert."

I said, "Well right now it seems to be mostly a matter of everybody signing the President's Re-employment Agreement and singing 'America the Beautiful' but later on there will be wage and hour and fair trade practice laws."

Mary said, "A man who sat next to me at the Ad Club luncheon yesterday, said that it is too late for the NRA and we might as well give up, because Standard Oil owns everything. He said they own Standard Brands, which in turn own Safeway Stores, which in turn own Pacific Fruit and Produce, which in turn has mortgages on all the farms. He says they are responsible for all the wars and that we are all just slaves being allowed to exist until the time comes when he can go into the trenches to protect Standard Oil."

Dede said, "Eeny, meeny, miney, mo, Standard Oil or the Communists—what do you want: a soldier's uniform or white fur on your skating costume?"

Mother said, "In Butte people used to say there was no use going on because the IWW's controlled everything."

Rhodsie said, "Let's heat up the coffee and have one more cup before we go in. We'll drink to the New Deal for America and Betty's new job."

Mother said, "That's a fine idea. Alison, you and Anne and Joan start carrying in the dishes."

While we waited for the coffee we sat at the cluttered picnic table and watched a thin little moon come up over the fir trees at the end of the alley. Shrill cries of "Alle, alle outs in free" came winging over from the children playing in the next street and overhead the leaves of Rhodsie's cherry tree rubbed against each other with soft rustling noises like old tissue paper. The air, fragrant with new-cut grass, rose up from the ground thick and warm like steam from the dishpan.

Rhodsie said, "Well, you've got the world by the tail now.

You're all healthy and Betty's got a job with the Government. Government jobs are awful good for women. You get sick leave and annual leave and you can cash your checks anywhere."

Dede said, "The only flaw I can find is that I'll have to take Betty's place with Mary. I can hear her now. 'Dede, dear, stop whatever you are doing and come right downtown immediately. I have a marvelous job for you. It's working for a perfectly darling man in a diamond mine in South Africa and the cattle boat leaves Sunday morning.'"

Mary said, "A job like that would be too good to give away, I'd take it myself."

Everybody laughed but I felt sad. As sad as a poor but carefree girl who has married a big, dull, rich man and knows that security can never take the place of romance.

I stayed with the NRA until the office closed on December 31, 1935, and true to Mary's predictions I rose from a four-dollar-a-day typist to a one-hundred-and-twenty-dollar-a-month secretary, to a clerk at $135 a month and finally to a labor adjuster at $1,800 per annum.

Those were vital, exciting times, my work was intensely interesting, I could bask in the warmth and security of accumulative annual and sick leave and old age retirement, and best of all, better than anything, I was at last on the other end of the gun. Somebody else was now worrying about getting my thoughts down in her notebook. That to me was success.

I could tell the day I started to work there that the Treasury Department and I were worlds apart. In the first place they had people working for them *who had never made a mistake;* in the second place they chose to ignore all previous experience not gleaned in the department and started everyone, no matter who they were or what they had done, even brilliant former labor adjusters who had their own secretaries, at the very bottom, and in the third place they thought that all Treasury Department employees, even those crawling around on the bottom, owed loyalty and should be at attention ready for a call twenty-four hours a day.

"We do not allow mistakes," I was told and so my hands

shook and I made lots of mistakes. All mistakes were immediately noticeable because the wrong person got the bid and the angry low bidder pounded on the counter in the outer office and wanted to know what in hell was going on around there.

This was the Procurement Division of the Treasury Department and we were buying supplies and letting contracts for the WPA, which was a very large order.

From the Award Section I progressed very slowly to the Contract Section where the atmosphere was much freer but there was ten million times more work and no more money.

Even though we worked a great deal of overtime, we were always behind in our work and got many little penciled letters on lined paper, addressed to the Treasurer of the United States and pleading for the money long overdue for rental of a team. "I can't buy no more oats and I need new harness. Please send me my money," Charlie Simpson would write and I would get tears in my eyes as I took out his file and found that we were returning his invoice for the fourth time because he had only sent one copy, or had not put on the certification or hadn't signed it.

For months I worked overtime and almost gave myself ulcers trying to make our contractors do things the Treasury way and trying to make the Treasury do things in a way not quite as frenziedly hurried as glacial movement but not quite as slow as the decomposition of ferns into coal.

Then finally I became resigned and became a regular but happier Treasury employee. When a pitiful letter came in pleading for long-overdue payment, instead of getting choked up and running from department to department, I would callously toss it into the enormous ready-for-payment stack, say, "Old X-3458962 is screaming for his money again," and go out for coffee.

I had been working for the Treasury Department a little less than a year when it came time to make my Christmas cards. I drew a nice little design, bought an enormous stack of paper that would take water color, obtained permission from the office boy to use the office mimeoscope and stylii, one stencil and the office mimeograph, and one night my friend Katherine and I stayed on after work and ran off my Christmas cards. The paper I had bought was too thick and had to be fed through the machine by hand so by the time I had run off my usual four or five hundred cards, which I wouldn't have time to paint and didn't have enough friends to send to, it was after midnight and all the janitors and watchmen had gone home.

The next morning when I arrived at the office, flushed with accomplishment and bearing a painted sample of my art work, I was greeted by furtive looks and whispered conferences. "What in the world's going on?" I asked, thinking they had at last uncovered some enormous bribe or misappropriation of funds.

"Someone broke into the building and used the mimeograph last night," a frightened co-worker whispered. "They're holding a conference about it downstairs now."

"Well, I used the mimeograph," I said. "I got permission from the office boy. I'd better go tell them."

"I wouldn't if I were you," she said. "It's a pretty serious offense and everybody's very upset."

"Nonsense," I said. "I'm going right down."

Just then the office boy came tearing into the office. He was pale and frightened. "Don't tell them I gave you permission," he gasped. "Please don't."

"Okay," I said. "But why?"

"There's a big meeting going on downstairs," he said. "They're going to send for you in a minute."

They did and I went down and was confronted with the evidence—a spoiled Christmas card saying "Merry Christmas and a Happy New Year—Betty Bard."

"What do you know about this?" the officer in charge of mimeographing said.

I said, "It's my Christmas card. I stayed down here after work last night and ran them off on the mimeograph."

He said, "Betty, that mimeograph is Government property—it is against the law to use Government property for private use."

I said, "I asked permission to use the mimeograph—anyway I always used the mimeograph at the NRA to make my Christmas cards."

He said, "*That* was the National Recovery Administration. *This* is the Treasury Department."

I said, "Well, I'm sorry, I didn't know I wasn't supposed to."

He said, "Being sorry isn't enough."

I said, "Well, I'll pay for the stencil and the ink, then."

He said, "I can't accept payment because there is no proper requisition or purchase order authorizing you to purchase them from the Government."

I said, "Well, what do you want me to do?"

He was so solemn about it all that I thought for a moment he was going to hand me a pistol and tell me that he would leave the room while I took the only way out. He didn't though. He looked out the window. Stared straight ahead. Leaned back in his chair and jingled coins in his pocket and finally said to me, "Well, I'm going to forget the whole thing. I'm just going to pretend it never happened. But don't . . . ever . . . let . . . such . . . a . . . thing . . . happen . . . again . . . while . . . you . . . are . . . in . . . the . . . employ . . . of . . . the Treasury . . . Department."

I took great pleasure in sending one of the Christmas cards to every single person in the entire Treasury Department, many of whom I didn't know. I could just see them burning them in ash trays and burying the telltale ashes in old flower pots.

I finally collapsed with tuberculosis and was wheeled away from the Treasury Department. When I got well again I went to work for the National Youth Administration.

PART III

12

I Have a Little Shadow—Who Don't?

GETTING TUBERCULOSIS in the middle of your life is like starting downtown to do a lot of urgent errands and being hit by a bus. When you regain consciousness you remember nothing about the urgent errands. You can't even remember where you were going. The important things now are the pain in your leg; the soreness in your back; what you will have for dinner; who is in the next bed.

By background and disposition some people are better suited to being hit by a bus than others. For instance Doris, who had worked in a Government office with me. Her mother had a little tumor, her father had a "bad leg," Doris had a great deal of "female trouble," and they all were hoping that Granny had cancer. Doris, her brothers and sisters, her aunts and uncles, her mother and father, her grandmother and grandfather, all of them, had begun life as barely formed, tiny little premature babies carried around on pillows and fed with eyedroppers. If they did manage to pull through the first year, and they often did, life from then on was one continuous ache, pain, sniffle and cough. When Doris or any member of her large ailing family asked each other how they felt, it wasn't just a pleasantry, they really wanted to know.

To Doris and her family tuberculosis would have been anticlimactic but a definite asset. So of course it was not Doris but I who got tuberculosis, and the contrast between our families was noticeable.

In the first place our family motto was "People are healthy and anybody who isn't is a big stinker."

In addition to good health, my family possessed a great capacity for happiness. We managed to be happy eating Gammy's dreadful food or Mother's delicious cooking; in spite of cold baths and health programs; with Gammy's awful forebodings about the future hanging over our heads; in private school or public; in very large or medium-sized houses; with dull bores or bright friends; with or without money; keeping warm by burning books (chiefly large thick collections of sermons, left us by some of the many defunct religious members of the family) or anthracite coal in the furnace; in love or just thrown over; in or out of employment; being good sports or cheats; fat or thin; young or old; in the city or in the country; with or without lights; with or without husbands.

This enjoyment of life, no matter what, was Mother's idea and she taught us early to despise "saddos" (sorry-for-themselves) and to make the best of things. How she managed this with Gammy around busily making the worst of everything is beyond my powers of comprehension. It could have been that Mother realized that as children's whole lives are made up of threats of one kind or another—"Just wait until Daddy gets home"; "Step on a crack and break your mother's back"; "Eat another piece of cake and you'll burst"—we wouldn't take Gammy's morbid prophecies very seriously, which we didn't.

When I finally got tuberculosis, thus achieving the goal Gammy had set for me early in life, we were all being happy and making the best of things in our brown-shingled house. Mary and Cleve were married and Gammy had died several years before, so at that time "we" meant Mother, me, my ten- and nine-year-old daughters Anne and Joan, my younger sisters Dede and Alison, an adopted sister Madge and as many other people as we could jam inside the bulging walls.

Madge was brought to the house one Sunday evening along with about forty other people, introduced as a friend of somebody's roommate. She played the piano, was instantly recognized as one of us and a week later moved in and was adopted permanently as a member of the family.

Our casually increasing household was such a source of amazement to a dear little neighbor who had a well-ordered life and only one child, that she used to hurry over on Sunday mornings to count us and see who or what had been added.

In this friendly crowded house illness was unwelcome. "Thank God we're all so healthy!" we said during the depression when we had meatloaf three hundred and forty-two times running. "At least we have our health," we used to say laughingly when the Power Company turned off the lights.

Now I was ashamed because suddenly I didn't seem to have my health. In January I began having a series of heavy colds, one right after the other. They would begin as head colds and I'd stay in bed and drink water and take aspirin for a day. Then the cold would move down into my chest and because my eyes and nose had stopped running I'd decide I was well and go back to work.

At work I'd notice vague pleurisy pains in my back so I'd move out of draughts and take more aspirin. If my cough was deep and shattering I'd get some cough medicine from a reliable druggist and after a while the cold would be gone. For a few weeks I would be apparently all right and then bang, another cold. I couldn't figure out where they were coming from or why, but I did know that each one left me thinner and tireder. In fact my tiredness became so constant that I ceased to notice it and thought that I felt well and had energy when actually I was merely not as tired as usual.

By spring I began getting up in the morning feeling dead tired and after dressing, drinking a cup of coffee and smoking a cigarette, I would feel like going back to bed instead of straining at the leash to begin the day's activities. By having another cup of coffee and a cigarette when I got to work and another cup of coffee and cigarette at ten o'clock, I managed to scoop up enough energy so that I felt quite brisk by noon. During the afternoon my energy receded rapidly until by four o'clock I used to be so tired that I would go out to the restroom and stretch out on a hard wooden bench for a blissful five minutes of rest.

I couldn't understand it. My job was hard but it was interesting and I liked the people I worked with, but every day I had to force myself to go to work. On weekends when I gardened, cleaned house and took the children for walks, I felt quite well so I reasoned that my lassitude had something to do with my job and everything would straighten out when I had my vacation.

From January on I noticed also that I had stars in front of my eyes when I bent over. Reaching down to get a file from a low drawer I would straighten up to a blinding kaleidoscope of stars, whirls, flashes and round black dots. Biliousness, I thought, and took calomel and tried not to bend over any oftener than I could help. I thought also that it was probably a combination of my tiredness, my job and the calomel that gave me the indigestion. People who are very nervous and eat so fast they rarely taste what they eat have indigestion but only big bores talk about it, so I ignored mine.

By the time I had gone through my sixth cold, I noticed that I seemed much more nervous, that I slept badly and that I had a heavy feeling over my heart and occasional sharp pains in my lungs. I attributed the heavy feeling and the pains to my indigestion and my indigestion to my nervousness and my nervousness to my job.

This sounds, I know, as though in addition to many symptoms of tuberculosis, I had also all the symptoms of a very retarded mentality. I hadn't. It was just that I was operating under the impression that I was healthy and I thought that everybody who worked felt as I did. It never occurred to me that my complaints were symptoms of tuberculosis. (Actually they all were.) From Gammy's training, the movies I had seen and the books I had read, I thought that the only real symptoms of tuberculosis were a dry hacking cough and a clean white linen handkerchief delicately touched to pale lips and coming away blood-flecked.

I was almost thirty years old, had been married and divorced, had two children, had raised chickens and seemed to have normal intelligence but what I knew about tuberculosis, its symptoms, its cause and its cure, could have been written on the head of a pin. It was just that nobody in our family had ever had tuberculosis. None of my friends had ever had tuberculosis, and it is not something that you read up on just for the pure joy of the thing.

The ironic thing is that, although I knew nothing about tuberculosis and never entertained the thought that I might have the disease, for two years I had been very concerned about a co-worker of mine in the Government service, who looked like a cadaver and coughed constantly, with a dry little hacking cough, much of the time in my face. "I think that man has tuberculosis," I finally told my boss excitedly. "Who don't?" was his laconic reply.

When I entered the sanatorium and filed a compensation claim against the Government, naming the cadaverous co-worker as a possible source of infection, he was sent through the t.b. clinic and found to have had active, communicable tuberculosis for nineteen years. He knew he had it and apparently liked it, for it was much against his will that he was finally sent to a sanatorium.

Four or five of us, who had worked with him, went to sanatoriums with t.b. but the Government paid none of the compensation claims. Whoever it was in charge of compensation claims in Washington had the same attitude as my boss. "All these girls have tuberculosis," read our claims. "Who don't?" came back the reply from Washington.

In March I still had January's cold so I surreptitiously consulted an eye, ear, nose and throat specialist. Having had little to do with doctors and having been convinced since infancy that I was healthy, I was ashamed to tell him all the little things that seemed wrong with me so I limited my symptoms to his field and told him about the cold and the chest pains. He examined my eyes, my nose, and my throat and said that there was nothing wrong with me. He patted my shoulder and told me to try infra-red on my back. Sometime later the cold went away.

In May the attacks of indigestion became so frequent and so severe that I went to an internal medicine specialist. I gave him the symptoms which fitted his field. I told him about the indigestion and stars in front of my eyes. He examined my stomach and abdomen and said that there was nothing wrong with me. He patted my shoulder and told me to drink less coffee.

By July I coughed a lot. Also in July I had a complete physical examination for $5,000-worth of life insurance. I told the examining physician about my cough and he said, "Cigarettes, haha, I have one too." I told him about the tiredness and he said, "You should have this job." I answered truthfully all the questions about who died of what and "has anyone in your family ever had tuberculosis, syphilis, Buerger's disease, large swelling of the spleen, a steady job, etc.," was considered a good risk and given the life insurance.

In spite of my increasing debility, there seemed to be nothing wrong with me. I was like the frail creatures in the olden days who for no apparent reason wasted away and died. I continued to take aspirin for the colds and chest pains; calomel for the stars and bismuth for the indigestion, and to attribute the other discomforts to my job, which was arduous in itself and, like all Government jobs, made more so by politics and conflicting personalities (chiefly my own).

In September I became afflicted with hemorrhoids (according to the dictionary you can have but one hemorrhoid—more than one are piles, which I consider an indelicate word). Hemorrhoids should not be glossed over or ignored, so I called my sister Mary, and she sent me at once to her husband, a pathologist. Inasmuch as the study of pathology seemed to embrace the entire human body, I told him all of my symptoms, even the nervousness and the insomnia. He listened gravely, examined my back and chest; tested my sputum, had my lungs x-rayed and sent me to a chest specialist.

I was at the chest specialist's all afternoon. He listened to my breathing and coughing, tested my sputum, examined my throat and fluoroscoped and x-rayed my lungs. He was showing me the x-rays when he gave me the diagnosis. He said, "This shadow is the tuberculous area in the left lung. You have pulmonary tuberculosis." I didn't know that pulmonary tuberculosis meant tuberculosis of the lungs. I thought it was some strange quick-dying type. He concluded, "You will have to go to a sanatorium."

Sanatorium, I knew what that meant. I had seen Margaret Sullavan in *Three Comrades* and I had read *The Magic Mountain*. Sanatoriums were places in the Swiss Alps where people went to die. Not only that but everyone I'd ever heard of who had had tuberculosis had died. I was undoubtedly going to be in excellent company but I didn't want to die.

For one who had just pronounced a death sentence the chest specialist seemed singularly untouched. He was whistling "There's a Small Hotel" and looking up a number in the telephone directory. He found his number and began to dial. I got up and went over to the window. It was nearly five o'clock and the September evening fog had begun to drift up from the waterfront. A car tooted its horn irritably in the street below. In the lighted windows of an office across the court I watched the girls jam things quickly into drawers, slam files closed and hurry into their coats and hats.

I said to the doctor, "What about my job?" He had hung up the phone and was leaning back in his chair. He was well tanned and very handsome. He said briskly, "Oh, you won't be able to work for a long time. Complete bedrest is what you must have. You're contagious too," he added comfortably. I began to cough and he automatically reached down into the drawer of his desk and handed me a Kleenex. I covered my mouth as he had told me to do, and as I had not done for the four or five months I had been coughing, and felt neat and very sad. I said, "How much does a sanatorium cost?" He said, "Thirty-five to fifty dollars a week." My salary had just been raised to $115 a month. I said, "How long will I have to be in a sanatorium?" He said, "At least a year—probably longer." I picked up my purse and gloves and said good night. As I went through the waiting room I could hear him whistling "There's a Small Hotel."

Mary's husband was waiting for me in his office. In a shaky voice and close to tears I told him about the diagnosis, the sanatorium and the $35 to $50 a week. He said, "The Pines, one of the finest sanatoriums in the world, is an endowed institution and free to anyone who needs care and cannot pay. There is a waiting list of over two hundred but mothers with small children are usually taken right in. I'll write a letter to the Medical Director." He took a sheet of paper and began to write. His writing was scratchy and entirely illegible, but he seemed very satisfied with it and anyway it was going to another doctor. He folded the letter and handed it to me. He said, "Be at the clinic at eight-thirty tomorrow morning. Here is the address. Give them this letter and tell the doctor to call me. As soon as Mary gets here I'll drive you home." He also was very handsome but, more important, he was interested and he was kind.

Mary came in then and in five minutes told me so many big lies about tuberculosis, who had it, where they got it, and so forth, that I was immediately cheered up. She said that practically everyone on the street had tuberculosis, that she couldn't go to a party without seeing at least four far-gone cases, that actually it had gotten to a point where she was ashamed to admit she hadn't t.b. because everyone who was anyone—look at Robert Louis Stevenson and Chopin—had had t.b. Anyway with or without t.b. she wished someone would order *her* to go on complete bedrest—she hadn't had any sleep for so long that the muscles of her eyelids had atrophied. She thought a slight case of t.b. should be the aftermath of every pregnancy so that the poor mother could get a little sleep. She thought a lot of things and she thought them out loud, which was soothing and made it unnecessary for me to talk and so I didn't cough all the way home.

Instead I worried about how to tell the family and if I should tell the children. I toyed with dramatic little scenes in which I went quietly into the house as though nothing had happened, smiling often and bravely, and then Mary told them. I entertained the idea of telling just Mother and when I had gone upstairs, smiling often and bravely, she would gather them all together, preferably around her knee, and tell them about my "trouble."

I needn't have wasted the effort. When we stopped in front of the house the entire family, including the children and the dogs, came bursting out. They already knew. Mary had called them while I was at the chest specialist's office. I was to go right to bed in Mother's bed, the fourposter in which we had all been born, and had had all of our illnesses.

There was a fire in the fireplace. There was fresh hot coffee. There were infinite love and abundant sympathy. There may have been too much sympathy because after a while I became almost overcome with my own bravery, selflessness and power of mind over body. To think that for the whole past year I had been going my way, working, playing and laughing, while all the time I was seriously, perhaps fatally, ill. I wallowed in self-pity. Instead of admitting to myself that it was a great relief to know what was wrong with me and that I was really sick instead of ambitionless and indolent, I dripped tears on Mother's blue down quilt as I created doleful mental pictures of little Anne and Joan putting flowers on Mommy's fresh grave. I was a big, no-sense-of-humor saddo. I coughed all night long and enjoyed doing it.

Instructions from the clinic were that new patients must arrive at The Pines between the hours of three and four-thirty in the afternoon, "after rest hours and before supper." Mary was to drive me out and Madge and Mother were going along. We had planned to leave about two o'clock. We had also planned to send the children to school and to keep everything very normal.

I awoke early to milky windows and foghorns. The hollow echoing footsteps of the paper boy followed by the thump of the paper on the porch. A streetcar clanging past, high-spirited and empty on its first trip. A window slamming shut across the street. The thud of the front door and several sharp joyful barks as Mother let the dogs out. The complaining groans of the starter on a car somewhere down the alley. The rumbling thunder of another streetcar crossing the bridge over the park ravine two blocks away.

Finally Anne asked bluntly, "Are you going to die, Betty?" I said of course not. How ridiculous. Joan said, "Bessie had tuberculosis and she died." Bessie was a school friend of Alison's, and until this moment her illness and death had been tactfully kept from me. I said, "She must have been a great deal sicker than I am." Anne said, "Will you be home for Christmas?" I said that I didn't know and then Joan said, "Mr. Bartlett takes out his teeth and washes them in the hose." The good-byes were over. It was time to get up.

In spite of our good intentions, the children did stay home from school and everything was very abnormal but I managed somehow to tie up most of the odds and ends of my life, and to have a permanent wave and a very short haircut before two o'clock. Then the thin autumn sunshine and the rollicking dogs gave a picnicking air to the good-byes, but even so as I walked down the steps of the old brown-shingled house I remarked morbidly to Dede that I felt like a barnacle that had been pried off its rock. Glancing briefly at my short, too-curly hair she remarked drily that I looked quite a lot like one too.

As we drove off I turned and waved and waved to the children. They stood on the sidewalk, squinting against the sun. Young, long-legged and defenseless. I loved them so that I felt my heart draining and wondered if I was leaving a trail behind me like the shiny mark of a snail.

The Pines was several miles out of the city and it was a lovely day for a drive but horrible little phrases such as "The Last Mile" and "The Last Roundup" kept creeping drearily into my thoughts as I looked at gardens blazing with dahlias, zinnias, Michaelmas daisies and chrysanthemums. At lawns blatantly green from damp fall weather, lapping the edges of the sidewalks. At full-leaved Western trees hesitantly turning a little yellow on the edges, while imported Eastern trees blushed delicately as they dropped their leaves in the soft, warm autumn air.

After a while we left the city and drove along the shores of the Sound. As we progressed the autumn colors grew braver and so did I. The bloodless lukewarm sunshine, too weak to lift the fog from the silky gray water, at least made the greens and yellows of the trees clear and brilliant, my outlook less doleful.

We entered The Pines by a long, poplar-lined drive. On either side were great vine-covered Tudor buildings, rolling lawns, greenhouses and magnificent gardens. It might have been any small endowed college except that there were no laughing groups strolling under the trees. In fact, the only sign of life anywhere at all was a single nurse who flitted between two buildings like a white paper in the wind. We parked the car, distributed the luggage among us and went up the brick steps of the main building.

The entrance hall was large and dim with tall leaded windows, a tiled floor and dark woodwork. Feebly lit mysterious corridors radiated from this central point and we all stood uncertainly wondering which to take. There was no one in sight anywhere. No sound. Mary said, "I didn't realize that your arrival would create such a sensation," and a nurse bobbed up from behind a high counter and said, "Shhhh!" This startled Madge so that she dropped the four large books she was carrying. They crashed to the floor and noise rolled along the corridors like spilled marbles.

The nurse swelled her nostrils and drew in her lips. I hurried over to the desk and explained that I was the patient. She said, "We were expecting you." Her voice held the same wild enthusiasm generally bestowed on process servers. She said, "What is your full name, Mrs. Bard?" I said, "It's Miss Bard. Miss Betty Bard. You see I have always used my maiden name in business and . . ."

The rest of what I was about to say went dribbling back down my throat for the nurse was looking at me with eyes that could have been taken out and used to replace diamond drills. She said, "You have children, haven't you?" "Yes," I said almost adding, involuntarily, "Mr. District Attorney." She said, "You're Mrs. Bard, then."

Then she took my history, probing deep, questioning all my answers and in general giving the impression that she was building up a case to prove that tuberculosis was really a venereal disease. When she had finished she gave me some papers to sign; a little book called, "Rules of the Sanatorium"; and some salient facts about visitors. She threw these facts into me like darts into a target.

They were: 1. The children could come to see me once a month for ten minutes only. 2. I could have three adult visitors on Thursdays and Sundays from two until four o'clock. 3. If my visitors came too early, stayed too late, were noisy, broke rules or exceeded the allotted three in number, my visiting privileges would be removed for an indefinite length of time.

Then Florence Nightingale leaned over the counter and directed us with her pen down one of the dark corridors to a waiting room.

The waiting room had large casement windows, a lovely view of the gardens, overstuffed furniture, a virginal fireplace with its firebricks washed and waxed clear up into the chimney, and no magazines, no ash trays. We put down the suitcases, chose places, sat down and were immediately engulfed in silence. The kind of all-embracing silence that makes the snap of a purse clasp sound like a pistol shot, the scratch of a match like the rasp of a hacksaw blade. Mary said at last, in a strained unnatural voice, "Napoleon Bonaparte had tuberculosis but I don't suppose you care. I certainly don't."

The silence settled down again like wet newspapers. Finally Madge, who was young and healthy but a terrific hypochondriac, said in her deep, slow voice, "God this is a depressing place! It would cheer me up just to hear somebody choking to death. I've got a pain in my chest, Sydney, do you think I've got t.b.?" Mother said, "Madge, you know that if this were an orthopedic hospital the pain would be in your leg." Madge laughed and dropped all the books again. The clatter was muted by the rug but we all looked guiltily toward the door. No one came. Nothing happened. Just the silence.

Like wax figures in a store window we sat motionless in unnatural attitudes on the unyielding furniture, all facing each other and the empty grate. The quality of the whole scene was so dreamlike that I looked at Mother and Mary, side by side on a mustard-colored love seat in front of the window, and expected to see large cobwebs attaching them to each other and to the casement back of them. I felt that we had all been there forever.

Then from far off, down one of the dim passageways we heard the creak of a wheelchair and the slap, slap of approaching footsteps. At once we came to life, stood up, checked over the luggage, embraced each other tenderly and said all the things we'd been trying so hard not to say for the past thirty minutes. I said, "Only once a month for ten minutes—I won't even know them." Mother, with tears in her sweet brown eyes, said, "I can't

I Have a Little Shadow—Who Don't? 195

bear to say good-bye to you, Betsy." Mary said, "Don't worry about money." Madge said, "I hope the rest of the place isn't as depressing as this."

A nurse came in pulling a wheelchair behind her. She was blond, cool and efficient. She said, "Which of you is Mrs. Bard?" I stepped forward. She did not smile. She looked at me, then at my luggage with expressionless granite eyes. She said, "Get in the wheelchair. Don't bring any books, you won't be able to read for a long time." She didn't acknowledge the presence of Mary, Mother or Madge. She merely piled my belongings in my lap and wheeled me out the door and down the corridor. I turned to wave good-bye but all I could see past her starched white uniform were waving fingertips, pale and blurred against the dark walls.

We left the main building, crossed a little vine-covered bridge, entered another building, took an elevator to the second floor and went creakily down a long, draughty, pale green hall, each side of which was partitioned off into rooms. Each room had two white-covered single beds in it and in each bed a head was raised as I went by.

At the end of the hall we went through a pair of swinging doors marked BATHROOM. Bathroom proved to be three rooms—a square center room with a single hospital bed in each corner, tall casement windows at the end and dark red block linoleum on the floor; a room to the left with three lavatories and two washtubs; and a room to the right, in which there was a large old-fashioned bathtub. The nurse was busily filling this with boiling water. I explained to her that I had had a bath not three hours before but she didn't even look up. She said, "Makes no difference, rule of the Sanatorium is that all incoming patients must have a bath. Get undressed."

As I undressed she opened my suitcase and took out soap, washcloths, pajamas, slippers and robe and accompanied each movement with a rule. She acted as if she were reading them off the bottom of the soap, in my bathrobe sleeve, from the hem of the washcloth. "Patients must not read. Patients must not write. Patients must not talk. Patients must not laugh. Patients must not sing. Patients must lie still. Patients must not reach. Patients must relax. Patients must—" I was ready for the bath so I interrupted to ask if I might put a little cold water into the steaming tub or if there was a rule that patients must be boiled. She gave me the full impact of her granite eyes and let a little cold water into the tub.

While I bathed she unpacked my bags, holding up everything in two disdainful fingers and saying, "Why did you bring this?" I answered truthfully that some of the things such as extra sweaters, I thought I would need; other things, such as a little sewing box made me by Anne and a calendar with the picture pasted on upside down, made me by Joan, some sachet bags and a little cactus plant, I had brought to remind me of home.

After I was well scrubbed and beet red from the boiling water which, I judged, was at least one third disinfectant, I was told to put on my pajamas and report to the washtub. Knowing that it would be wasted effort, I told Granite Eyes that already that morning I had had two shampoos, one before and one after my permanent wave.

She looked without interest at my hair, which had been painstakingly arranged in flat curls close to my head, and said, "It's a rule of the Sanatorium that all incoming patients must have their hair washed." This she proceeded to do, aided by a great deal of green soap, her own strong fingers, and more boiling water. "At least she didn't delouse me," I thought bitterly as she hauled out the drier. The drier was very hot and had enough force to strip the spring growth from any tree at fifty yards.

When my hair was as dry as excelsior the nurse handed me a comb and a mirror. One glance at my exploding head and I felt like breaking the comb in little pieces and throwing them over my shoulder. I made a few futile dabs but it was like trying to part and arrange a thistle. The nurse offered no suggestions. She put away the bath things, then wheeled me down the hall and into a four-bed ward.

The ward was large and square. The walls were a pale Oscar Wilde-ish green. The floor was dark red. Across the east end of the room were four casement windows, curtainless and blindless and opened wide. In each corner of the room were a bed, a bed-

I Have a Little Shadow—Who Don't?   197

side stand and a chair. Each bed had a white muslin slipcover, called a windshield, over the head, a white cotton spread and a folded dark green blanket on the foot. The bedside stands had white porcelain tops. In three of the beds there were patients. The fourth, in the southeast corner by the windows was turned down for me.

The nurse helped me off with my bathrobe and motioned me in. After the scalding bath and the hot blasts from the hair drier, reaching my legs down into the clammy depths of the bed was like pulling on a wet bathing suit. I asked for a hot-water bottle. The nurse had just put it, along with my clean pajamas and washcloths into the cupboard of the bedside stand. She didn't take it out and she didn't answer.

She put the bath powder, soap, toothpaste and toothbrush in the drawer. To a bar on the side of the stand she fastened, with large safety pins, a heavy brown paper bag neatly folded down at the top. Inside this she put a smaller brown paper bag, also neatly folded down at the top. "All used paper handkerchiefs must go into this bag," she said. "You must put in a clean bag every morning." Beside the used-napkin bag she pinned another heavy brown paper bag. Into this she put a large package of new paper handkerchiefs. She said, "Always cover your mouth when you cough. Use these handkerchiefs."

On the top of the stand she put two glasses of water on a neatly folded paper napkin. Also a waxed cardboard sputum cup. She said, "Keep nothing on your stand but your water glasses; and sputum cup. Never keep pictures or flowers on your stand." She put extra brown bags, extra sputum cups and extra paper handkerchiefs in my stand drawer, saying, "Keep your stand neat and clean. An orderly patient is a helpful patient." Then pushing the wheelchair out of the way she stepped back and looked me over. Coolly, impersonally.

I said again, "May I please have my hot-water bottle filled?" Granite Eyes said, "It is a rule of the Sanatorium that hot-water bottles are never filled until October first." I said, "I'm cold. My teeth are chattering." She said, "October first," and left. This was September twenty-eighth. Three days to go. Well, I could hold out if my teeth would. I pulled the covers up to my chin and looked around.

Across from me was a woman apparently in her early thirties, thin to the point of emaciation, with thick short curly brown hair, a small triangular face, feverish cheeks and enormous luminous brown eyes. Her name was Sylvia Fletcher she told me. She was very sweet and very hoarse. She said in a whisper that sounded like walking on spilled sugar, "Don't worry about the cold. You'll warm up eventually. I know because I've had t.b. for twenty years."

In the southwest corner was a small, very pretty dark woman also in her early thirties and also very thin. Her name was Marie Charles and she informed me immediately that she hated everything about The Pines and everyone in The Pines. She said, "It kills me when I think how anxious I was to get in this place. I had read too many books and I thought all sanatoriums were like those in the Swiss Alps. What a laugh! The only thing Alpine about this place is the attitude of the nurses." Sylvia said, "Now, Marie, you must be patient. The cure of tuberculosis is all discipline. Patience and discipline." Marie flounced over and turned her face to the wall.

In the northwest corner was a little Japanese girl with delicate pale brown hands folded demurely on her chest. Her name was Kimi Sanbo. She had thick straight black hair parted in the center and pulled severely back with two blue barrettes, sharp black brows that tilted toward her temples and large, very bright buttonhole-shaped black eyes. Her cheeks were pink and shiny. She said nothing.

At four o'clock we had supper. First an ambulant patient came around and propped up the beds so that we were sitting up; then nurses dealt out trays, set with silver, napkins, salad, bread and butter, dessert and little slips of paper with beautiful thoughts on them. Then the food carts were wheeled around and we were served spaghetti, soup and tea by the Charge Nurse. The food was well seasoned and very good but cold. The beautiful thought on my tray said, "If you must be blue, be a bright blue."

While we were eating supper the Charge Nurse and House

Doctor made a rapid tour of the room and asked us how we felt. I said that I felt cold and the Charge Nurse, who was Nordic and beautiful, said, "Hot water bottles October first," and they left. Half an hour after supper we took our temperatures. Temperatures seemed to be very important and as each of my wardmates took the thermometer out of her mouth she solemnly reported the results. Sylvia's was 102°, Marie's 101°, Kimi's 101.6° and mine was 99°.

At five o'clock the radio, which was controlled and set at the office, with a speaker in each ward, began drooling forth organ music. Organ music of any kind depresses me and added to that was the fact that I had no bed lamp. A bed lamp apparently was not considered a necessity and had not been on the list of requirements. My corner was dark. My thoughts gloomy.

It was hard to remember how anxious I had been to enter The Pines; how grateful I had been to the Medical Director for putting me ahead of the long waiting list; how wonderful it was that I was being cured and cared for for nothing. I was cold and lonely and I missed my children and my family. The ward was very quiet and little wisps of fog crept through the wide-open windows. If only I could read, or write, or talk or do anything but lie there and listen to that awful organ music.

The organist was playing "Hills of Home." I couldn't stand it. Large tears rolled out of the corners of my eyes, across my temples and into my ears. I looked at my three wardmates. They all seemed relaxed and contented. Sylvia said, "The first hundred years are the hardest," and a nurse, coming in just then to give us back rubs, said, "Patients are not allowed to talk. Roll over, Mrs. Bard."

At seven o'clock we had hot cocoa, hot milk or cold milk. At nine o'clock the lights were turned out by a main switch in the hall. The night nurse operated by flashlight. Up and down the halls she went with her flashlight like a firefly dancing over each bed, resting for a second on each face. When she left our room the darkness, silence and cold settled down again like a shroud.

The dark-haired woman coughed, drank water, reached in her stand for something, turned over and coughed again. Sylvia wheezed faintly. Her bed creaked and I heard the thump of her water glass on the stand. There was no sound at all from Kimi's corner. I drank some water and tried turning on my stomach but in so doing I missed the original slightly warmed place where I had been lying and hit virginal, ice cold, fog-dampened sheet. I almost screamed as I quickly turned back and snuggled down into my original lukewarm nest. The night went on and on and on and I grew progressively colder and sadder. There's one thing to be said in favor of life at The Pines, I thought, as I tried futilely to warm a small new area at the bottom of the bed. It's going to make dying seem like a lot of fun.

13

I'm Cold and So Is the Attitude of the Staff

THE STAFF at The Pines had but one motivating factor—to get the patients well. This motivating factor, like a policeman's nightstick, was twirled over our heads twenty-four hours a day. And by necessity too, because a tuberculosis sanatorium is a paradox. It should be a place where the patients are striving to get well, aided by the doctors and nurses, but is actually a place where the patients are trying to kill themselves but are prevented, in many cases, by the doctors and nurses.

In the beginning the staff at The Pines had undoubtedly been more sympathetic, more understanding, more interested in each patient as an individual, but years and years of working with people who clutched their tuberculosis to them like a beloved old shawl and dared the doctors and nurses to get it away from them, or took the attitude that the staff was secretly injecting them with tuberculosis to keep them on to perform small tasks like putting up beds or pushing tray carts, had finally worn off any little facets of sympathy and tenderness and left the system smooth, efficient and immutable. "We are going to make you well and the shortest distance between two points is a straight line," we were told. "Here is the line, either follow it or get out."

The shortest distance between two points in waking people up in the morning is to bong them on the head with something. The Pines had the next best thing, the washwater girls. The washwater girls were female patients with eight hours up, who were testing their strength and endurance (and the bedrest patients' nerves and stamina) by doing a little work around the hospital.

That first morning, in the bleak, low vitality period between five-thirty and six, they suddenly came careening in our door, snapped on the overhead lights and brought their cart, loaded with basins and pitchers, to a crashing halt in the center of the room. The blare of light and the shattering noise were like being exploded.

I was jerked out of sleep and into wakefulness with one blow and sat up quivering, trying to bring the room into focus. A short, round girl with black curly hair and surprising, light blue eyes, slammed an aluminum basin down on the porcelain-topped stand with a resounding wham and told me in a loud cheerful voice to put one of my water glasses into the basin. I did and she filled the glass with hot water, putting a very small additional amount into the basin.

She told me that her name was Estelle Richmond and that she had been at The Pines for three years and was "real bad." As she was plump and pink cheeked and looked much healthier than most of my friends, I said, "But you look wonderful." She said, "Oh, I get along fine for a while and then I break down and back to bed I go. I've been in this ward five different times. Are you very bad?" I answered truthfully that I didn't know but that I hoped to go home in a year. "A year!" She was scornful. "Nobody gets out of here in a year. It even takes longer than that to die. You better plan on longer, kiddo." Kiddo didn't dare tell her that she had been secretly planning on six months, dead or alive.

The other washwater girl, a very thin young blonde with a gold tooth and a maroon sweater, was giving Sylvia, Marie and Kimi the news about the rest of the sanatorium. "Mary Haley had a hemorrhage and is back at Bedrest. Katherine Fay had a chest exam yesterday but the doctor told her she had to stay on three hours up. She's been on three hours for two years. Poor kid! Hazel Espey's going to have an operation and John Hennigan was caught smoking and lost his town leave, his first in two years."

I noticed two things: all the news was depressing and the patients spoke of two, three and five years with a casualness usually associated with minutes. I asked Sylvia if she knew how long the average patient stayed at The Pines but she was brushing her teeth and didn't answer, so I pushed the question to one side and took up a weightier one of whether to wet my hair first and wash in comby water, or to wash first and wet my hair with spit.

Always cross and irritable in the morning, I was now also sodden with fatigue and cramped with cold and when I had finished washing in the small puddle of already lukewarm water, my face felt as pulled and dry as though I had on a mud pack. I reached in my stand drawer for my bottle of rose water and glycerin and found that the nurse who admitted me had evidently considered it medicine and sent it home.

I took out my hand mirror and prepared to do something with my hair but one look at my dry gray face and sphagnum-moss hair made me want to bang my head against the back of the bed and scream. I took out my lipstick and Sylvia said immediately, "No, no, Betty, patients are not allowed to wear makeup except on visiting day." This made me want to bang her head against the back of the bed and scream. To make matters worse my blood was all crouched shivering in the vicinity of my heart instead of coursing warmly down into my icy extremities. I slammed the drawer of my stand shut and lay back and hated morning.

After the washwater girls had collected the basins, we all removed the brown paper bags of used handkerchiefs from our stands, unfolded the edges, twisted the tops and threw them to

I'm Cold and So Is the Attitude of the Staff 203

the foot of the beds. Then we put in carefully folded clean bags, marked our sputum specimens with the name, date and whether it was an eight- or twenty-four-hour specimen, assembled our new sputum cups, tidied our stands and listened to Marie complain.

Marie had pains in her chest, gas on her stomach, aches in her joints, was sure she had bedsores, and was constipated. She thought all doctors were quacks because they hadn't diagnosed her tuberculosis while it was in its early stages, and though I learned that this complaint was common among all the t.b. patients and stemmed undoubtedly from the fact that too many doctors wouldn't know tuberculosis if it was coiled around their legs, in Marie's case picking early tuberculosis out from among her hundreds of other ailments would have been as difficult as picking one lone violet in a field of vetch.

Marie said that all patients were supposed to be moved out of the four-bed ward and up the hall into one of the cubicles at the end of one month, yet she had been at The Pines five weeks and they hadn't moved her. She said that all the other patients were allowed to read and write fifteen minutes a day and walk to the bathroom once a day at the end of the first month, but not she. The Charge Nurse didn't like her.

Kimi said, in her small high voice, "It has been my observation that, in all things in life, the man is favored. Here at The Pines, in the Men's Bedrest Hospital, which is one floor below this, a man may read all the daily paper from the day he enters." Sylvia said, "Men are stronger than women. They don't need such complete rest." Kimi said, "Nonsense, it is because the Medical Director is also a man. He thinks, 'The woman's mind is little. She can lie twenty-four hour a day for thirty day, a total of seven hundred and twenty hour, doing nothing. The man's mind is big. He must give it something to think about. I will let him read the paper immediately.'"

Marie said, "How did you get so smart in only seventeen years?" Kimi said, "I will be eighteen tomorrow and anyway I have not been popular. I have had plenty of time to observe and think." As Kimi was very beautiful, I was curious to know why she had not been popular. She said, "The Japanese are a race of small people. I am tall. I used to go to parties but I would spend the evening sitting alone on the couch. Like a giant Buddha I smiled and smiled as I watched the antics of the little people."

At twenty minutes past seven the same ambulant male patient who had come in the evening before, put up our beds for breakfast. The beds operated like lawn chairs and, after he had helped us to sit up, he adjusted the backs of the beds according to our comfort. The evening before he hadn't spoken a word so I presumed that talking to us was against the rules. Unfortunately it wasn't.

As he put up the back of my bed he said, "My name's Charlie Johnson. You're new here, ain't you?" I said yes, so he said, "Well, I been here five years and I seen 'em come and I seen 'em go. Some go out on their feet but most of 'em go out in a box. How bad are you?" I said that I didn't know but that I only expected to stay a year. "Ha, ha!" he laughed mirthlessly. "A year. That's what they all say when they first come. Ha, ha! The only one who ever got out in a year was a woman who had cancer of the lungs. They let her out in three months—feet first. Ha, ha!"

Laughing Boy's appearance was as morose as his outlook. His putty-colored cheeks had deep little gullies running from the bridge of his nose down past the corners of his drooping mouth, as if his face had been eroded by a constant flow of tears from his small watery eyes.

Charlie moved slowly and resentfully, as though the little tasks he performed for the institution would be the death of him and he and the institution both knew it. It was our misfortune to be the last room to be served food, so Charlie was in no hurry. He lingered on and on as depressing as an open grave. At last the nurses came with the breakfast trays.

Breakfast, at seven-thirty, consisted of half a grapefruit, oatmeal and cream, toast, boiled eggs and coffee. It was very good and very cold. The Charge Nurse, who served the food, said, "You may have as many eggs as you wish, Mrs. Bard, and you may have them either hard- or soft-boiled." I chose two hard-boiled

I'm Cold and So Is the Attitude of the Staff   205

and when she had gone Marie whispered loudly. "That's a laugh. 'Choose what you wish.' All the eggs are hard-boiled and if you take less than two, old Gimlet Eyes will say you are not a co-operative patient and you'll get a warning letter from the Medical Director." She also said that the coffee was fifty per cent saltpeter and that if I didn't find a cockroach on my tray it was just beginner's luck. She wrinkled her nose with distaste, took one bite of the grapefruit, two sips of coffee and pushed the tray away.

After we had eaten breakfast, the Charge Nurse made rounds to see what we had eaten and to hear our complaints. As we were all as immobile as blobs of dough in rising pans when she flashed in our doorway, she was very pleasant to us. Sylvia complained about pains in her stomach and diarrhea, Marie complained about pains in her stomach and constipation, Kimi said nothing.

My only complaint was that I was cold. A dank shivery cold that lukewarm coffee had done nothing to dispel. I said so. The Charge Nurse smiled blandly and said, "October first we have hot-water bottles." I said, "How about an extra blanket?" She turned back my spread and saw that I had two woolen blankets and a night blanket. She said, "You should be warm, Mrs. Bard." I said, "I'd like to be but I'm not." She looked at me sternly for a few minutes, as though I were deliberately not circulating my blood, then went away.

After she had gone Charlie came back to let down the beds and to tell us about two hemorrhages in the Men's Bedrest Hospital. "I'll probably be next," he finished gloomily.

A nurse came in and put a thermometer on each bedside table. "Take your temperature in half an hour," she told me. "Put the thermometer under the tongue and leave it in the mouth five minutes." Another nurse came in with bedpans. Past the door went a parade of lucky month-or-more patients on their way to the bathroom. Their long housecoats, measured tread and serious demeanor made them look like bridesmaids. Occasionally the illusion was spoiled by a nurse helping a new patient on her first trip, or by some brave patient who waved and smiled at us.

When the bathroom parade was over we took our temperatures. They were low. A nurse came in to count pulses and collect the thermometers. I asked her if everyone's temperature was low in the morning but she didn't answer. Just looked at me blankly and wrote on her chart.

When she had gone Sylvia got out bath powder, towels, washcloth and soap. It was her bath day she explained. Baths were given once a week and bath days assigned on entering. Shampoos were given once a month, and judging from my still excelsior-like hair, even this was too often.

As the nurse helped Sylvia into her robe, I saw how frighteningly thin she was, realized for the first time how much too bright her eyes were, how flushed her cheeks. It gave me an unpleasant feeling, as though someone had hit me hard in the pit of the stomach. I felt my own body and noticed how tight the skin was on my ribs, how my pelvic bones stuck out like hooks in a coatroom.

I looked out the window. I could see sky and the tops of the poplars that lined the drive. The sky was gray and puffy with rain. The poplar trees were yellow and limp. It was not very stimulating. I looked out the door and saw a nurse wheel by a patient on a bed. The woman's eyes were closed. Her face as white as the pillow. I wondered why she didn't ride in a wheelchair like the rest of us. If she was dying. Where she was going.

Two nurses came in to change the sheets on Sylvia's bed and to make the rest of our beds. As they made my bed, they instructed me to cover my mouth with a handkerchief and to roll from side to side. They made the top of the bed then the bottom. I asked them why the woman had been wheeled by on a bed instead of in a wheelchair, where she was going. They didn't answer. They left me apprehensive, the bed plump, smooth and chilly.

A small withered man in a dirty white cap and clean blue coveralls came in to sweep the room. His name was Bill, he said. As he swept he sniffed loudly and looked longingly out the windows instead of at his pushbroom, which left wads of gray dust under the beds. I asked him if he was a patient and he turned his small sad face from the window and said, "Patient, that's rich. I been a patient here off and on for nine years." Nine years! Dear God! Was there no limit?

When he had gone I asked Kimi if all the male patients were old and sad like Bill and Charlie. She said, "No, most of the male patient are young but because of sex the young virile men are not allowed in the Women's Bedrest Hospital and, vice versa, the young pretty nurse are not allowed in the Men's Bedrest Hospital." I asked her what the young men did and she explained that they worked in the greenhouse, laboratory, x-ray and shops where there was close supervision. I thought of Bill's yearning glances out the open window and wondered if he was longing for sex or work in the greenhouse.

At nine-thirty a nurse offered us either hot chocolate or cold milk. She explained that we did not have to take this nourishment but I was already hungry and still cold so I took hot chocolate gladly. So did Kimi. Marie and Sylvia had nothing. The nurse, coming back a little later to pick up the cocoa cups and to bring us clean, filled water glasses, explained that we must drink lots of water, as it was very important in the cure of tuberculosis.

At ten-thirty the Charge Nurse, with a wheelchair, appeared suddenly by my bed. Without a word, she helped me into my bathrobe, my slippers and the wheelchair and wheeled me out the door. I asked her where we were going but she only smiled, said, "Shhh," and took me down another corridor and into a small examination room where a young doctor gave me a chest examination. When I came back everyone was eager to know where I had gone and what they had done to me. They seemed disappointed that it had not been the removal of some large organ, something more exciting than a chest examination.

At eleven, Miss Hatfield, an assistant charge nurse and a gay friendly girl, brought medicines to cure the complaints of the morning. At eleven-fifteen Charlie came in, sagging with bad news, to put up the beds. At eleven-thirty we had dinner.

I was very hungry and the delicious, well-seasoned food, much to my surprise, was hot. There were roast pork, applesauce, bread-and-butter pickles, mashed potatoes and gravy, string beans, lettuce with French dressing, tomato soup, served for some strange reason after the main course, hot rolls and butter, baked custard and tea. Marie looked at her tray, said, "Ugh, pork again," and pushed it away. Sylvia said nothing. Kimi covered everything on her tray but the custard with shoyu sauce, a large bottle of which she kept in her bedside stand. When the Charge Nurse returned to offer us second helpings, I asked for more meat and applesauce and was immediately shamed by incredulous stares from Sylvia and Marie.

While we were eating, a nurse brought in the mail. As this was the only reading matter allowed any of us, we were eager for a letter from anybody, no matter how boring. I was too new to have mail so the nurse informed me that I could read the little book of rules given me at the desk the day before, "but," she added sternly, "patients are not allowed to open or read mail until they have eaten their dinner." Thus assuring the Charge Nurse that if the news from home was sad, we would bawl on full stomachs.

The little book of rules began, "Everything that is not rest is exercise." The writer elaborated. . . . "If you had a broken leg you would not walk on it. The same applies to your lung. In order to heal, your lung must have rest. Talking, laughing, singing are all exercise which can be avoided." This all seemed very logical and easy to understand. The next part struck me as a trifle odd. "Please," the writer of the little book begged, "do not steal out of other patients' lockers and *please* do not spit on the floor." Apparently sex and over-optimism weren't the only characteristics of people with tuberculosis.

From twelve-thirty to two-thirty were rest hours. "The strictest rule of The Pines is observance of rest hours and any infraction of the rule for absolute rest during these two hours, means instant dismissal," it had stated in the book of rules. It also stated: "Getting well depends on the patient. Rest, fresh air, good food, and later, regulated and supervised exercise, all help but if the patient doesn't have the will power, honesty, and character to obey the rules, nothing will save him. . . . If you cannot pay the price and feel that you will not be a good influence on others, go home and give your bed to someone who will be of value."

I'm Cold and So Is the Attitude of the Staff

During the rest hours, I lay in my clammy bed and looked at the pale green walls and tried to think about will power and honesty and how grateful I was to be there; about the two hundred people on the waiting list, who they were and what they were doing. Marie and Sylvia and Kimi slept. Everyone else slept too, apparently. There was not a sound. Occasionally, with terrifying suddenness, a nurse would appear at the door to see if we were resting. One time it was a cheerful nurse. She winked at me and disappeared. Through the windows I could just see the tip of one of the poplars. Its yellow leaves were motionless, like paper leaves hung by threads to an imitation tree. The sky was a dirty white now, the air steel blue with fog.

It seemed so strange, this stillness. It was daytime and there should at least have been the tapping of a distant hammer, the bark of a dog, the slam of a door. It was as though we were all dead. I took a drink of water and it had the acrid, slightly warm taste of bathroom water. I wondered why kitchen water and bathroom water never tasted the same. I moved my feet around to try and find a warm place in the bed. It was as futile as feeling around on a cement floor to find a soft place to lie down. I looked at my watch. One o'clock: an hour and a half to go.

I closed my eyes and tried to relax, joint by joint, muscle by muscle, according to an article I had recently read on charm. This relaxing was supposed to have been done by the hostess just before a dinner party and while the capon was roasting, the wild rice was steaming and the pistachio ice cream cake was hardening. My reaction at the time had been that she should have had cheaper food and more help, but now I was grateful for her suggestions on how to relax. The article had said, "Think of your big toe. It is heavy. It is limp." I thought of my big toe but it was cold and stiff and there seemed to be a short circuit between my brain and my lower extremities. I tried my fingers, arms and shoulders. I was no more successful.

A girl in the next room began to cough. Her cough was deep and resonant and was a welcome relief from the silence. It was like a signal, for immediately up and down the corridors there were more coughs. Small dry coughs, loose phlegmy coughs, short staccato coughs, long whooping coughs. The hospital began to seem peopled and cheerful.

A nurse flashed in the doorway. She said to me, the others being asleep, "Patients must control their coughs. A cough can be controlled." I didn't say anything because I hadn't coughed and I knew if I spoke I would. She looked at me penetratingly for a minute and then flashed away again. I noticed that the coughing had ceased. Apparently she had stopped at each door and turned it off, like the radio.

I looked at the green ceiling again and tried to be honest and grateful. I thought of that terrible evening when the chest specialist had told me that I had tuberculosis; that if I wanted to get well I would have to go to a sanatorium; that sanatoriums cost $35 to $50 a week. I remembered how I had stood and looked at him, feeling like a mouse in an apple barrel—no way out. Around and around—no way out—no way out—no way out.

Now here I was in a hospital, being cared for, being fed, being watched over, being cured, I hoped. Yet the institution had to remind me to be grateful. I had to remind myself to be grateful because my instinct was to be resentful. Resentful of the rules, resentful of the nurses who enforced the rules. I looked at my watch. It was one-seven.

I looked back at the ceiling and tried to relax my fingers but my heart was pounding and I felt like a skyrocket about to explode into a million jagged stars. I turned my pillow over and took another drink of the tepid water. I closed my eyes and pressed my fingers against the eyeballs. Brilliant, blinding kaleidoscopic pictures appeared. It was infinitely more interesting than the green ceiling but according to the little book, not very honest or grateful.

I reached out and got my damp cold washcloth and put it over my eyes. That was better. I thought, "That is my big toe. It is heavy." But all I could see was that pistachio ice cream cake. I'll bet it was heavy. I took the washcloth off and turned over so I could see the poplar tree again. While I watched, one small leaf let go and dropped limply through the misty air. Compared to

I'm Cold and So Is the Attitude of the Staff   211

the hospital it seemed like an act of hysterical activity. I watched for a long time but no other leaves fell off the tree.

The girl in the next room began to cough again. It was muffled as though she were trying desperately not to cough but I heard the low murmur of the nurse and "Patients must control their coughs." My heart began to pound again, senselessly, as though I were climbing a steep hill. I turned over and lay on it and could feel its thudding clear to the top of my head. Thump, thump, thump, thump. I turned back again and it pounded harder.

When the nurse looked in I motioned to her. She came quickly to the bed on soundless feet. I said, "My heart's pounding." She looked at my chest and held my wrist for a minute then said, "Palpitations. Very common with t.b. Go to sleep," and left. I turned on the right side and my heart quieted a little. I closed my eyes but my thoughts, like a skidding car toward the railing of a bridge, immediately veered toward home and the children. I quickly opened them again.

I drank some more water and thought, "I haven't even been here a full twenty-four hours yet and I have at least a year yet to go." Again my thoughts careered dangerously toward home. Keeping away from homesickness was like walking across a rock slide. Every step was insecure and the very next one might bring the whole mountain down on me. If only I had a hot-water bottle. How long could people stay dank and cold without mildewing? How long was two hours anyway? Was being cold all the time part of the cure or was it the easiest way to keep patients quiet and under the covers? Why weren't frail little creatures like Sylvia cold? She said she was always warm. Maybe that was the fever.

I reached under the covers and tried massaging some warmth into my feet. It was as unproductive as trying to get sparks by rubbing two wet sponges together. I made up my mind that before that day ended I was going to have a talk with the Charge Nurse. I was going to ask her if keeping the patients half frozen was part of the cure; what the term "taking the cure" meant;

what tuberculosis was, what the germ looked like; what its effect on the lung was; what rest had to do with the cure; if t.b. was actually curable; why some people, like the man in my office, could have t.b. for twenty years and live normal lives while others, like me, in less than one year became completely incapacitated; why I couldn't rest during rest hours; why I was so nervous; if, as time went on, I would become more restless or more well-adjusted. There were hundreds more questions I could ask but these would do for a start and would give me something to go on.

Trying to memorize the questions I wanted to ask took up the last long dragging minutes of the rest hours and at last there was a gentle clink-clank down the hall and in the door came a nurse with the nourishment cart. Thank God, I thought. Hot cocoa! But the choice was ice-cold milk or ice-cold buttermilk. "What, no fans?" I said bitterly under my breath, as I chose ice-cold buttermilk. Kimi took plain milk, Sylvia and Marie nothing.

After nourishment a nurse filled our water glasses again, another nurse took orders for supplies, such as toilet paper, paper handkerchiefs, sputum cups, etc., and told me to order enough for a week, as supplies were only given out on Saturdays.

After she had gone a nurse came in and asked us questions and wrote the answers down on a chart. The frequent detailed discussions of sputum, its amount and color, often made me wish for a more dainty ailment like diabetes or brain tumor. After she had gone the nurses brought wash water and in a little while Charlie put up the beds and it was time for supper.

Except for rest hours the day had gone by quickly. The long spaces of time had been well broken by small activities. For supper we had cold beef, scalloped potatoes, vegetable soup, banana salad, bread and butter, cookies, beautiful thoughts and hot tea.

I had just taken a large bite of meat and was reading my beautiful thought which said, "I have often regretted my speech, never my silence," when Sylvia threw up. I don't know whether she choked or was suddenly sick or had just read her beautiful thought, but she threw up all over her supper tray and down the side of the bed. It made me very sick. I quickly drank some tea

I'm Cold and So Is the Attitude of the Staff 213

and looked to see how Marie and Kimi were taking it. They weren't taking it any way. They were eating their supper as though it hadn't happened. I drank a little more of the tea.

Sylvia tapped with her spoon on the stand and eventually a nurse came in and cleaned her up. When she had finished, the nurse turned to me and said, "Eat your supper, Mrs. Bard. You must learn to ignore these things." She brought Sylvia another tray and some more tea and she ate her supper and so did I.

When the Charge Nurse and the doctor made their rounds, they came only to the doorway and said, "Everybody fine?" and so I put off asking the questions about tuberculosis until the next day. Half an hour after dinner we took our temperatures, mine was 98.6°, Marie's 102°, Sylvia's 101°, Kimi's 99°, and almost simultaneously the radio came on.

First there was a program of dinner music, then a play, then music, then a play. The radio flowed on until lights out at nine o'clock. The music was very nice but the plays and programs were very irritating because the volume was kept so low we could only hear occasional words. At seven o'clock we were given nourishment again, hot chocolate or cold milk. At seven-thirty the day staff went off duty and two evening nurses came on. Immediately there was a low distinct hum of talking from all over the hospital. It was a soft undercurrent noise like the hum of a refrigerator but it stood out in the absolute quiet.

We talked too. I asked Sylvia how she got tuberculosis. She said that she had had it since she was a child, that all her life had been lived in sanatoriums. She had been in Switzerland, New York, Arizona, Colorado, New Mexico and California.

I asked her if The Pines was like any of the other sanatoriums. She said, "No. In all the other sanatoriums they have the rules but only in The Pines do they enforce them." I asked her if being cold was part of the cure. She said that she didn't think so. That she wasn't cold.

I asked Marie and Kimi if they were cold. Marie said only part of the time, Kimi said that she was cold all of the time. She said, "I have instructed my family to bring heavy sock, many sweater and mitten." I made a mental note to tell my family to bring sock, sweater and mitten too. Also a bed lamp and a stand bag.

The stand bags, made of bright chintzes, were like shoe bags with large pockets for writing paper, bedroom slippers and hand mirror and smaller ones for pens and pencils, combs and brushes and cosmetics. They were pinned to the towel bar on the stand by safety pins and their accessibility eliminated a lot of reaching.

At eight o'clock a nurse brought medicines. At eight-thirty we brushed our teeth with drinking water, spitting in our bedpans and Sylvia and Marie began to talk about bedsores. Sylvia told about bedsores in Europe, in New York, in California, in Colorado, in Arizona and New Mexico. Marie told about her grandmother's bedsores and her own. At nine o'clock the lights were switched out.

I pulled the clammy sheet up around my neck, stuck my feet timidly down into the icy regions at the foot of the bed and thought longingly of delightful hot climate diseases like leprosy, cholera and jungle rot.

The next morning I was awake with my eyes open and feet braced when the lights blared and the washwater girls came crashing into the ward.

By breakfast time a very consumptive sun had begun to peer wanly out from under its hood of fog and we all said hopefully that there would probably be sunshine for visiting hours. I wondered sadly if anyone would come to see me. Kimi said, "I certainly hope my family received all my letter. My mother is so rattle-brained at times. Always writing poetry and forgetting my instruction." I asked what her instructions were. She said, "The instruction were about the heavy sock and sweater and mitten. But it would be just like my mother to forget all about the warm clothing and bring me one of her beautiful poem about the spring."

There was a terrific clatter in the hallway and two nurses pushed in a large pair of scales, for in addition to its being Sunday and a visiting day, this was also the last day of the month and weigh day. As each of us was helped out of bed and onto the scales, the room was tight with hope, for gaining weight signified at least a foothold on the climb to health. Losing weight meant a

I'm Cold and So Is the Attitude of the Staff 215

sliding backward and we could almost feel Sylvia's wild desperate attempts to grab something that would keep her from slipping farther down toward the yawning chasm, as with scared eyes and indrawn breath she watched the impersonal nurses adjust the weights and push the balance back, back, back. Sylvia had lost six pounds. Marie had lost three pounds, Kimi had gained five pounds and I weighed the same as I had at the clinic, which was twenty-three pounds underweight for my age and height, according to the chart.

For a time after the scales had gone the room was still and heavy with despair. Even the sunshine seemed to have lost its promise and was watery and without warmth. Sylvia looked ahead at nothing and plucked nervously at the sheet. Marie twirled the knob of her stand drawer with one thin finger. Her cheeks were flushed, her eyes dark and angry. Kimi examined the palms of her hands. I watched the wind flitter the corner of the paper napkin on which my water glasses stood.

Then from Kimi's corner there was a small sound. I looked over and saw that she was crying and blotting her eyes with her bed jacket. I asked her what the trouble was and she said in a forlorn voice, "I am not happy to be the only one who has gained. It makes me feel like a beeg lonely hog."

Just after nourishment the Charge Nurse moved Marie and Sylvia. As we kept our same beds, bedside stands and chairs all the way through the Bedrest Hospital, moving the patients was simple. The Charge Nurse put their chairs on the foot of their beds and wheeled them to a new location. Another nurse came for their bedside stands and flowers. We asked this other nurse if she would move Kimi's bed up across from mine, where Sylvia's had been. She said suspiciously, "Did the Charge Nurse order it?" and Kimi said, "Would we ask you if she hadn't?" The nurse moved us grudgingly and when she had gone, Kimi said, "I hate to resort to trickery but sometimes it is the only way I can get my wish."

After dinner Kimi put on a little lipstick, while I put on quantities of liquid suntan makeup, mascara and bright pink lipstick. It made me look like an old sick Madam but raised my spirits several notches.

Kimi's family came on the stroke of two. Her father with an armload of yellow chrysanthemums as big as grapefruit, her mother with a poem but also the sock, sweater, mitten and other presents, and her brother, George, a tall handsome young Japanese, with some sweet and sour spareribs, which he ate himself because he thought Kimi was too fat.

My visitors were late and Kimi's dear little mother, thinking that I had no friends or judging from my appearance that they were all cheap transients, brought me half of the yellow chrysanthemums and arranged them beautifully in a square white vase. She had just put the vase on the stand and had said in her gentle voice, "For you," when Granite Eyes came in to fill the water glasses. She said, "Patients are not allowed to keep flowers on their stands," and clunked the vase to the floor.

Then she said, "Patients may not talk to other patients' visitors, Mrs. Bard. If you break the rules your visiting privileges will be taken away." As Kimi's mother spoke only a little English and apparently did not understand what the nurse was saying, she smiled and bowed to Granite Eyes and said, "Thank you very much, it is a lovely day." Kimi's brother, who had been watching, turned and spoke to Kimi and her father in Japanese. They all laughed. Granite Eyes stalked out of the room but her back looked self-conscious.

Just then Mother, Mary and Jim, Mary's husband, came in. Jim walked purposefully up to the bed and immediately handed me everything he had in the way of conversation. He said, "You look fine." The rest of the two hours he spent looking longingly out the window or examining me from different angles, as if I were a building site.

Mary brought me a huge bunch of butter-yellow chrysanthemums with chartreuse centers. Mother brought a bed lamp and a stand bag (Mary had unearthed an old friend and old patient of The Pines who had told her I would need these) and a box of hot fresh cookies. They were so curious about everything in the institution and I was so curious about everything at home that the two hours were up almost at once.

When Charlie came in to put up the beds he said, "Well, I seen your two friends down the hall. They're in a cubicle together but they don't look too good to me. I doubt if either of them two ever gets out of here. Of course, they might send 'em home to die, but they'll never get out any other way." Kimi said, "Charlie, I think you are in the wrong work. I think your occupational therapy time should be spent in the morgue." This, for some odd reason, sent him into paroxysms of laughter.

Sunday night after supper the store girl came around and took orders. The store girl was an ambulant patient but always a *very trusted* one as she took orders from the men too. This store girl's name was Velma Martin and she had, in addition to her trustworthiness, a purple plaid coat, steel-rimmed spectacles, a nasal voice and a habit of working her tongue around the inside of her mouth as if she were looking for hidden crumbs.

After Velma came the nourishment cart bearing, in addition to the regular milk and cocoa, all the excess food brought patients by their visitors. The nurse offered us dry white cake, always referred to in our family as "choke cake," chocolate cake, cup cakes, cookies and candy. She said that any food we had been given that we couldn't eat by lights out must be put on the cart. I felt it was a sacrilege to put mother's cookies on the cart with the dry cupcakes and the choke cake and was wondering what to do with them when the night nurse solved the problem by eating them all while she talked to us.

She told us that her name was Katy Morris, she was twenty-four years old and very interested in t.b. because her brother had died of it. Kimi said, "I suppose that most of the patient here will eventually die." Katy said, "Nonsense! Most of the patients here will get well. A few will die certainly, but most everyone who does what he is told and tries to get well, gets well."

Just before she left Kimi said, "Just on the chance that I may be one of the few who die, will you turn the radio up just a leetle." There was a radio control in our ward and Katy, winking at me, turned it up until we could understand all the words.

I thought that evening, and again and again in the weeks to come, how fortunate I was to have gentle, intelligent, considerate, witty, beautiful Kimi for a roommate.

Being suddenly thrust with perfect strangers and forced to live with them without any privacy at all for twenty-four-hour period after twenty-four-hour period is as much a problem in adjustment as a planned marriage but without the impetus of curiosity or the surcease of sex.

I like people but not all people. I'm neither Christian enough nor charitable enough to like anybody just because he is alive and breathing. I want people to interest or amuse me. I want them fascinating and witty or so dull as to be different. I want them either intellectually stimulating or wonderfully corny; perfectly charming or hundred per cent stinker. I like my chosen companions to be distinguishable from the undulating masses and I don't care how.

From my stay at The Pines I learned that a stiff test for friendship is: "Would she be pleasant to have t.b. with?" Unfortunately, too many people, when you try separating them from their material possessions and any and all activity, turn out to be like cheap golf balls. You unwind and unwind and unwind but you never get to the pure rubber core because there isn't any. When I started unwinding Kimi I found that under her beautiful covering she was mostly core. She said, "It is not character on my part, Betty, it is just that if you have to have tuberculosis it is easier to be Japanese."

Monday, immediately after rest hours, Kimi and I were handed a new problem in adjustment. Her name was Eileen Kelly and she was young and pretty with very long red hair and very long red fingernails. With disapproval radiating from her like heat, Granite Eyes wheeled Eileen in and helped her out of the wheelchair.

Eileen took off her robe, which was pale blue and leaned far from the required warm sensible bathrobe and heavily toward a peignoir. She had on sleeveless, backless, black satin pajamas and an anklet. Granite Eyes took her by the bare arm disdainfully as though she were holding her up in two fingers and disposing of her.

Eileen, not at all disturbed, leapt nimbly into the bed, but as she slid down between the icy sheets she let out a yell. "Jeeeeesus God, this bed's cold!" Like a shout in any empty church the yell

I'm Cold and So Is the Attitude of the Staff 219

bounced against the walls of the completely quiet Bedrest Hospital. At once the Charge Nurse was projected in the doorway. Eyes flashing, lips stretched tight with disapproval, she demanded an explanation of this very unorthodox noise. Granite Eyes said, rather inanely, we thought, "Miss Kelly's cold." The Charge Nurse said, "Miss Kelly, patients of The Pines do not shout."

She noticed a bare shoulder. Then turning back the covers, as though she were looking for maggots in a sack of flour, she revealed the rest of the bare and satin-clad Miss Kelly. Her nostrils swelled almost to the bursting point. She said to Granite Eyes, "Miss Murdock, go to the lockers and get a pair of outing flannel pajamas." She turned to Miss Kelly. "Did you read your list of requirements?" Miss Kelly said that she had. "Then," said the Charge Nurse, "why have you come here wearing *silk* [she breathed out heavily as she said this loathesome word so that it came out "suh-hilk"] pajamas and nail polish?" Miss Kelly said wisely, "I don't know."

Just then Granite Eyes came puffing back with a very ragged pair of blue and white flannel pajamas which, Kimi pointed out to us later, had probably belonged to a patient who had died. The Charge Nurse snatched the pajamas and sent Granite Eyes back for oil of peppermint. Then she removed Eileen from the black satin and stuffed her into the outing flannel with purpose and dispatch; with sharp surgical scissors, which she carried in her pocket, she cut about half an inch from the long pointed blood red fingernails; removed the polish from the remaining stubs with oil of peppermint; and informed Miss Kelly that the next morning her hair would be cut to within one inch of the ear lobe. Her stiff white uniform switched angrily through the door and she was gone. Miss Kelly sat bolt upright in her bed, a deadly sin, and stuck out her tongue at the retreating Charge Nurse. Then she turned round hostile blue eyes on Kimi and me and said, "Jesus, what a dame!"

When the House Doctor and the Charge Nurse made rounds a little later Eileen complained of the cold and asked for a hot-water bottle. The Charge Nurse said quickly, "Hot-water bottles are filled at eight-thirty in the morning and at seven-fifteen in the evening." Eileen said, "I wasn't here at eight-thirty this morning and I'm cold now." The Charge Nurse said, "Your hot-water bottle will be filled at seven-fifteen this evening."

It was unfortunate that on that of all evenings the hot-water bottle filling should have been assigned to Miss Muelbach, who was so slow that even if she had put hot water in the bottles, which she never did, they would have been cold by the time she got them distributed. She threw mine onto the foot of my bed, dripping and cool. I looked over at Eileen. She said a very bad word and threw her hot-water bottle on the floor. It lit with a resounding clunk but, with Miss Muelbach on hot-water bottle duty there were so many resounding clunks up and down the ward, this one passed unnoticed.

Eileen waited for a few minutes, eyes on the door, then turned her face to the wall and bawled with loud slurping sobs. I felt desperately sorry for her. I knew how cold, unloved and unwanted she felt. I knew how hateful everyone at The Pines must seem but I couldn't think of anything to say that wouldn't sound like a beautiful thought or a quotation from the book of rules. Kimi solved the problem by saying, in her small sweet voice, "Eileen, all crying will do is to make your pillow and sheet wet and colder. When Katy, the evening nurse, comes on duty she will fill your hot-water bottle. Don't be sad, we are your friend and are in sympathy with you."

Kimi's speeches always sounded as though they should have been on parchment with a spray of cherry blossoms or a single iris painted across one corner.

Friday after rest hours another new patient was wheeled in. She was twenty-four years old, very thin, very blond and very Southern. Her name was Minna Harrison Walker. She had large, slightly prominent, pale blue eyes, white eyelashes and she blinked when she talked. When the nurse thrust her into bed and told her to keep warm with rules, she smiled up at her and said, "Ah declah, Miss Swenson, you ah the sweetest thing. Ah'm so lucky to be heah. Pore little ole me would have died if that nice doctah hadn't taken me in heah."

Eileen looked over at Kimi and me and held her nose. Miss

Swenson was murmuring to Minna. Minna said, "Of course Ah don' want you to get in any trouble, you sweet lil ole thing, but Ah've got this awful pain in my tummy and Ah suah could use a hot-water bottle." She got it.

When the Charge Nurse made her rounds that evening Minna said, "You know that ole list didn't have a bed lamp on it and it's so dahk and lonely heah in the cohnah. Ah wrote mah Sweetie-Pie to bring me a bed lamp but it won't be heah until next visitin' day. Ah suah am lonely." The Charge Nurse brought her a bed lamp, which had probably belonged, Kimi gently reminded her, to some patient who had died. At that time Eileen didn't have a bed lamp either and she was furious. As the Charge Nurse finished attaching Minna's lamp, Eileen said, "Well, Jesus, honey, it's dark ovah heah too," but all she got was a cold look.

The next day it rained. Cold, wet, gray, chilling rain. It blew in the windows and under the covers and Kimi and Eileen and I were cold and miserable. Granite Eyes filled Minna's hot-water bottle twice. During rest hours Eileen read movie magazines under the covers, but Minna read the Bible and let herself be caught doing it.

It was a little new nurse who caught her or the punishment would have been more drastic. She rattled the pages just as the nurse came to the door and the nurse threw back the covers and there was little Minna clutching her Bible and looking up with big, scared, pale blue eyes. The nurse said, "Reading during rest hours is forbidden, Mrs. Walker. Any activity during rest hours is forbidden, Mrs. Walker. New patients may not read or write for one month, Mrs. Walker." Minna said, "Oh honey, Ah'm so sorry. The other girls were readin' so Ah thought it was all right. Oh, hush mah mouth, what have Ah said? Ah didn't mean to tell."

She looked over at us. Kimi was asleep. Eileen had slipped her movie magazine under her mattress. The new little nurse said, "Well, I won't report you this time but next time the Charge Nurse will hear about it." She rustled self-consciously out. Eileen reached down and got out her movie magazine again, then looked over at Minna and said, "Bitch." Minna had her eyes closed. The Bible was conspicuously placed on her bedside stand.

On October fifth, Kimi had an x-ray and the next day was given fifteen minutes a day reading-and-writing time. The Charge Nurse came in before rest hours and said, "Miss Sanbo, you may read and write for fifteen minutes a day," and Kimi said, "Thank you very much, but I do not think I will have the time." Eileen said, "When can I have reading-and-writing time?" Minna said, "Oh, Ah thought you already had youah readin'-and-writin' time." There was a terrible silence and Minna covered her mouth and said, "Oh, hush mah mouth, what have Ah said?"

After supper the Charge Nurse took Eileen to her office for a little talk. She delivered her back in about a half hour, red-eyed and defiant. After the Charge Nurse had left, Minna said, "Ah declaah, honey, Ah didn't mean to tell. Ah really thought you did have readin'-and-writin' time." Eileen said wearily, "Oh, shut up!" Then she crawled to the foot of her bed and turned the radio very loud.

Minna had only one visitor but he came on the stroke of two each visiting day and stayed the full two hours. It was "Sweetie-Pie," her adoring husband. Sweetie-Pie was about fifty years old, bald, fat and doughy-faced, but he brought Minna flowers and candy and bath powder and fruit and bath salts and jewelry and perfume and bed jackets. She always referred to him as though he were a cross between Cary Grant and Noel Coward and said often, "Ah just don' know how I was lucky enough to get that big ole handsome husband of mine."

Once, right at first, Eileen had said, "You can stop right after the 'big old,'" and strangely enough Minna began to cry. She said that "she loved that big ole handsome man" and that he was her "Sweetie-Pie" and after that nobody said anything. After all if it made her happy to think doughface was handsome, that was the important thing.

The day after she gave Kimi her reading-and-writing time, the Charge Nurse told her she could walk to the bathroom once a day. Kimi was ecstatic until after breakfast when she stood up to put on her robe. Then Minna said, "Oh, honey, youah so tall, youah just enohmous! I had no idea you were so big!"

Kimi, looking as though she had been slapped, said, "The Japanese are such little fellow, already I felt like Gulliver with the Lilliputian." I said, "But you're not very tall, Kimi." Kimi said, "Oh, yes, already five and one half feet and probably still growing." I said, "But I'm five feet seven," and Eileen said, "And I'm five feet five." Minna said, "And poah little me can't reach five feet with high heels. Its shuah lucky foh me that Sweetie-Pie says that good things come in small packages." Eileen said, "And I can get just as sick to my stummick on a little of your guff as I can on a whole lot." "And the bite of a little rattlesnake is just as deadly as the bite of a big one," Kimi said, moving slowly and regally out the door.

14

Deck the Halls with Old Crepe Paper

EXACTLY TWO WEEKS, to the day, after I entered the sanatorium I slept the whole night through and the next morning I didn't cough at all when I woke up. By ten o'clock my sense of well-being was so great it was almost choking me. I had energy, my brain was clear, I didn't ache any place, and I loved The Pines and everyone in The Pines. The depression and terrible sense of foreboding I had been wearing around my shoulders since the night I learned I had tuberculosis, had been mysteriously lifted off during the night and though it was a cold foggy morning and both the wash water and my hot-water bottle had been lukewarm, I brushed these off the day like a crumb off the bedclothes. I felt well!

At noon Miss Muelbach, whom Eileen had christened Gravy Face, brought the mail and threw it at us so that a letter from Mother went into my cup of tea. Poor thing, I thought as an aura of sweetness and light flared up around me, probably tired. I smiled benignly at Miss Muelbach and she glared stonily back at me. I started to wipe the tea off Mother's letter but she said, "You know you're not supposed to read your mail until you've eaten your dinner." "Oh, I'm not going to read it," I said so sweetly I was almost singing. "I'm just wiping the tea off it." "Well, all right then," said Gravy Face and stumped out of the room on her gray hairy legs.

Mother's letters have always been a delight and she is such an untiring and fluent letter writer that the family often refers to her as "Scrib." In my letter writing I usually take some small incident and by a process of lies and poor descriptions build it up and up into something dull but very long. Mother never bothers with such deceit. She merely sits down at her desk and writes what is going on at the moment.

This letter told me that one of the dogs had run a thorn in his foot. That a neighbor was just outside the window improving the shining hour by cutting the last living branch from his wife's poor little prune tree. That she had just baked an applesauce cake. That Anne was begging her to find a school that did not include "rhythmetic" in its curriculum. That large boys of sixteen and seventeen knocked at the door constantly to ask if Joan could come and pitch for their baseball teams. That Dede was making a coat and with her usual hardheadedness was not taking any advice from anyone. Mother wrote, "It is quite difficult for me to sit quietly by, evening after evening, watching her try to force the sleeves in upside down." That Alison was still surrounded by "the locusts," as mother called her high school friends, who descended on the house after school and ate everything that wasn't metal or hadn't been baked in a kiln. That Madge was just then playing piano very beautifully in spite of a bandage almost to the shoulder on her right arm. Mother said that Madge hadn't yet revealed whether the bandage denoted t.b. of the bone or that she was preparing to get off work, later in the week. That everyone missed me terribly but the children were becoming very well adjusted to my absence.

The whole letter was as much a part of Mother as though she had snipped off a piece of herself and sent it to me. I read it for the fourth time just before rest hours and that day, at last, I was able to think of home and the children without the slamming of a coffin lid as an off-stage noise. I spent the rest hours making plans for the future and they differed from any previously made because they were based on a premise of "when I get well" instead of "if I die." The rest hours still seemed two hundred hours long and I was still cold but there was some reason for it now.

When at last the nourishment cart came clanking down the hall, I didn't have my usual end-of-rest-hours nervous frustration. I felt relaxed and refreshed.

The room was very quiet. Eileen was writing a letter under the covers, Minna was sleeping and Kimi was using her fifteen minutes' reading-and-writing time to look at some movie magazines, generously delivered in person by Eileen early that morning. I listened to the faint scratch of Eileen's pen, the soft little swish as Kimi turned a page. Suddenly the Charge Nurse was in the room. She was angry and her really beautiful blue eyes sparked. She said, "It has been reported to me by other patients that there is noise in this ward in the evening. Is that true, Mrs. Bard?" I said, "Why, er, uh, er . . ." Eileen said, "Who's the snitcher?"

The Charge Nurse turned and gave her a look like a dipper of ice water. She said, "I want to know if the report of noise in this room at night is true." Kimi said, "How many people have reported this noise?" The Charge Nurse said, "What difference would that make, Miss Sanbo?" Kimi said, "If many people have reported the noise it must be the radio because if the noise were sufficient for many people to hear, the nurse would also hear it and stop it. We occasionally exchange pleasantry in the evening but not for the ear of the whole ward." The Charge Nurse looked completely baffled. She said, "But this patient said," and we knew then that it was one particular patient, "that she could hear you laughing and talking." Not one of us said anything. The Charge Nurse said, "She said that she heard you very plainly, Mrs. Bard."

I said, "But I haven't spoken out loud since I got here. How could she recognize my voice? All whispers sound alike you know." Eileen said, apparently to herself but in a very audible voice, "Dirty little snitcher." The Charge Nurse said, "You will hear more of this!"

I noticed that not once had her accusations included Minna. I also remembered that Minna had that morning gone with her for a throat examination. I could almost hear that "hush mah mouth, what have Ah said?" I looked over at her but she was feigning sleep with her white eyelashes lowered over her pale eyes. I was sure I hadn't talked any more than anyone in the hospital and certainly not one millionth as much as Eileen, but I was frightened. What if I should be sent home for breaking rules? Me, a grown woman. Whether or not I had broken the rules was unimportant, the important thing was the implication that I hadn't been intelligent enough to see what was being done for me.

Eileen said, "It seems goddamn funny to me that the Old Dame never once looked at Little Eva. It also seems goddamn funny that Little Eva was with the Old Dame this very morning. Hush mah mouth, what did you say, you dirty little snitcher?" Minna kept her eyes closed but her lids twitched noticeably. Kimi said in a voice as gentle as breath, "In Japan, I believe it is customary to pour boiling oil over the tongue and down the throat of a betrayer." Minna turned her face to the wall.

My beautiful sense of well-being was gone and in its place was such a feeling of dread and depression that it shriveled my stomach and tied my intestines in knots. When the House Doctor made rounds and asked how I felt, I told him I felt as if I'd swallowed an outboard motor. He laughed, punched me in the stomach and ordered a sedative. The Charge Nurse compressed her lips and wrote it down.

After pulses she came for me in a wheelchair. She took me down to the examination room and told me that there was no room in the hospital for ungrateful patients who did not obey the rules. I told her that I had not broken any rule. She said that the patient who reported me had said that she could not rest in the evening because I made so much noise. I said that that was obviously ridiculous and for her to ask the night nurse. She said that she was going to take the matter up with the Medical Director and I said that I didn't see what she had to take up. She didn't answer, merely swelled her nostrils and wheeled me back to bed.

When Katy brought my sedative, I told her the whole childish incident. She said, "You know that's one thing that's wrong with this place. They forget how important peace of mind is in resting. Oh, well, the worst you'll get will be a letter from the Medical Director, so drink this and have a good sleep." After lights out and just before we went to sleep, Kimi said, "I forgot to tell you that Indians used to stake an informer to the ground, then press on his eye socket and pop out his eyeball like a grape."

The next day I got my letter. It was a quotation: " 'Suppose it were perfectly certain that the life and fortune of every one of us would, one day or other, depend upon his winning or losing a game of chess. . . . The chess-board is the world; the pieces are the phenomena of the universe; the rules of the game are what we call the laws of Nature. The player on the other side is hidden from us. We know that his play is always fair, just, and patient. . . . To the man who plays well, the highest stakes are paid, with that sort of overflowing generosity with which the strong shows delight in strength. *Anyone who plays ill is checkmated—without haste, but without remorse.*' " The letter was signed by the Medical Director.

That night my stomach was in knots again and the House Doctor ordered another sedative. When Katy brought the sedative, she read the letter and passed it to Eileen and Kimi. Eileen read it and said, "I only play checkers myself." Kimi said, "I cannot believe in the omnipotence of one who never overlooks a mistake, particularly since I have been taught that 'to err is human, to forgive divine.' " Katy said, "And a grudge will soon rot the pocket you carry it in. What do you say we wipe the slate clean and start tomorrow off fresh?"

I was glad to, Minna was pitifully eager, Kimi agreed but Eileen said, "You don't remove a skunk's smell by paintin' out his stripe." Katy said, "Come on, honey, for the sake of the cure, let's have peace." Eileen said, "The first time you get a knife in your back it's the other fella's fault. The second time it's your fault. Little Eva's had her knife in my back about three times. From now on she's strictly poison." Katy winked at Kimi and me and left. Eileen crawled down to the foot of the bed and turned the radio so that it was clear and loud.

The next day was a visiting day and Sunday and bright with sunshine so the incident was forgotten and the ward was peaceful until Velma, the store girl, came after supper to take our orders. She said, as she pulled her mouth over to one side and massaged her upper gums with her tongue, "I heard through the grapevine that the Charge Nurse caught all you kids out of bed playing checkers." This seemed to put the proper light on the whole silly episode and for a time, at least, we all harmonized and did not need sedatives.

My great sense of well-being returned but this time it was accompanied by a terrible restlessness and irritability. I felt perfectly well and it drove me insane to lie there hour after hour, day after day, doing nothing. Absolutely nothing.

So far, no one in our ward had had any treatment other than rest and Eileen certainly hadn't had much of that, but we all seemed to be progressing favorably. I didn't cough at all, now; Kimi never had; Eileen coughed only in the morning and when she talked and laughed, and Minna only when she exerted herself unduly, discussing rumors or case histories. We all had voracious appetites and took any and all food that was offered and as much as they would give us. Our letters home were always pleas for more food, and on visiting days our ward looked like a delicatessen.

Then one day without warning, Minna was wheelchaired away during rest hours and given pneumothorax. We had heard of pneumothorax, always referred to as "gas," from the ambulant patients but we weren't sure what it was and we thought it was only for the very sick.

When Minna came back she told us that the Medical Director had explained to her that pneumothorax was to a tubercular lung what a splint was to a broken leg. That it was the introduction of clean air into the pleural cavity, which in turn forced the lung to collapse through its own elasticity. It was like forcing air between the covering and the bladder of a football so that the bladder couldn't expand. She said that the Medical Director had told her that she was very lucky to be able to take artificial pneumothorax as it could not be given to many patients due to adhesions (places where the lung had grown to the pleura).

Then she told us that she didn't want to alarm us unduly, but it was her impression from her lengthy and illuminating talk with the Medical Director, that patients who weren't taking any form of treatment were so far gone that the institution didn't dare risk it. With this cheering remark she closed her eyes and went to sleep.

By bedtime that night, however, she had changed her mind about who were the lucky ones, for Charlie had told her about spontaneous collapses. A spontaneous collapse, according to Charlie, was almost always fatal and happened very frequently. Minna said, "He told me that some patients' lungs ah just full of holes, mine probably ah, and when pressuh is put on the lung through pneumothorax, the lung collapses like an old tiah with a blowout. Charlie says that patients are dyin' like flies around heah with these spontaneous collapses."

A tuberculosis sanatorium, like a boarding school, is rife with gossip and rumors. But the gossip and rumors at The Pines, instead of being about cheerful things like boys and parties, were always about poor little patients who were mistreated by the staff.

The rumors were all based on a little bit of truth but turned out like the whispering game we used to play as children where we sat in a circle and the starter whispered something to the person next to him and that person whispered it to the one next to him until it had gone all around the circle.

I asked Katy Morris about some of the rumors and she told me that the janitor supposedly forced to janitor while hemorrhaging was actually a very lazy patient who always had some excuse for not getting his supervised exercise. His hemorrhage was in reality a very slight nosebleed caused by blowing his nose too hard. The mother and daughter, who were separated and died of broken hearts, was actually a case of a very stupid mother and a very sick daughter. When they were in a room together the mother talked to her daughter constantly and gave her all kinds of forbidden food. When they were separated they sulked and complained. They both died eventually of advanced tuberculosis and lack of cooperation.

Katy said, "There's nothing as dumb as people with t.b. You tell them, 'Now if you do this you'll get well but if you do this you'll die,' and they always try to do the thing that will kill them." She looked over at Eileen, who was lying on her side, her red hair fanned out on the pillow, her deep blue bachelor-button eyes round and bright with interest. Under the covers she had her writing paper, her fountain pen and five movie magazines. Kimi said, "Katy, if the nurses were all like you, it would be much pleasanter for the patient." Katy said, "Kimi, if the patients were all like you it would be much pleasanter for the nurses."

Minna was given pneumothorax every other day and her lungs didn't burst or blow up and she continued to sleep twenty-three hours out of the twenty-four, but when poor old Sweetie-Pie came bouncing in on visiting day, wreathed in smiles and loaded with packages, she entertained him for two hours with her operation, her suffering and the horrible things that had happened to other patients and that might and probably would happen to her. We watched him droop and sag like a melting snowman.

After he had gone, Minna sat up and ate every crumb of her supper including two helpings of the main dish. Kimi looked over at her, wearing a new pink angora bed jacket and happily eating soup, while the mournful steps of the deflated Sweetie-Pie dragged along the corridor, then said softly, "With what a vast feeling of relief he will close the lid on your coffin." I choked on my soup and Eileen shouted with glee. Minna said only, "Next week he's bringin' me a pink hood to match this jacket."

On October nineteenth, Kimi and I were moved. Just after rest hours the Charge Nurse suddenly materialized in our room and without a word put my chair on the foot of the bed and wheeled me up the hall into a cubicle on the east side of the building. I was pleased, for the last week had been very tedious and any change was welcome. I said to the Charge Nurse, "Oh, I'm glad you moved me today." She said only, "I have put you near the office where I can give you more supervision." Then, "I'm putting Miss Sanbo in with you, if you don't mind." Mind! I was delighted. She said, "Some people would object to sharing a room with an Oriental." I said that I would prefer it, so she went to get Kimi.

Our new little room was just large enough for our two beds, placed with the heads to the windows and tight against each wall, our bedside stands and chairs. By stretching only a little we could pass things to each other.

On October twenty-eighth, a wild and stormy Sunday morning, the Charge Nurse came into our cubicle and said, "Mrs. Bard, you have been here one month today. The doctor says that you may read and write for fifteen minutes a day and you may walk to the bathroom once a day." She smiled and said, "I have brought you the Sunday papers. Do not exceed the time."

A few minutes ago our little room had been cold and depressing with the wind howling through the windows, the rain splatting on the sills, the green walls dank and confining. Now, with my first assurance that I was getting well and the delightful prospect of walking to the bathroom, the whole picture changed. I turned on my bed lamp and snapped open the funny papers. How cozy everything seemed.

On the stroke of two I opened my eyes and there were Anne and Joan and Mother. Anne and Joan had on new dark blue coats and their own shining faces and were beautiful.

Anne said, her eyes filling with tears, "I would like to kiss you." Joan said, "I can do a figure eight on my roller skates." Anne said, "The nurse said that we couldn't even touch your bed." Joan said, "I can do a figure eight on my roller skates."

I said, "Don't you think this is a beautiful hospital, girls?" Anne said, "It smells!" Then added tactfully, "Like medicine. When can you come home, Mommy?" Joan said, "When you come home you can see me do a figure eight on my roller skates." Kimi's family came in then and the children were fascinated and had to be turned around and faced in my direction.

I asked about school and Anne told me about what "a terrible cheater Charlie Thomas is but the teacher loves him so much she lets him cheat—even helps him," which sounded unlikely. Joan asked, "What is cheating?" I said, "Oh, asking other people to help you with your work, copying off other children's papers, looking in the book during tests." Joan said, "Oh, I do those things all the time. Everybody does. Only I get so mad at Marilyn because when I copy her arithmetic paper she has all the answers wrong. I did two figure eights on my roller skates yesterday." Anne said, "Oh stop talking about those old figure eights." Joan said, "Well, Grandmother told us not to talk about being Japanese." Then the Charge Nurse came and the ten minutes were up. The children threw me kisses and went away with the nurse, taking my heart with them.

After supper, in that most depressing and lonely time of day, early evening, the radio seemed possessed and concentrated on tunes like "Sonny Boy," "My Buddy" and "Boy of Mine," all played on the organ. Our little room was morbidly quiet and sorrow was heaped in my corner like dirty snow.

I was staring at the ceiling and going over a little scene in which Anne went from door to door in patched shoes taking orders for greasy doughnuts that I baked at home and Joan skated in the street to show me how she could do a figure eight on her roller skates and was hit by a truck, when Kimi said, "I would rather have beautiful children I could see but once a month than ogly little monster I could see all the time."

I have always liked any special day, be it Mother's Day, Groundhog Day or Bastille Day and the big full-bodied holidays like Christmas, Thanksgiving and Easter fill me so full of feeling and spirit that I can get tears in my eyes just looking at a fruitcake.

Lying in bed at The Pines day after day, week after week, month after month, engaged in pursuits such as listening to the split, splat, splat of the rain hitting the gutter outside my window or waiting my turn to have my lung collapsed, should have increased this feeling for holidays about a billionfold. It didn't. The days were all so exactly alike and followed each other with such monotonous regularity that I lost all interest in holidays as such.

I knew them only as "gas" day, bath day, fluoroscope day, visiting day, supply day or store day. It was in part infiltration into sanatorium life, divorce from normal living. It was also in part the childish self-centered attitude of an invalid. What I was doing, how I felt, what was to happen to me became more and more important to me as time went on.

At first when my visitors told me of happenings in the outside world I was vitally interested and relived each incident vividly with the telling. Then gradually, insidiously, like night mist rising from the swamps, my invalidism obscured the real world from me and when the family told me tales of happenings at home, I found them interesting but without strength, like talk about people long dead. The only real things were connected with the sanatorium. The only real people, the other patients, the doctors, the nurses.

At home Thanksgiving had always been a delightful occasion even when we were being thankful for meatloaf shaped like a turkey. We thought about Thanksgiving, planned for Thanksgiving and talked of Thanksgiving for weeks beforehand, but the evening before the actual day was the best time of all. Then the house seethed with children and dogs, with friends and cooks, and with delightful smells of baking pies, turkey stuffing and coffee. Every time the doorbell rang we put on another pot of coffee and washed the cups and by the time we went to bed we were so nervous and flighty that when accidentally bumped or brushed against, we buzzed and lit up like pin-ball machines. Thanksgiving morning usually found us all quite nasty and with too many things planned for the oven, but even the fighting was fun. Warm, family fun.

At The Pines I awoke the morning before Thanksgiving to darkness and drumming rain and thought only, Shampoo, today. I wonder which nurse I'll get. In the bathroom after breakfast, I overheard Sheila telling Kimi that we were having turkey and coffee without saltpeter for Thanksgiving dinner. "Thanksgiving?" I said. "When is it anyway?" "Tomorrow," Kimi said with obvious disgust. "Surely you have not forgotten how, with tear streaming from your motherly eye, you begged the Charge Nurse to let Anne and Joan come four day early so that you could see them on Thanksgiving." I remembered then and was lightheaded with joy at the prospect of seeing my darling Anne and Joan, but I had no feeling about Thanksgiving until after supper that night.

The ward was very quiet. The radio had been turned off and the smooth surface of the evening stillness was broken only by the faraway clatter of the nurses washing nourishment cups and the dreary slip, slop of the rain. I tried to read but kept losing my place and reading the same paragraph over and over again.

Every magazine story seemed to be about a girl who was nauseatingly little, nauseatingly thin and said "Jeepers." As I was only interested in stories about large plump women with tuberculosis, and had always nourished an overwhelming desire to kick in the groin anybody, no matter how tiny, who said "Jeepers," I threw the magazine to the foot of the bed and turned off my bed light. "Pulitt, pulatt, pulitt, pulatt," said the irritating rain on the roof of the porch. There was no other sound from anywhere.

I lay and thought about the quiet until it finally dawned on me that this was the night before Thanksgiving, that everyone was thinking about home, that the air was so thick with longing, so crowded with memories that it was difficult to breathe. Someone across the hall pushed aside the heavy curtain of remembering to draw a long shuddering breath. There was a sigh from the room next door.

Thanksgiving Day dawned cold and rainy. Our trays were set with little baskets of candies and the nurses were very pleasant, even closing the windows before dinner in honor of the day. The Pines had certainly done their share in trying to make the holiday a success but in spite of good intentions, I ate little and without relish. I longed for meatloaf shaped like a turkey and my warm loving family.

On the stroke of two, my dear unselfish, faithful mother brought Anne and Joan, with new raincoats, shining eyes and fresh damp curls. They were all in determinedly high holiday spirits and I thought what a trial it must have been for Mother to have to leave her family, her warm house and open fire, to come miles and miles in the rain by bus to that chilly cheerless hospital; to sit in a draught and listen to me complain. It was hard on Anne and Joan too, who, though they loved the ride on the bus and looked forward to each visit with me, had to spend one hour and fifty minutes in the dreary fireless reception room.

I asked them how they would pass the time while waiting for Mother, and Anne said, "I brought along the *Mexican Twins* and I'm going to read to Joan." Joan said, "She said she was going to read to me whether I wanted her to or not." Then Anne presented, in an intensely dramatic fashion, a play they were rehearsing at school. She took all the parts, throwing herself into each with such fervor and abandon that at the finish there was applause from some of the nearby cubicles.

Joan had brought out a book of interesting facts and at each pause in Anne's recital she produced an interesting fact. Anne: "No, no, you wicked queen, you'll never marry the Prince!" (Pause for character change.) Joan: "Betty, did you happen to know that the earthworm has a life span of seven years?"

By December I had been moved across the hall to a two-bed cubicle, I had one hour reading-time, I was taking pneumothorax but once a week and I was colder than I had ever been before. Our bedpans and water glasses froze solid each night and we wore woolen mittens and woolen hoods even at mealtimes. My new roommate, Eleanor Merton, was an inspirational patient and on silence, which was as near as you could get to being by yourself with someone four feet away from you twenty-four hours a day.

Also by December first I knew the entire Bedrest Hospital routine by heart and could tell exactly what was going to happen every minute of every day. This made the time move with glacial slowness, made me even more restless and crotchety. Things which I had grown to accept as part of being institutionalized suddenly became unbearable and, I regret to state, I began to complain constantly about everything, finally even developing small vague aches and pains which I eagerly reported, morning and evening, to the long-suffering Charge Nurse, who gave me meaning looks and aspirin.

Of course the major irritation of all was my roommate, who

was so damned happy all the time, so well adjusted. She loved the institution and the institution loved her. She loved all the nurses and all the nurses loved her. She loved all the other patients and all the other patients, but one, loved her. That one used to lie awake in the long dark cold winter nights and listen hopefully for her breathing to stop.

One night the maxim on my supper tray was: "Dare we face the question of just how much of the darkness around us is of our own making?" The Official-in-Charge-of-Beautiful-Thoughts was not only Miss Bartlett of Bartlett's *Quotations*, she was psychic.

On December twelfth Kimi was given a chest examination and three hours' time up; Sheila was moved to the Ambulant Hospital and Eileen had a hemorrhage. Molly Hastings brought me the news and she was grave about Eileen. She said that for weeks they had suspected Eileen of shaking down her thermometer, of not reporting her cough, that the hemorrhage had been severe and was a bad sign. She also said that Eileen was not like herself, that she was sullen and quiet and seemed to have lost all her spirit.

I said passionately, "It's because she's alone. It's horrible to be alone. Look what it's done to me." Molly said, "But you're not alone now," and she smiled at Eleanor who looked inspirational and smiled back. I said, "Why don't they move Eileen in with me, I know I could make her want to get well." Molly was very unenthusiastic. She said, "Neither of you would get well and you'd probably both be thrown out. In tuberculosis it's each man for himself."

Each man for himself or not, I wrote Eileen a long and probably unconvincing letter, telling her about Kimi's time up and how much fun it would be when we were all at the Ambulant Hospital. I didn't get an answer from Eileen, who was not allowed to write, but I had a note from Minna that should have been bordered in black. Minna said that her pneumothorax was not successful, as she knew it would not be, that she was scheduled for a thoracoplasty operation, but she had little hope of its success as she was so tiny and delicate and the doctors were so incompetent. Then she told me about Eileen's hemorrhage. She said, "I knew it would happen some day. Eileen won't take care of herself, won't obey the nurses. They've got her down now with sandbags and ice packs on her chest, but I suppose this is the end."

I also had a note from Kimi. She wrote, "I have had my chest examined and have been granted three hour time up, but I feel no joy with Eileen so sick and the grim raper [I gathered that she meant reaper] so near. I also have occupational therapy time . . . one half an hour a day. The occupational therapy teacher is forcing me to crochet. She says it will release tension. I have made a chain eleven feet long. It is knotty with released tension and dirty with sweat which I find releases more readily than tension."

That night, after confused dreams, I awoke in the cold, early night to the dark stillness of the ward. I always hated The Pines at night. It was so much a hospital where anything might happen, anyone might die. My pajamas and three sweaters were in a lumpy uncomfortable mass under my ribs, so moving slowly and carefully I tried to straighten them out. Everyone was asleep with faint buzzing snores sounding faintly at intervals. My right leg grew lumpy with a cramp and I had to turn over quickly. Finally everyone seemed to be awake and there were coughs up and down the halls like a relay race. A grim terrible race with Death holding the stakes. I thought of Eileen cold and alone with sandbags on her chest. Sylvia had said that hemorrhages were very frightening. That the blood was bright red and foamy.

Someone was tapping on her stand. It was the way to summon a nurse but never used, especially at night, except in an emergency. The tapping went on, clink, clink, clink, clink. The nurse didn't come. I could hear her in the office telephoning. The elevator door clanged shut. The tapping went on, clink, clink, clink. It seemed to come from down the hall where the private rooms were. Eleanor said in a whisper, "Something's happened. I hear a doctor."

I grew panicky and thought of course that Eileen was worse. The tapping on the stand grew louder, more insistent. Everyone was awake now. There was a low hum of voices, the carrying sibilance of whispering. The elevator door clanged again. The tapping on the stand was now demanding, bang, bang, bang! No one heeded.

Morning came at last, dark and wild with wind and rain lashing and clawing at the windows. The ward was oppressively quiet. The day staff came on duty, cheerful and brisk, bringing breakfast. I gulped two cups of warm comforting coffee but I couldn't shake off the horror of the night before. I felt as though I'd been in a dark filthy cellar and must and cobwebs still clung to me.

As I walked down the hall to the bathroom I thought I detected an ominous undercurrent. There was a furtiveness to the whispering. In the bathroom I learned, from one of the older patients, that a girl in emergency had died during the night. I had never seen the girl, didn't even know her name but it was my first death. My slowly built-up confidence and assurance of recovery were kicked from under me. I shivered uncontrollably. My windows had framed a magnificent expanse of sunlit sky, mountains and ocean, but when I looked out I saw only the hideous leering face of a Peeping Tom.

On Sunday, December eighteenth, Mother, Mary and Dede came loaded with food and enthusiasm. I immediately skimmed the cream from their visit by telling them of the woman who died, of my preoccupation with death. Dede said, "For you to be worrying about death seems to me as asinine as someone who is tone deaf worrying about losing his voice." I said coldly that I didn't get the allusion. She said, "My God, haven't you looked in the mirror lately? You're so big and healthy you're frightening." We all laughed and I cheered up a trifle.

Then I told them about Eileen's hemorrhage. Mother asked if the sandbags were a punishment and I explained that they were to keep her lung compressed. My sister Mary said, "You knew from the very first that Eileen was resisting every effort to cure her t.b. The only reason the Medical Director is keeping her here is because tuberculosis is contagious. Now for heaven's sake close the door of that vault and cheer up, Christmas is coming and so is another spring!"

On her rounds after supper the Charge Nurse informed us that we would draw names and exchange small Christmas presents, that we were not allowed any kind of a Christmas tree, not even imitation ones, as it made too much work for the nurses. She said that the institution would decorate the wards. She also said that any presents sent by us to the outside world would first have to go through fumigation.

Having seen the results of fumigation on my sweaters and pajamas I realized that this limited my gift selection to objects of stone but I didn't care, Christmas was in the air at last and I borrowed Eleanor's two-year-old Sears, Roebuck catalog and spent a happy evening roaming from plows to perfume. I slept all night that night and never again became obsessed with death.

The next afternoon two nurses fulfilled the Charge Nurse's prediction and decorated the wards. I had counted on cedar boughs and pine cones and waited breathlessly for their spicy scent to vie with the lysol for domination of the ward. What I got were limp festoons of red and green crepe paper (obviously well fumigated) and red cardboard bells, hung slightly askew in each doorway. In my new happiness, I didn't care, it was something and it spelled Christmas.

The day before Christmas it began to snow. The flakes were big and wet and thudded straight to the ground, where they surprisingly did not melt but soon coated the lawns, the trees and the buildings of The Pines in a most Christmas-cardy way.

Christmas Eve my brother Cleve, calmly ignoring every rule of the sanatorium, suddenly loomed in my doorway large and handsome, smelling deliciously of cigarettes and out of doors and bearing a huge carton overflowing with presents from the family. The evening nurses arranged our presents in exciting heaps on the foot of our beds but instructed us not to open them until morning.

Except for large wrinkly packages, bearing thousands of Christmas seals, which were easily identified as being from Anne and Joan and brought quick tears and a large lump to my throat, it was like Christmas Eve in boarding school. We drank hot chocolate, talked and laughed furtively and listened to the clear sweet voices of carolers coming up the drive.

There were several groups of carolers and they wandered around the grounds stopping by the porches and under the windows and singing all the lovely familiar Christmas songs. "Hark! the Herald Angels Sing," "Joy to the World," "Silent Night," "Adeste Fideles," "Wind Through the Olive Trees," "We Three Kings of Orient Are," "O Little Town of Bethlehem," "Once in Royal David's City," "Oh, Holy Night," and "Away in a Manger." They were apparently volunteers from church groups or good-hearted local people, for their voices were untrained and discorded occasionally in a homely, friendly way.

As they moved around the grounds the songs came to us now loud, now faint like songs from a campfire or over still water on a summer evening. When they sang under the windows of our ward, the melody was interwoven with sounds of deep sorrow, weeping and long broken sighs, for some of the patients were spending the second, third, even sixth Christmas away from home and a few knew they would never be home for Christmas.

But in spite of wet snow and thick dark the carolers sang with spirit and vigor, and "Joy to the World" came streaming joyously in every open window and soon drowned out the sighs and strangled sobbing. When the carolers left, the ward was perfectly still, frosted with peace and good will.

On January sixth the Charge Nurse invited me to The Pines moving picture show, but she handed me the invitation so thickly encased in rules it was like being given a present of one smelt wrapped in the Sunday *New York Times.*

She said in part, "You are on the list to go to the movie tonight, Mrs. Bard. You may wear makeup, if you wish, but you may not talk or laugh. You are to be ready by seven o'clock, in your robe and slippers, with your pillow and night blanket. You will be called for by a *male* [she said male in a low throbbing voice as though it were some dangerous new sex] ambulant patient but you are not to speak to or to laugh with your escort. Your temperature and pulse will be taken as soon as you return to bed and if your temperature or your pulse has increased you will not be allowed to go to the next moving picture show." I thanked her, promised not to speak or to pulsate and she left.

Deck the Halls with Old Crepe Paper 241

When she had gone I dug down under the thick depressing wrappings and found that my little present was still there, I was going to the movie!

After supper I was so excited my heart pounded like a jungle drum and my hands were as fluttery and unmanageable as freshly caught sole, but I smeared on lipstick, wet my hair with drinking water and thought, This is living!

Eleanor, who was also going to the movie, remained, of course, as unruffled as a turnip. I had been dressed, twitching on the edge of my bed, for half an hour so of course she was called for first. Her escort, large, handsome and cheerful, stopped at the door, smiled at both of us but read Eleanor's name from his little slip of paper.

When I finally heard my name being read in a high uncertain voice at the doorway of the wrong room, I knew that Eleanor had had the evening's luck. My escort had nothing in common with Eleanor's. He was not handsome, he was not cheerful and he wasn't a man. He was about seventeen years old, approximately six feet six inches tall, two inches thick, greenish and so shy that I was afraid that speaking to him would have the same disastrous melting effect as putting salt on a snail.

Resignedly I took my night blanket and pillow, climbed into the wheelchair, signaled that I was ready and away we went, silently and swiftly like a cold draught, in and out of elevators, through long dark tunnels, up and down ramps, in and out of buildings and there wasn't a word between us. The Charge Nurse would have been so proud of me. When we reached the auditorium my escort kicked open the swinging doors, tipped me out like a sack of coal and melted back into the dark tunnel before I could turn and give him one of my inspiritional smiles.

Feeling like a package that has been left on the wrong porch, I clutched my night blanket and pillow and looked around. The auditorium was brightly lighted, rather small and rapidly filling to capacity. There were beds with the backs propped up along both sides and in the back of the hall, ordinary seats in the middle. I was wondering where I was to sit when an unsmiling strange nurse gripped my arm, steered me along the wall on the left side, helped me up onto a front bed beside Eleanor, stuffed my pillow behind my head, covered me with my blanket and told me not to talk.

As always at The Pines, the sexes were carefully sorted. The men all on one side, the women all on the other, the space between carefully patrolled by gimlet-eyed nurses with powerful flashlights to make sure that the sexes didn't mingle in the dark.

I found that sitting on a bed with a pillow behind my head was the most comfortable way ever devised for seeing a motion picture but I thought the picture itself rather a tactless choice for the joyous entertainment of patients in a tuberculosis sanatorium. It was Greta Garbo in *Camille*.

Just to show me that in tuberculosis there is no sure thing, that all the paths of the tuberculous lead over quicksand, Monday morning, three days after I had gone to the movie and taken that first firm step toward normal living, I was informed that I was to go to surgery the following Thursday. My pneumothorax doctor, no longer the Medical Director but one of the regular staff, told me very casually after my pneumothorax that I was to "have some bands cut," an intrapleural pneumolysis, to be exact. He said that I had one or two large adhesions and until they were cut I could not have a proper collapse of the lung.

I spent the morning of January tenth in x-ray, posing with one arm above my head, one hand on my hip, both hands on hips, both arms above my head, and the evening listening to Eleanor tell of recent deaths at The Pines. As she had never before talked to me in the evening, I knew that she was only talking about death because I was going to have surgery, but I listened anyway in fascinated horror.

She said that when patients, usually unsuccessful surgery cases, were going to die they got violent diarrhea and nausea, grew thinner and thinner, weaker and weaker, and were finally visited by the Medical Director and told to put their affairs in order because they were going to die. She said that more men than women died at The Pines because of a distressing tendency on the part of wives to divorce their poor sick husbands and thus remove their incentive for getting well. I asked her if men didn't also divorce their sick wives but she said no, that men never divorced their wives, no matter how long the wives were at The Pines. I was amazed at this demonstration of "the faithful old male," especially as my experience with men in the business world had led me to believe that many men forgot all about their wives when away from them for very short periods, like all day at the office. Eleanor concluded that all some women seemed to want out of life was to paint their faces and go to nightclubs. It was with difficulty that I refrained from saying, "I'll say, kid!"

At eight o'clock, an evening nurse delivered a note from Eileen Kelly. Ordinarily I would have grabbed it and ripped it open for Eileen's letters, no matter what her condition, were always amusing, always made me laugh. But this evening Eleanor and her morbid predictions had me stuffed so far down in my crypt that I could not summon the courage to open and read what I was sure was Eileen's farewell letter. I put it on my stand unopened and continued to look out into the dusky hallway and think about my operation.

Just before lights out Katy stopped at our door and said, "Isn't it fine about Eileen?" I said, "What about her?" She said, "Didn't you get her letter?" I said, "Yes, but I didn't read it." She waited while I opened the letter and read that Eileen was much better, that she had been given half an hour of occupational therapy time and expected time up very soon. Katy said, "You see what being a good girl does for you?" and left. I said to Eleanor, "Well, there's one that won't die." She said, without looking up from her knitting, "I wouldn't bank on it if I were you."

The next afternoon Eleanor was moved, thank God, but her discussions of death, like the smell of flowers after a funeral, lingered behind her. After supper my apprehension was increased by extensive preparations for surgery and a large sleeping potion.

The next morning at seven-thirty, like a picador toward a bull, Miss Muelbach came charging at me with a hypodermic needle. "I'm allergic to morphine," I said mildly but she already had the needle in and was bearing down on the plunger, so I didn't pursue the matter further. Instead I put on the sterilized white stockings, white cap and white gown she handed me and when she had gone I looked in the mirror. My reflected all-white image was so much like a young weevil emerging from a sack of flour that I expected to see a flour manufacturer's label embossed in blue on the bedspread.

I decided to put on some mascara. This was strictly against the rules but I thought the situation warranted it. After all if I died I didn't want my body sprayed with Black Leaf 40 and dumped on some compost heap. After I had put on plenty of mascara I looked again and found that I now looked like a weevil who hadn't slept. I was contemplating the removal of the mascara when two strange nurses wheeled in a stretcher, transferred me to it with one jerk of the sheet, and wheeled me rapidly to the surgery on the top floor of the Administration Building.

Because of my allergy the morphine, instead of dulling my senses, had made me very bright, alert and nervous. Very conscious of every sound, every smell, each new face. The surgery was high and very light with shiny white-tiled walls. Waiting for me were two doctors looking like wrinkled Ku Kluxers in their surgical caps and gowns, and three surgical nurses wound and bound in white. One of these identified herself as an operation artist, and a friend of my sister Mary.

I was transferred from the stretcher to the operating table and turned on my right side with both arms over my head. Then after a great deal of scrubbing and painting on my back and chest, novocain was injected in my left side under the arm and in my back in the vicinity of my shoulderblade.

The doctor who usually gave me pneumothorax explained what they had done, were doing or intended to do. "We are now making a hole under your arm. In this incision we will put a little light so that the surgeon can see what he is cutting from the incision he has made in your back." The operation artist, who was peering in the holes and drawing what she saw, also made comments. "Your lung is the prettiest shade of blue," or "You should see the neat job the doctor is doing."

It was very hot in the surgery and I was extremely nervous. Before long little rivulets of perspiration began running off my forehead and down into the mascara on my eyelashes. The mascara ran into my eyes and stung fiercely. Tears streamed down my cheeks. I tried to tell the nurse stationed at my head to wipe my eyes but every time I spoke the doctor told me to shut up as they were cutting my lung and talking apparently moved it.

The nurse finally noticed my tears and thinking that I was crying from pain or fear or both, hurriedly held spirits of ammonia under my nose which made my eyes water more and released more mascara.

After what seemed like years the doctor explained that they had anesthetized for two adhesions but had found four and were going to have to cut them anyway. I was to be brave, he said, and was not to flinch. I was very brave and didn't flinch but only because the slight burning from snipping the unanesthetized adhesions was nothing compared to the torture I had already endured from the mascara.

At eleven-thirty I was wheeled back to the Bedrest Hospital and put, in spite of loud protestations on my part, into the light room, reserved, according to Eleanor, for the sure-diers. At two o'clock Mother and Mary brought me an armload of spring flowers and I blanched when I saw them for I had forgotten that it was a visiting day and thought they had been sent for.

By four-thirty I had been moved back to my own room and only by a slight soreness under my arm and in my back and by my very red-rimmed eyes could I tell that I had spent the morning in surgery. I had been instructed to eat lying down for a few days but Charlie came to see me anyway. He gripped my right hand and said, "When Kimi told me you'd went to surgery I said to myself, 'Say good-bye to a good kid, Charlie.'" I said, "Why Charlie, there wasn't anything to it. I feel perfectly wonderful." He said, "You better wait until the next few days are over. There's many a slip 'twixt the cup and the lip."

My first slip came about seven-thirty when I noticed a peculiar scrunchy feeling in my left wrist. When I doubled my fist or flexed my fingers it felt like crumpling tissue paper. I asked the evening nurse about it and she looked frightened and immediately produced the House Doctor who gave me a sedative. In the morning the scrunchy feeling was gone. I asked the Charge Nurse what it was but she only smiled and asked me who had given me my hypodermic the morning before.

At noon Charlie, who acted very surprised that I had pulled through the night, asked me how I felt. I told him about the tissue paper in my wrist. He said, "Air in your veins. That's the way they kill rabbits at the laboratory. Shoot air in the veins and stop the heart. That bubble of air you got in your veins might get to your heart anytime now. It'll stop just like that." He snapped his fingers. "Well, you won't know what hit you, that's sure," he concluded comfortingly.

Two days after my operation I was given a new roommate. A girl named Katherine Harte, who had curly black hair, large green eyes, dimples and empyema. Kate was twenty-five years old, had been in The Pines for two years, had eaten almost nothing for two weeks, had to have her bed propped up day and night, and was ready to die. She told me that she felt as if she were floating about six inches above her bed and that she saw everything through a thick gray mist.

The next day after Kate moved in was a visiting day. As I put on makeup after dinner, Kate advised me that she had told her family to stay home because she intended to spend the visiting hours with her eyes closed floating in the gray mist. I didn't say anything. I felt guilty because I was so well and she was so sick and because I knew that Mother, Mary and Madge were coming to see me and my visiting hours were bound to be a delight.

Even when Mary, Mother and Madge came in and cheerfully unloaded an armload of forsythia, two books by Humphrey Pakington and a large box of oatmeal cookies on my stomach and while Mother told me about the children, the happenings at home, at school and in the garden, Kate lay as still as death, her eyes closed, apparently floating in her mist.

Then Mary told about entertaining a doctor from Boston who was so reserved, so Eastern and so disapproving of the informal West that after two days of him she had become so self-conscious about being Western that every time she walked she could hear her spurs jangle and when she spoke she had to check herself to keep from whirling her lariat around her head and calling him Pardner. Mary's stories were always funny but even if they hadn't been she was so warm and vivid herself that just having her in the cold rainswept little room was as comforting as a bonfire.

Before Mary finished the story the Charge Nurse stopped at the door and warned Kate and me about laughing. Surprised at the inclusion of Kate, I looked over at her. Her green eyes were open and she was wiping away tears of laughter. I introduced her to the family. Madge said, "My God, you're beautiful! Why do you have to sit up like that?" Kate, carefully watching the door for nurses, explained that she had empyema, an infection of the pleural cavity, and added casually that she was dying. Madge brushed the dying aside as unimportant. What she wanted were the symptoms of this empyema, the details of how Kate had gotten tuberculosis, what her first signs had been.

Mary said, "Nonsense, you're not dying. Millions of people have empyema—common as measles," which was entirely untrue of course but seemed to cheer Kate, who told Mary about the floating and the gray mist. Mary said, "Malnutrition, very usual symptom. Your stomach has probably shrunk to the size of a crabapple. Here, eat a few of these cookies."

Being married to a doctor, Mary felt that she knew more about medicine than the American Medical Association but the only people she was allowed to treat were her family, who knew that no matter what their symptoms, she would diagnose them as being indicative of whatever disease she happened to remember from the latest medical journal. When Dede was cutting her wisdom teeth Mary told her she had every symptom of a rare South American virus disease, and when Alison broke her leg skiing, Mary, who had just heard about psychosomatic medicine, told Mother that Alison could wear a cast if she wanted to but the whole thing was purely a manifestation of her psyche.

She had apparently abandoned the psyche for little crabapple stomachs and empyema as common as measles, but it made no difference what it was because it cheered up Kate, influenced her to eat several cookies and all of her supper, and evidently changed her attitude toward dying for she never mentioned it again.

It was probably the natural progression of the disease but it might have been, as Kate insists it was, the effect of my cheering visitors that made her temperature begin to go down the very next day, made her start to get well and was responsible for our both being given three hours' time up on the twenty-first of February.

15

Ambulant Hospital

MARCH TWENTY-FOURTH was a spring day. A nice regulation spring day patterned after a picture in a Second Reader. The sunshine was direct and warm and gave the straight pale green poplar trees and the small well-stuffed white clouds neat black outlines against the flat blue sky. Over all were pleasant usual spring noises. An airplane busily humming through the serene atmosphere, a boat whistling conscientiously as it threaded its careful way through the little islands of the Sound, a rooster crowing, the rhythmic ringing of a distant hammer, the whirring of a lawn mower, the hurried click of hedge clippers.

It was a day to hang out clean white clothes, to dig in the garden, to try out new roller skates, to put up a swing, but Kate and I had to be satisfied with lounging in lounge chairs on the porch, doing fancywork and taking our time up. We had reached our full three hours the evening before and we felt like eager fledglings teetering on the edge of the nest waiting for the push that would make us try our wings. From now on anything might happen, the Ambulant Hospital, a tub bath, a trip to the beauty parlor, work in the occupational therapy shop, six hours' time up—anything. All we had to do was to sit quietly and wait.

The sun now had one or two of its beams aimed at my back, which made me feel like a frozen roast just slipped into a hot oven. I knew I should get up and move but I was hypnotized by the delicious warmth. I leaned back and closed my eyes and let the dangerous sunshine flow over me like warm oil. I was jerked from my lassitude by the Charge Nurse's voice. It quivered with horror as she said, "Mrs. Bard, you're sitting in the *sun!*" I said, "I'm sorry, I must have dozed. I'll move right away." She said, "No need to move, you and Miss Harte are to go for chest examinations." Chest examination! That meant the Ambulant Hospital! I wanted to shout with joy but I tried very hard not to register anything other than blind obedience. The Charge Nurse said, "You may walk to the examination room," and left the porch.

I had gained twenty pounds in the five months I had been at The Pines and I felt like a tank as I lumbered uncertainly up the long hallway, on legs unsteady with disuse and excitement. Once I stumbled and, when I grabbed at a cubicle wall for support, it gave way under my tremendous impact and wavered indecisively over the head of a sleeping patient.

When we reached the examination room the Charge Nurse was waiting for us. She sent me in first. The doctor examined my chest and lungs very thoroughly but said nothing. When I came out my face was hot with excitement and I was afraid the Charge Nurse would think I had the dread t.b. flush. Before Kate went in she said in a tense little voice, "Pray for me hard."

While Kate was examined I shuffled slowly back to my bed, now in a four-bed ward at the opposite end of the building from the entering ward. I climbed into bed and for once the icy sheets felt soothing to my excited, flushed body. I looked in the mirror and my face, as I had feared, was a mottled tomato red. I put my cold, damp washcloth over it and closed my eyes. My heart was pounding boom, boom, boom, and my unused muscles twitched convulsively like a dying chicken, so of course the Charge Nurse chose that time to take my pulse and temperature. After a minute or so she said, "You're excited, I'll come back later." Then, "Better get that pulse down if you want to go to the Ambulant Hospital this afternoon." She sounded stern, but she was smiling and I knew that she was happy over my progress and no doubt glad to get rid of me.

Kate came in then and the Charge Nurse told her that she too was to go to the Ambulant Hospital that afternoon. She said that we were to rest quietly until the move. It was like asking someone to rest quietly on her wedding day, but we tried.

Of course I couldn't sleep during rest hours, but because I knew that I would be under close observation and would have my pulse and temperature taken as soon as I woke up, I kept my eyes shut and tried to relax. Each minute seemed like an hour, and each hour like a century but finally it got to be two-thirty and the nourishment cart came clanking in, closely followed by nurses with carts for Kate's and my belongings and bedding, and the Charge Nurse with a wheelchair for me. We took the usual route to the basement and the tunnels, then taking all turns to the left instead of to the right, which led to x-ray, we came at last to a low rustic building which housed the dining room, the examining rooms and the Ambulant Hospital Charge Nurse's office.

This Charge Nurse, according to a letter from Kimi, who had gone to the Ambulant Hospital three weeks before, was "the most terrible creature living—soft-spoken but exuding venom from every pore of her short lumpy body." Therefore I was not too surprised after the Bedrest Charge Nurse had left, to have her say, "You have been a problem, Mrs. Bard." I said, "I'm sorry." She said, "Being sorry is not enough, Mrs. Bard. We must have proof of your desire to cooperate. Proof of your trustworthiness. Proof that we will be proud to have you in our hospital."

I didn't know what she was getting at. How could I, sitting in a wheelchair in my blue woolen bathrobe, suddenly produce evidence of good citizenship? I said, "I don't know what you mean. What kind of proof?" She was acting as though she expected written references. She said, "You're going to have to change that attitude, Mrs. Bard." I said, "I'm sorry but I don't know what you want me to say." She said, "If you don't know what to say then we haven't been able to teach you very much."

I said, "I don't understand what you're talking about and I don't know what you want me to say." She smiled at me blandly and said, "I just want you to say that you intend to do your best to be an obedient, helpful, cooperative, industrious patient." I said, "I do" meekly in spite of a poignant longing to say, "The hell I will!"

The welcome over, we started for the hospital. I had a slight premonition that life from then on was not going to be any gambol on the grassy turf, so, as the Charge Nurse wheeled me to my new room, I asked about the rules. Were they the same as those at the Bedrest Hospital? If not, what were the rules of the Ambulant Hospital? The Charge Nurse said, "We do not tell the patients the rules, Mrs. Bard. We find that the trial and error method is the best way to learn them." I said, "But how can I be obedient, cooperative and helpful if I don't know what I'm supposed to do?" She said, "We do not allow arguing, Mrs. Bard. I am in authority and I do what I think is best for the patients."

We entered the Women's Ambulant Hospital. The building, brick and of modern architecture, was two stories high, had gentle ramps instead of stairs and was designed like an ocean steamer with all the accommodations outside cabins, opening on screened promenade decks about ten feet wide. The Charge Nurse wheeled me into an apartment on the south side, first floor, facing a cherry orchard, told me supper would be at four-thirty, that a nurse would call for me with a wheelchair, that I was to be ready, and left.

My bed had already been made and my belongings were in cartons on the floor. My new roommate, Sigrid Hansen, said, "You are to have the two bottom drawers in the bureau, the right-hand locker in the bathroom." I said, "You mean we have our own bathroom?" She said, "Yes, over there. It is warm and we dress in there." I went over and opened the door. The dressing room was deliciously warm and contained two large metal wardrobes and a wash basin. At the end there was a little lavatory. No more bedpans, wheee!

I put my clean pajamas and sweaters in the bureau drawers,

the rest of my stuff in the bedside stand, and got into bed. The bed was very cold. I asked Sigrid if we were allowed hot-water bottles. She said, "Sure, fill it yourself in the bathroom. Fill it every ten minutes if you want to." I immediately got up and filled my hot-water bottle with scalding water. What bliss!

Toecover is a family name for a useless gift. A crocheted napkin ring is a toecover. So are embroidered book marks, large figurines of a near-together-eyed shepherdess, pin-cushion covers done in French knots, a satin case for snap-fasteners (with a card of snap-fasteners tactfully enclosed so you won't make a mistake and think it a satin case for hooks-and-eyes or old pieces of embroidery thread), embroidered coat hangers, hand-painted shoe trees (always painted with a special paint that never dries), homemade three-legged footstools with the legs spaced unevenly so the footstool always lies on one side, cross-stitched pictures of lumpy brown houses with "The houfe by the fide of the road" worked in Olde Englishe underneath, hand-decorated celluloid soap cases for traveling with tops that once off will never fit back on the bottom, crocheted paper knife handle covers complete with tassel, bud vases made out of catsup bottles, taffeta bed pillows heavily shirred and apparently stuffed with iron filings, poorly executed dolls whose voluminous skirts are supposed to cover telephones.

A toecover is not a thing that follows economic cycles. During the depression when everyone was making her own Christmas presents, toecovers abounded. In good times toecovers are not made at home but are bought in the back of Gifte Shoppes whose main income is from the lending library in the front.

On May third, I made my first trip to the women's occupational therapy shop and discovered it to be a bubbling source of toecovers presided over by the most enthusiastic advocate for and producer of the toecover in this era, Miss Gillespie.

Miss Gillespie was physically and mentally exactly what you'd expect the producer of hand-painted paper plates to be. She had a mouth so crowded with false teeth it looked as if she had put in two sets, firm, obviously dyed black hair, spectacles, wide hips and her own set of rules. One of these rules was that women patients could not use the basement lavatory because "the men will see you go in there and *know* what you go in there for." Another forbade the pressing of men's trousers by women, on the grounds that such intimate contact with male garments was unseemly.

On my first morning, I was directed by Miss Gillespie to sit at a table and roll bandages. She said, "Go over THERE! No, there! No, THERE! No talking. Quiet, must have QUIET. Work, work, no need to talk! Talking is bad for the lungs. Quiet, must have quiet!" I sat down next to Kimi who said, "Pay no attention to her, Betty." As Miss Gillespie was standing directly behind Kimi I hissed, "Be quiet, she'll hear you." Kimi said, much louder, "Oh, no she won't, for she is deaf as a stone."

For three days I rolled bandages under the hysterical supervision of Miss Gillespie and found it not unpleasant for it was useful work and the occupational therapy shop was large and light with green walls and furniture and a nice view of the cherry orchard from its south windows.

On the fourth morning when Sheila, Kimi and I reported for work at eight-thirty, Miss Gillespie screamed, "Typing! Typing. Must have typists! Magazine to get out! Quiet, must have typists, must have quiet!" Kimi, Sheila and I could all type, so we were made associate editors of the sanatorium magazine which meant merely that we typed from eight-thirty to ten-thirty anything that Miss Gillespie handed us.

As the ward news often contained "I seens," "he don'ts" and "we done its," we at first attempted to make a few editorial changes. Miss Gillespie compared the copies with the original and went wild. "Right from the heart," she yelled pounding on the original manuscript with her ruler. "Right from the heart, don't change a word. Type. Type. After all everyone don't talk like you." "No, he don't," Kimi said gently, smiling at Miss Gillespie who couldn't hear a word she was saying, "but I only done the best I could. I seen the mistakes and I fixed them." Miss Gillespie said to Sheila and me, "Why don't you try to act like Miss Sanbo. She is quiet. She don't argue. Now everybody to work, quiet! Quiet!"

From ten-thirty to eleven-thirty was our own time but we were supposed to learn useful occupations so that there would be a place for us in the great industrial world into which we were soon to be dumped. A few of the trades offered by Miss Gillespie were the manufacture of little crocheted baskets to hang by the sink to hold wedding and engagement rings while the owner washed the dishes, clothes-pin curtain retainers, rooster pot-holders, hand-painted paper plates, embroidered combing jackets, kewpie doorstops, crocheted needle books, crepe-paper lampshades, crocheted book marks, imitation crepe-paper sweet peas, holders for paper towels made out of old candy boxes decorated with forget-me-nots and marked "This looks like a towel, This feels like a towel, This is a towel, Use it."

I asked Miss Gillespie if I could use my time to brush up on my shorthand, but she, evidently having never heard of shorthand and supposing it to be some sort of game like volley ball, yelled, "No! No! Too noisy!"

On May tenth I was sent to the Bedrest Hospital on flower duty. My flower partner, a tiny little woman who wore old corsages and referred to her husband as "Big Daddy," and I walked to Bedrest at nine o'clock and reported to the Charge Nurse who was very cordial, complimented us on our time up but couldn't resist the old impulse to warn us not to talk as we took our empty carts and started up and down the wards gathering up all the vases of flowers.

I was shocked to find Eileen very thin and white and listless. She had had another hemorrhage, she told me, and was running a temperature all the time. The only time she showed even the faintest glimmer of her old fire was when she told me about the crush she had on the new store boy.

Minna was in one of the private rooms, tickled to death because one of her kidneys had become infected and the doctors were contemplating removing it.

My first try at washwater duty was five days later and began rather unfortunately. Harassed by Miss Gillespie's screamed warnings that I was to be in the dining room at five-thirty and not a second later, I hurled myself across the lawns in the cool gray of the dawn and arrived at the dining room breathless and ready for work at four-twenty. The night nurse, glad of company at that dreary hour, fixed coffee and fruit juice and we talked until we were joined at five-thirty by my washwater partner, a small pleasant Eskimo girl named Esther.

As my first morning at The Pines was still clear in my memory, I tried to wake the patients gently and Esther and I made many trips and gave everyone a full basin of hot water. Eileen seemed better and more cheerful as she told me that she and the store boy were engaged and would be married as soon as they were well. Minna rubbed her thick white eyelids, blinked and said, "Ah'm soooooo sleeeeeeepy," and for a minute I was back in the four-bed ward and wanted to pound her on the head with the water pitcher. Marie was cranky and said that she didn't like so much or such hot water; Eleanor said that she had heard that Margaretta was in emergency in a coma and wouldn't last through the day, that the little thirteen-year-old girl, Evangeline Constable, had had a spontaneous collapse and was not expected to live, and had I heard about Eileen's hemorrhage; old Gazz-on-Her-Stummick asked me if I wouldn't please fill her hot-water bottle as she had so much gazz on her stummick she hadn't closed her eyes all night, so I did and she said that the hot-water bottle was too hot and wouldn't I please put a little cold in it and while I was there would I hand her her sweater and if I saw the nurse would I send her in and would I bring her a glass of fresh water as she didn't like the taste of water after it had stood and could I pour just a little water on her flowers as they seemed to be drooping and . . . I grabbed her basin and fled.

On Hospital Day, May twelfth, we could have as many visitors as we liked from nine to twelve-thirty and from two to four in the afternoon.

The day was warm and clear, the poplars along the drive sparkled and swayed in the breeze and by eight-thirty the whole hospital was filled with expectation and the smell of new-mown grass. Anne, Joan, Mother, Alison, Mary, Madge, Cleve, Margaret, friends from out of town, everyone came.

Anne and Joan, very proud in new dark blue coats, spent the entire five and a half hours asking me if they could have wooden shoes, and I had a strong feeling, that if I died, their chief sorrow would be not getting the wooden shoes. Just before dinner I dressed and took the children around the promenades and introduced them to my friends and after the first four or five introductions I didn't have to push so hard on the tops of their heads to make them curtsy.

Kimi had the first town leave. On May thirteenth at noon her family came to get her and Sheila and I stood on the dining-room terrace and waved and waved, the tears running down our foolish faces.

I awakened on the day of my town leave to leaden skies and driving rain which I didn't mind in the least as it meant a fire in the fireplace at home. On the stroke of twelve Mary drove up and out spilled Anne and Joan followed by Mother carrying my tweed coat. I ran down the ramp and was engulfed in embraces and my old tweed, then to the car and away. The thrill of going through the gates, rounding the bend and losing sight of the sanatorium was never to be forgotten.

When we drove up in front of the house, sisters Dede, Alison and Madge, the dogs and the cats were on the steps to greet me. We all went in, Anne and Joan glued to each side, and then I had cups and cups of delicious, strong, hot coffee. I felt peaceful and content and so happy. Then Madge began to play the piano. She played "Tea for Two," "Night and Day," "Body and Soul," "Judy," all my favorites, and I was overwhelmed. It was all too wonderful. I wept and the children cried too, and the dogs barked and everyone else tried in loud voices to be cheerful. Mother hurriedly served lunch.

We all sat down at the table and everything was very gay for a few minutes. Then Joanie put down her soup spoon and began to bawl. With sympathetic tears streaming from my own eyes, I asked her what the trouble was. She gulped and said, "I was just thinking about showing you my new shoes and I remembered they have dye spilled on them." I finally persuaded her to get them anyway and she came down with a very large pair of Mexican huaraches with a pinpoint of black dye on one side. I exclaimed over the beauty and wondrous size of the shoes and everything was peaceful until lunch was over.

Then brother Cleve, his wife Margaret and son Allen, dear neighbors and their children, the "old baby" now a little boy who shook hands and talked plainly and solemnly, and neighborhood children came to see the returned invalid. The very foreign atmosphere of lovingkindness proved too much and again I wept and the children chimed in. When the visitors had gone we piled logs on the fire, made more coffee and prepared to make the most of the fleeting eight hours.

Unhappily I raised the question of where I would sleep when I returned, which brought to light the fact that the-always-ice-cold but with-its-own-bath-downstairs bedroom, instead of being filled with flowers in crystal vases awaiting my return, had not been touched since I left. In fact was being used as a storeroom. "Just as though you didn't expect me to come home ever," I said brokenly. "Oh, we knew our good luck couldn't last forever," Dede said putting her arm around me. The issue of who was to clean the back bedroom before I came home ended in a tremendous and very vigorous family fight involving every injustice done to any of us as far back as we could remember. In the midst of this emotional upheaval I was horrified to find that I was weeping and TATTING!

I was in the office on the stroke of eight o'clock and rather disappointed to find that my pulse and temperature were perfectly normal. As I had returned laden with hot ham sandwiches and a chocolate cake, I was greeted by my tubercular friends with great enthusiasm.

After lights out I lay in the dark and thought about the day. I was certain that my family hadn't the least idea of the meaning of the words rest and quiet; that they thought because I looked much healthier than any of them that I must be equally strong or stronger; that it would be impossible to observe rest hours or to adhere to only eight hours' time up at home. I was very tired, quite unhappy and bewildered and didn't care that I had lost my next town leave.

The next morning Kimi and Sheila were informed that their next town leaves had also been canceled on the grounds that the Charge Nurse thought that they thought they were superior to her. They said that they didn't care.

As there was a perfect cloudburst during rest hours and immediately before visiting hours, Mother arrived very wet and very cross. She denounced me soundly for weeping on my day at home, said that everyone had planned a happy day for me and that I was a most unsatisfactory guest. I explained that tears were brought on by joy but she merely sniffed and intimated that I was a big "saddo" and very spoiled. She said, "You have been concentrating on yourself for eight months, now it is time you began to think of someone else."

I wish that I could say that I immediately began thinking of other people and was consequently much happier. I didn't. As soon as visiting hours were over I told Kimi and Sheila how very un-understanding my family were. They retaliated with similar tales of hard-heartedness on the part of their loved ones. After supper we sat in the bathroom, drinking tea, eating cake and talking about how difficult it was going to be for delicate, emotionally frail us to get the proper care in the big cruel outside world.

16

"Let Me Out! Let Me Out!"

THE MEDICAL DIRECTOR of The Pines made himself personally responsible for all admissions to and discharges from the sanatorium. He never admitted as a patient anyone who could afford to go to a private sanatorium and he never gave an honorable discharge to a patient until he was sure that patient was well enough to resume normal living.

Patients at The Pines paid nothing or what they could and only the Medical Director knew who paid what. People who can reach out anytime and touch death have little false pride and the nothing-payers, by their own admission, were in the great majority. The Medical Director ruled his sanatorium and the patients with a rod of iron, said constantly that people with tuberculosis were ungrateful, stupid, uncooperative and unworthy. Then, carefully screening himself from his own kindness the way he screened his patients from their operations, he loaned those same ungrateful, stupid, uncooperative and unworthy patients money, bought them bathrobes and pajamas, took care of their families and children, listened to their problems, helped them get work and fretted twenty-four hours a day over their welfare.

We patients at The Pines differed in color, nationality, political beliefs, IQ, age, religion, background and ambition. According to the standards of normal living, the only things that most of us had in common were being alive and speaking English, but as patients in the sanatorium we had everything in common and were firmly cemented together by our ungratefulness, stupidity, uncooperativeness, unworthiness, poverty, tuberculosis and longing for a discharge.

Discharges were announced on Mondays directly after rest hours. As a patient was never told anything about the progress of his tuberculosis cure and was never warned of impending dismissal, a discharge was supposed to be a complete and wonderful surprise. Actually, every Monday from five-thirty A.M. until three o'clock, all eight-hour patients were jumpy with anticipation and lay in their beds during rest hours, stiff and prickly with hope, listening for the slap, slap of the Charge Nurse's feet.

June twelfth was a beautiful summer morning. The pergola over the dining-room walk was quilted with pink roses and purple clematis. Long ribbons of purple and blue violas bordered all the beds in the formal garden and in every corner were clumps of great, heavy-headed peonies. The air was moist and scented and a tender breeze gently flipped the leaves of the poplars, now silver, now green. The brightly robed patients moving slowly and sedately toward the dining room were so like figures in a pageant that I expected a chorus to come out from behind the privet hedge.

Over our morning coffee, Sheila, Kimi and I decided that from that day forward we would maintain stoic calm and complete indifference toward the Charge Nurse and Miss Gillespie. Kimi said that she was also toying with the idea of starting a rival sanatorium magazine to be called "Over the Sputum Cups." We asked Miss West, a friendly little nurse, if she thought there was a chance of our getting our discharges that day, but she said that we should settle down and forget such nonsense, as patients were never discharged under a year. A year would mean August for Sheila and Kimi, September for me.

At two-thirty we heard the slap, slap, slap of the Charge Nurse and it meant nothing to us. She turned in to Kimi and Sheila's room, then came to me and told me to report to the dining room. I was in my robe and was on the rustic walk before I noticed that I was barefooted. I ran back up the ramp to my room, grabbed my slippers but didn't stop to put them on. When I got to the deserted dining room Sheila was sitting at a table clasping and unclasping her hands. Kimi was with the Medical Director. I was the last to be called.

The Medical Director was sitting at the Charge Nurse's desk. He told me to sit down and I fell weakly into a chair. He said, "How would you like to go home this afternoon?" I couldn't answer. I just looked at him. He then told me that my sputum had been negative since October, that I was in fine condition, that I would have to take pneumothorax for from three to five years, that he had had a most difficult time teaching me that I had tuberculosis and that he still wasn't sure that I realized how serious my illness had been. I said, "If my sputum has been negative since October I must have started getting well almost as soon as I got here." The Medical Director said, "You have made a very rapid and splendid recovery and you are fortunate in having great recuperative powers. All are not similarly blessed. The important thing for you to remember is not that your sputum has been negative since October but that you had a cavity in your left lung and a shadow on your right lung. You have had serious tuberculosis, do not forget it." I asked him if I could be with the children and he said, "Certainly, you're not contagious." I tried to thank him for all he had done for me but he brushed it aside. "Take care of yourself," he said. "Show me that you have learned something about tuberculosis, that's all the thanks I want." We shook hands and I returned to the hospital where I found Sheila and Kimi sitting on their beds and looking dumbly at each other.

Miss West came in, hugged us all and offered to run over to the office and call our homes. Patients came from all sides to congratulate us and we told them all we would be packed and gone in a maximum of twenty minutes. The Charge Nurse had told me that I didn't have to send my things through fumigation so I tossed everything helter-skelter into cartons and was fully dressed and ready to leave in twelve minutes.

Sheila's family came about thirty minutes after Miss West called them. Kimi and I put on our coats and walked to the car with her. We expected our families within the next few minutes so we thought we'd just stay on the walk by the dining room. It was three-ten. At four-thirty they still hadn't come but we disdained offers of supper and returned to the promenade. I ran the gamut of things that might have caused the delay and at last came to the bitter conclusion that they didn't want me. I saw my future as a long series of trips from one sanatorium to another, a trail of enemies behind me.

The deep twilight settled down and Kimi and I could hardly see the road. A single car wound slowly around the bend. Kimi and I jumped up and began assembling our bundles. The car passed our building and went on up the drive. We sat down again. We could hear nurses calling to each other as they went off duty; the doleful splash of the fountain, the soft pad of slippered feet in the hallway. Why didn't they come? Would we have to face the humiliation of begging the Charge Nurse for just one more night under her roof? We decided to walk to the office and call again.

Kimi's mother answered the phone at her house and was so

excited at hearing Kimi's voice and so bitterly disappointed not to have been home when the first call was made, that she began to sob. Kimi spoke crisply in Japanese for a few minutes then hung up the phone and translated for me. "Mama is so emotional, she is a poet you know and so of course slightly unbalanced, she began to cry when she heard my voice so I said, 'Please don't waste time crying, Mama, just get hold of Papa and drive out here as fast as you can.'"

There was no answer to many long, long rings at my house. In desperation I called a neighbor who told me that the entire family were across the lake on a picnic and she had no idea when, if ever, they would return. I left word that I would be waiting all night if necessary but they must come.

At nine o'clock the family came for me and after reaching home, we stayed up until three o'clock drinking coffee and eating leftover sandwiches. When I climbed into bed in the uncleaned back room my stomach felt like a just-hooked marlin, but I was happier than I had ever been in my life.

It took me the whole summer to learn that you do not dispose of eight and a half months in a sanatorium just by leaving the grounds. I had had to struggle and bleed to adjust to sanatorium routine and I had to struggle and bleed to adjust back again to normal living. Certain marks of sanatorium life, like the prison pallor, disappeared with time; some, only concentrated effort erased; a few, like the scars from surgery, remained forever.

When I first came home, I dreamt about the sanatorium every night and awoke every morning when the five o'clock streetcar clanged past, expecting the washwater girls. At first I used to get up, stealthily retrieve the paper from the front porch, make a large pot of deliciously strong coffee and luxuriate in the breakfast nook until around seven when the family began seeping downstairs. After a month or so I would wake up, realize that I was at home and go back to sleep.

At first I had no inclination to resume old friendships, and I kept up an enormous correspondence with my sanatorium friends. I clung to Sheila and Kimi as though we were all lepers trying to live in a non-leper colony. Sheila disengaged herself from us after the first few weeks and became very normally interested in her coming marriage. Kimi and I clung together. She came to the house frequently and we walked in the park and talked about The Pines, Miss Toecover and the patients.

Kimi said that she was very lonely and unhappy, that her former friends treated her as though she were violently contagious, and boys, who before had been merely too short for her, were now like "mites" in comparison. I tried to cheer her with stories of my lonely, unhappy girlhood. Of how even without tuberculosis I had always been shunned. After the third chapter of "The Lone Wolf" in grammar school, high school and at college, Kimi said, "Enough of this lying. Let us face facts. I used to be full of fun and have many friends. Now I am oversensitive. I get hurt by everything and I do not find enjoyment in anything. I am hateful to my poor mother and father and I quarrel incessantly with my brother and sister. I am only happy when I am with you discussing the old day at the sanatorium." I told her that I was sure that this was all part of the adjustment from one life to another, but I felt much less sure than I sounded for I knew that I had become big and fat and whiny and the epitome of everything the sanatorium had warned us against.

Then my sister Mary invited Anne and Joan and me to visit her at their summer camp in the San Juan Islands. We left at a little after five, one still summer morning, and drove through miles and miles of rich, well-kept farmland, deep forests and along rocky shores. The camp, a series of small silver-gray cabins, was on a great curving sweep of sandy beach, sand dunes and tide flats covered with shells, sea-animals, driftwood and agates. We cooked and ate all of our meals out of doors and at night after supper we built beach fires, toasted marshmallows and watched the sun go blazing down behind the Straits of Juan de Fuca and the moon rise over the small dancing lights of the fishing fleet. After a day or so I stopped dreaming of the sanatorium.

After ten days we returned home loaded with agates and near-agates, vile-smelling shells, pretty stones and bright plans for the future.

Soon after coming home from the beach I spent my first evening among strangers and in an apartment. The evening was not unusually warm but the room seemed suffocating and the air smelled as if it had been rented with the apartment. Everyone looked very tired and seemed to me to be on edge and straining to have a good time.

After the first hour I too looked tired and was on edge and straining to have a good time for the apartment was heated to 90°, there wasn't a shred of oxygen left in the air, I was fat and my blood was attuned to a temperature of not over 50°. I coughed tubercularly a few times but all that got me was another offer of a drink. About eleven o'clock as I actually began to lose consciousness, I staggered across the room, mumbling apologies, raised the window two inches and opened the door into the hall. My hostess shivered a few times, then giving me an accusing look went in and got little sacks and jackets for the women. The men hunched their shoulders, looked for the draft and moved into protected corners. When I got home I sat out on the porch and breathed in great reviving breaths of fresh air and wondered how I was ever going to stand working in a hot stuffy office.

In July Mother left to spend a month on a friend's farm and I took over the housekeeping. I found that with hard work and activity my spirits soared, but I went down for my pneumothorax overflowing with apprehension for fear I had "overdone." The doctor collapsed my lung and told me that I was in fine condition and that I could stay up twelve hours a day.

Later in the week I went to a luncheon at a country club and was dumfounded to have everyone dumfounded to be in actual contact with a returned White Plaguer. During the luncheon there were many questions about the exact symptoms, the location of the first pain, etc., and before the afternoon had ended I was moderately certain that I had uncovered several hidden but far-gone cases of t.b.

When I got home Sheila called to tell me that two patients at The Pines had died. Immediately my trip to the beach, the luncheon, my household duties became vague far-away things and I threw myself headlong into the sanatorium. I called Kimi to give her the bad news and we talked and talked about patients who would die, had died and might die. That night I dreamed of The Pines again and awakened very early with the old depression hanging over me.

I decided that since my future was short and black, I should spend every minute with Anne and Joan. I arranged a crowded and gritty picnic in the park, including, in the heat of my enthusiasm, five very young neighborhood children as well as my own two and all the dogs. Apparently somewhere during my incarceration I had lost touch with that carefree spirit of young things, for the dogs ran wild, the park gardeners threatened to put us all out, the smallest children became entirely unmanageable and lay in the paths kicking and screaming, while the larger ones disappeared into the tops of trees.

I finally emerged from the park yanking in one hand, by the leashes, the three dogs who slid along on their haunches, and in the other hand, three little, red-eyed, snuffling boys tied together by their belts and led by my scarf. The four older children I had abandoned while they were still risking their necks in the trees. As I grimly headed toward home, I wondered if this was why the sanatorium was constantly warning its patients about being around young children when they got home.

At that time Anne and Joan and Anne's best friend Ermengarde spent the lovely summer days in their room with the doors and windows shut, playing Sonja Henie. Anne and Ermengarde took turns in an old green chiffon party dress and Alison's black hockey skates, stumping around on the linoleum floor, being Sonja Henie. But Joan was always Tyrone Power. Dressed in her Buck Rogers helmet, an old pumpkin suit with bloomer legs, long brown stockings and her red rubber raincoat she pursued Sonja on a pretend roller coaster, on a pretend Ferris Wheel, on pretend horseback, then finally caught her on the ice (or linoleum rug), always posing in a poorly executed very unsteady arabesque performed to the squeaky accompaniment of the Skaters' Waltz played on their little phonograph. I watched the performance one day much against their wills and made some suggestions about the costumes. The suggestions were not well received. Joan said that

I had been in the hospital so long that I apparently didn't recognize the fact that she was dressed exactly like Tyrone Power. Anne said that she and Ermengarde dressed and skated exactly like Sonja Henie and they could prove it by pictures.

When Joan had other plans, Anne and Ermengarde spent the lovely, sunny, summer daytime in their room with the windows and doors shut, playing opera singer. Crouched by the little phonograph they would listen attentively while Alma Gluck sang "Lo Hear the Gentle Lark" over and over and over again. Then Ermengarde would stand up and sing the song with Anne prompting from her crouched position on the floor, then Anne would sing and Ermengarde would prompt. This was a harmless enough activity except that Ermengarde was the type of singer who had a gesture for every single word. "Lo" she sang with her index finger pointed menacingly toward the audience; "hear" (her head was bent slightly to one side, her right hand cupped her right ear) "the gentle" (stroking motions) "lark" (bouncing and fluttering of wings) and Anne copied her exactly.

Anne's voice was sweet and true and she had perfect pitch; and it disturbed me to see her dressed in an old black lace party dress, her red curls pinned to the top of her head with hundreds of old jewels, standing on her little table and spoiling her sweet singing with the corny gestures. I said as much. Anne exploded. She said, "You've had tuberculosis and you don't know anything about singing opera. Ermengarde's grandmother was an opera singer and she taught Ermengarde how to sing and she said that all opera singers used gestures all the time just like Ermengarde."

Kimi said that she thought it would be a good idea to leave the children alone and to brush up on my shorthand. I retaliated by suggesting that she register for the University in the fall as a means of filling her idle time, occupying her mind and meeting new people. Kimi begged me to speak to her mother and father on behalf of the University idea as she feared that they thought her still too frail for such a venture.

So one evening I went over to her house and talked too much, about the University, in the high shrill voice I reserve for foreigners, but was apparently convincing for the next week Kimi obtained the permission of the Medical Director to take ten hours at the University in the fall. I registered at a business college for an evening class in shorthand.

Early in the fall Mary and I drove into the country to buy peaches and stopped at the house of an old school friend. We had forgotten that Old School Friend had ripened into the type of housekeeper who washes off banana skins with lysol before peeling them and we greeted her effusively and demanded food and coffee. She was most unenthusiastic. "Weren't you in a Tuberculosis Sanatorium?" she asked me through a small crack in the door. "She only got out June twelfth," Mary said, looking at me proudly. Old School Friend excused herself for a minute, firmly shutting the door in our faces. The day was warm but certainly not warm enough to warrant our being kept out on the porch as long as she kept us. When she did let us in, some time later, she produced coffee and food but we ate it quickly and over such a bedlam of noise that conversation was impossible. It was not hard to determine that while we waited on the front porch Old School Friend had gathered up her children and bolted them in some back room where they kicked and screamed and pounded on the door and demanded to be let out the whole time we were there.

As we drove away Mary said, "Don't you dare go back and live with her no matter how hard she begs. You just tell her she lives too far out in the country and you must keep in circulation." I laughed but I was bothered. What if I applied for a job and somebody in the office felt like Old School Friend? I asked Kimi if she had had any such unpleasant experiences. She said, "Oh my, yes. Sometimes they do not wait until I am out of the house before producing the Flit Gun and vigorously spraying everything I have touched."

The next morning, feeling very spiritless and shabbily neat, I boarded a streetcar crowded with the ten-thirty group of smartly dressed, refined-looking female suburban shoppers. I crouched up near the front and kept reassuring myself that it wasn't printed anywhere on me that I had had t.b. Then the streetcar hit a rather bad district near town and who should get on but Coranell Planter, the Bedrest occupational therapy teacher.

She saw me immediately and screamed, "Well for Gawd's sake, Betty, you're lookin' swell! A lot better than when you left THE SANATORIUM! You're sure FAT TOO! Ha, ha, ha!" Feeling hundreds of curious eyes on me I cowered into the corner and mumbled, "You look well too." Coranell yelled, "What did you say, honey? I can't hear over all this noise." I said, "You look well too." She said, "Feelin' grand. Just grand. Did you hear that Minna had her kidney took out? Just eaten away with t.b. Gracie is having the third stage of a thoro and Bill Williams just had another HEMORRHAGE! Gawd that poor kid has had a tough time. Eileen has had another HEMORRHAGE TOO. You know, kiddo, I don't think that poor little Eileen is going to pull out of it. Swell little kid, too, but she don't have any spirit any more. She says that she's never been happy since they moved her away from you and Kimi. Roommates are awful important when you're on bedrest and the Charge Nurse is a real good nurse but she don't realize that the most important thing of all is whom's with who."

When I finally got off the streetcar five blocks after Coranell, I decided that I would put off going to the employment office until after lunch. I was to meet Mary for lunch at an Italian food-importing place at one o'clock and though it was then only eleven forty-five and the restaurant was just around the corner, I went bleakly in, sat down at the counter and ordered a cup of coffee.

"Aren't you Betty Bard?" said a pleasant masculine voice at my elbow. "I used to be," I said turning around. Bill Wilson, an old friend of Mary's, was beaming at me. He said, "Well, this is pleasant!" He leaned back in his chair and looked me over with interest. "Weren't you at The Pines?" he asked. "Yes," I said, looking down, fumbling with my gloves and wishing that Bill didn't have such a loud voice. "When did you get out?" he asked in the same carrying voice. I told him. "You look wonderful!" he said enthusiastically. "Are you all well?" "Yes," I said, "in fact I came downtown today to look for a job." "You mean you haven't a job and you want one?" he asked eagerly. "Yes," I said. "Thank God," he said. "I've been interviewing secretaries for three weeks and I'd given up hope of ever finding one who wrote both shorthand and English. Can you come to work tomorrow?" I said, "I might consider it even if it means walking twenty miles in my bare feet over old Victrola needles every morning." My new boss laughed and ordered me a roast beef sandwich. He said, "How was it out there at The Pines? I've heard it's a pretty tough deal." "Oh, not at all," I heard myself saying. "I actually enjoyed it. The discipline is strict, of course, but it has to be in the cure of tuberculosis. . . ."

PART IV

17

Anybody Can Write Books

AT THE TIME Mary decided that anybody can write books, I was married, living on Vashon Island and working for a contractor with cost-plus Government contracts, making a very good salary.

Then an old friend of Mary's arrived in town and announced that he was a talent scout for a publishing firm and did she know any Northwest authors. Mary didn't so she said, "Of course I do, my sister Betty. Betty writes brilliantly but I'm not sure how much she has done on her book." (I had so little done on it I hadn't even thought of writing one.) The publisher's representative said that the amount I had done was not the important thing. The important thing was, had I talent? "Had I talent?" Why, Mary said, I had so much talent I could hardly walk. She'd call and make an appointment for him to just talk to me and see. She did too. That very afternoon at five and she called me at a quarter to five.

"Betsy," she said. "Forrest's in town and he is a publisher's representative and needs some Northwest authors so I've told him you were one. You're to meet him at the Olympic Hotel at five o'clock to discuss your new book."

"My what?" I yelled.

"Your new book," said Mary, perfectly calmly. "You know that you have always wanted to be a writer and Betsy, dear, you've got great talent."

"I have not," I said. "You know perfectly well that the only things I've ever written in my life were a couple of punk short stories, some children's stories, *Sandra Surrenders* and that diary I kept when I had t.b."

Mary said, "The trouble with you, Betty, is that you have absolutely [she said "ab . . . so . . . lute . . . ly"] no sense of proportion. Instead of using your great brain to write a book and make fifty thousand dollars, you in . . . sist on getting a mediocre job with a mediocre firm and working yourself to the bone for a mediocre salary. When are you going to wake up? When?"

"I don't know," I said, wondering if the switchboard operator had heard all that mediocre stuff.

Mary said, "I told Forrest you'd meet him at the Olympic Hotel at five to discuss your book."

I said, "But I can't write a book."

Mary said, "Of course you can, particularly when you stop to think that every publisher in the United States is simply dying for material about the Northwest."

"I never noticed it," I said sullenly.

Mary said, "Betty, listen to me. We are living in the last frontier in the United States. The land of the great salmon runs, giant firs, uncharted waters and unscaled mountains and almost nothing has been written about it. If you told the people in New York that salmon leaped in our front doors and snapped at our ankles they'd believe it. Most of the people in the United States either think we're frozen over all the time like the Antarctic or that we're still wearing buckskins and fighting Indians. Now personally I think it's about time somebody out here wrote the truth."

"If I wrote the truth about my experience in the mountains," I said, "I would only be proving that salmon snap at our heels and that there are still Indians."

Mary said, "What difference does it make? At least you'd be writing and using your great talent."

All that talk about my great talent was beginning to hit home. Up to that moment I had never shown any particular talent in anything except making Christmas cards and picking and cleaning chickens, and it was a nice feeling to sit there at my golden-oak desk littered with unchecked purchase orders and think that every publisher in the United States was foaming at the mouth with impatience waiting for me to write about the Northwest.

"What time is the appointment?" I asked.

"Five o'clock," Mary said. "You've only got five minutes so hurry."

As I put on lipstick and combed my hair, I told one of the girls in the office that I had to hurry as I was going to meet a publisher's representative at the Olympic Hotel to discuss my book. She said, "Gosh! Betty, are you writing a book?"

"Sure," I said with the casualness of great talent, "and this publisher's representative has come all the way from New York to talk to me about it."

"What's your book about?" she asked.

"About my experiences on a chicken ranch," I said.

"Oh," she said, with obvious disappointment and changed the subject.

Walking up to the hotel in the February rain, I decided that I would tell Forrest that I was going to write a sort of rebuttal to all the recent successful I-love-life books by female good sports whose husbands had forced them to live in the country without lights and running water. I would give the other side of it. I would give a bad sport's account of life in the wilderness without lights, water or friends and with chickens, Indians and moonshine.

The publisher's representative, who was very friendly anyway, liked my idea and told me to go home and write a five-thousand-word outline and bring it to Mary's dinner party the next night.

Having never written either an outline or a book, I was a little slow and found it necessary to stay home from work the next day to finish it. I called the construction office and told my best friend there that I had to stay home and write an outline for a book but would she please tell the boss I was sick. She said sure she would, wished me luck, hung up the phone and skidded in and told the boss that I was staying home to write a book and so I was fired and in one day transferred my great talent from construction to writing.

When I told my husband and daughters that I was going to write a book they were peculiarly unenthusiastic. "Why?" they asked. And I couldn't think of any reason except that Mary thought I had great talent, so I said, "Because every single publisher in New York wants me to, that's all." A likely story, they told each other as they tapped their foreheads and suggested that I take a nice long rest.

During that long, long year between the conception and birth of *The Egg and I*, I sometimes got so depressed I put the book away in disgust and went into town and applied for and got dreary little part-time jobs that seemed much more in keeping with my ability than writing. Then after a month or so, Mary would hear about it and call me up and demand that I quit and again unleash my great talent.

One Monday morning during the summer, I was hanging out the last of a huge washing when Mary called and demanded over the long-distance phone, "Betty Bard MacDonald, are you going to spend the rest of your life washing your sheets by hand or are you going to make fifty thousand dollars a year writing?" It didn't leave much of a choice so I got out the manuscript and got started writing again.

Toward the end of the summer, when the book was almost finished, Mary called and told me to write to Brandt and Brandt, literary agents whose name she had gotten from the former editor of the Seattle *Times*. All successful writers have agents, she told me, and Brandt and Brandt are the very best. I thought, Well, if they are the very best at least I'll be starting at the top and after they turn me down I'll go to the Public Library and learn the names of some others.

Mary said, "Be sure and tell them about the short stories, the children's stories and the t.b. book. Remember, Betty, nobody likes a one-book author."

Feeling exactly as though I were trying to join an exclusive club on forged credentials, I wrote to Brandt and Brandt and sent them the five-thousand-word outline I had shown the publisher's representative. In my eagerness to prove that I wasn't a stinking old one-book author I made it sound a little as though we had to wade through old manuscripts to go from room to room in our log house, and that I was a veritable artesian well of the written word. Much to my amazement and chagrin, Brandt and Brandt, immediately on receipt of my letter, wired me that they were delighted with the outline and to send every manuscript I had, which certainly wouldn't take long.

I called Mary and told her about the telegram and she said, "Now, bonehead, are you convinced that you're a writer or do you still want to work in some musty little office?"

I was on my way to town and had stopped at the mailbox on the way to the ferry and there nestled among a pile of bills, was this long white important-looking envelope. My first thought, of course, when I saw the Brandt and Brandt on the back, was that it was a letter taking back the telegram. I didn't have time to open it on the dock so I waited until I was installed in the Ladies' Cabin of the ferry before ripping open the flap and removing with trembling fingers the letter that rocked my world.

I read it over and over and with each reading it became more wonderful. My book, that nebulous product of Mary's faith in me, had suddenly materialized into an actual thing. I was a writer and I had to tell somebody. I hurried all over the upper deck of the ferry but the cabins were empty. I went down to the car deck but there were only trucks.

When we docked at the other side, I scanned the waiting cars for a familiar face and finally in desperation rushed over to a man and his wife whom I knew very slightly and told them that my book had been accepted. I couldn't have picked nicer people. They were as enthusiastic as though it had happened to them and I left them feeling very successful and terribly talented.

The next dandy thing that happened was the next spring when I was learning that the darkest, lowest period in a writer's life is that awful interval between acceptance and publication. I knew I was a failure, I knew the book was no good, I was sure I was going to get the manuscript back and I had spent all the advance.

I decided to go to town and look for a job. Preferably one involving the filing of the same card over and over and over day after day. I had found a reasonable facsimile of the job I had in mind and was making my weary way home along our trail, when Anne came running to meet me calling, "There's a telegram for you and you're to call Seattle operator twenty-eight right away."

It's come, I thought. They have decided not to publish the book and they're demanding their money back. "Hurry, Betty," Anne said. "Find out what the telegram is." "No," I said. "I'm going to wait until after dinner. I'd rather get bad news on a full stomach."

After dinner I called the operator and Whispering Sam, who was at that time relaying all messages to Vashon before burning the only copy, read me a very long wire of which I got about ten words. Three of these were "Atlantic Monthly" and "serialization," which I knew must be wrong, as the *Atlantic Monthly* represented to me the ultimate in literary achievement and I was certain they couldn't be interested in anything I had written.

I called Mary and she immediately changed her tune from best sellers, and trips to New York, to awfully important books, not very good sellers, and trips to Boston. She said she'd call Western Union for me and call me right back. She did in a matter of minutes and told me that I was to call Boston the next morning at eight o'clock and she thought I'd better get the next ferry and pick up a copy of the telegram which Western Union was reluctantly holding at the edge of their telegram burner. The next ferry left in sixteen minutes so I sent Anne and Joan up to stay with my sister Alison and I ran the mile and a half to the dock.

The main office of the telegraph company is located on a dark side street in the financial district in Seattle and as I got off the bus and walked in the rain across the deserted streets, I kept thinking, This is the most important moment of my life. I must remember everything. I felt enchanted and as though I should be leaving a trail of light behind me. My steps made no sound and I was as light as a petal when I entered the telegraph office and asked for my telegram. I read it standing by the counter and then, stuffing it in the pocket of my raincoat, I floated out to my sister Mary's.

18

Owner Desperate

THERE IS no getting away from it, life on an island is different from life in the St. Francis Hotel but you can get used to it, can even grow to like it. *"C'est la guerre,"* we used to say looking wistfully toward the lights of the big comfortable warm city just across the way. Now, as November (or July) settles around the house like a wet sponge, we say placidly to each other, "I love it here. I wouldn't live anywhere else."

I cannot say that everyone should live as we do, but you might be happy on an island if you can face up to the following:

1. Dinner guests are often still with you seven days, weeks, months later and sleeping in the lawn swing is *fun* (I keep telling Don) if you take two sleeping pills and remember that the raccoons are just trying to be *friends*.

2. Any definite appointment, such as childbirth or jury duty, acts as an automatic signal for the ferryboats to stop running.

3. Finding island property is easy, especially up here in the Northwest where most of the time even the *people* are completely surrounded by water. Financing is something else again. Bankers are urban and everything not visible from a bank is "too far out."

4. A telephone call from a relative beginning "Hello, dear, we've been thinking of you . . ." means you are going to get somebody's children.

5. Any dinner can be stretched by the addition of noodles to something.

6. If you miss the last ferry—the 1:05 A.M.—you have to sit on the dock all night, but the time will come when you will be grateful for that large body of water between you and those thirteen parking tickets.

7. Anyone contemplating island dwelling must be physically strong and it is an added advantage if you aren't too bright.

Our island, discovered in 1792 by Captain Vancouver and named Vashon after his friend Admiral James Vashon, is medium sized as islands go, being approximately fifteen miles from shoulder to calf and five miles around the hips. It is green, the intense green of chopped parsley, plump and curvy, reposes in the icy waters of Puget Sound, runs north and south between the cities of Seattle and Tacoma and is more or less accessible to each by ferryboat.

On the map Vashon Island looks somewhat like a peacock and somewhat like a buzzard. Which depends on the end you choose for the head and how long you have been trapped here. The climate, about ten degrees warmer and wetter than Seattle and vicinity is ideal for primroses, currants, rhododendrons, strawberries, mildew and people with dry skin who like to read. The population is around five thousand *people* and an uncounted number of sniveling cowards who move back to the city for the winter.

Because of its location and the fact that it rises steeply from the water into high plateaus, Vashon Island is plethoric with views. Across the west are the fierce snowy craggy Olympic Mountains and the magnificent untamed Olympic Peninsula, black with timber, alive with game and fish, soggy with lakes and streams, quivering with wildness. Separating Vashon from the Olympic Mountains and Peninsula is the narrow, winding, lovely West Channel of Puget Sound. To the east are the smoky purple Cascade Mountains and Seattle. North are other islands, Bainbridge, Blake, Whidbey and the Olympic Mountains. South of us is Mount Rainier, that magnificent, unbelievably shy mountain who parts her clouds and shows her exquisite face only after she has made sure Uncle Jim and Aunt Helen are really on their way back to Minneapolis. Mount Rainier is 14,408 feet high which is higher than Fujiyama but only half as high as Mount Everest. It has twenty-six glaciers, listed in the encyclopedia as quite an accomplishment, and was also discovered by Captain Vancouver who seems to have spent a great deal of time cruising around this part of the world discovering things. Except in the very early morning or rare summer evenings when the foothills show, Mount Rainier appears to be a mirage floating in clouds, appearing and disappearing (mostly disappearing) just above the horizon.

Everything on Vashon Island grows with insane vigor and you have the distinct feeling, as you leave the dock and start up the main highway, that you should have hired a native guide or at least brought along a machete. Alder, syringa, maple, elderberry, madroña, pine, salmonberry, willow, wild cucumber, blackberry, fir, laurel and dogwood crowd the edges of the roads turning them into green tunnels and only the assiduous chopping and slashing by the county and the telephone and power companies keeps this jungle from closing up the highways altogether.

From the water Vashon looks like a stout gentleman taking a Sunday nap under a wooly dark green afghan. The afghan, obviously homemade, is fringed on the edges, occasionally lumpy, eked out with odds and ends of paler and darker wools, but very ample so that it falls in thick folds to the water. Against this vast greenness, houses scattered along the shore appear small and forlorn, like discarded paper boxes floated in on the tide. The few hillside houses look half smothered and defeated, like frail invalids in the clutches of a huge feather bed.

The farmland of Vashon—Vashon is famous for its red currants, pie cherries, peaches, strawberries, gooseberries, boysenberries, loganberries, raspberries, chickens, eggs, goat's milk, Croft lilies and orchids—is gently sloping and covered with plump green and brown patchwork fields tucked in around the edges with blanket-stitching fences. Scattered here and there over the landscape are rather dilapidated outbuildings, placid cows and goats stomach-deep in lush pasture, and churches. The newly built, freshly painted houses are either along the main highway or on the beaches. Vashon is not a geranium-planted-in-the-wheelbarrow, wagon-wheel-against-the-fence, Ye Olde Tea Shoppe community.

Our ugliness is rawboned, useful, natural and honest. Our beauty is accidental, untampered with, often breathtaking.

Every road on Vashon leads to the water eventually. From almost every inch of the island we can see either the water or Mount Rainier or the Olympics or the Cascades or all four. All the edges of the island are fringed with the black spikes of virgin firs.

There are several very high points, perhaps a thousand feet or more above the water. From these places we can look down at the gray-blue Sound winding among islands dark and hairy with trees. The tides and currents show up in the channels like spilled ink. The ferryboats are white ducks waddling earnestly from shore to shore.

The town of Vashon, quite a typical western crossroads settlement, is small, flourishing, friendly, adequate and tacky. The stores have nothing in common with the early day, "hay, bacon, gasoline and soft drinks" country store. Our stores are modern, well stocked and obliging—if they don't have it they will get it. Only occasionally do they show signs of naïveté. Once when we first moved here I sent Don to get me some wild rice purposely forgetting to tell him it was $2.25 a package. He came home with eight boxes and after I had stopped screaming he explained defensively, "I only had one but the woman at the checking counter said that as long as they were two for a quarter why didn't I take a couple more, so I did. We can use it, can't we? She said 'Wild rice don't go good in Vashon. It's a slow-mover.'"

At night from the north end of Vashon we can see the lights of Seattle glittering on the horizon like a lapful of costume jewelry. From the south end the lights of Tacoma twinkle briskly along the water, then blaze up and mingle with the stars. We like this. We say, there just across the water is a city of almost a million—another of a quarter of a million is there. We can go *there* any time. It assures us that we are here by choice.

How is it we moved to Vashon Island in the first place? Well, it was just after Pearl Harbor and my husband, Donald, and I had recently met and married.

I was working for a contractor who was building something or other, very vital, for the government at terrific expense in Alaska. It seems to me that I have heard that it was a dock and somebody forgot to take the tides into consideration and so most of the time it stands thirty feet above the water.

Don, who was doing final test at the Boeing Airplane Factory, shared a rather dank, dark hillside duplex just off the campus of the University of Washington with an intellectual pal who read philosophy by candlelight, never shaved, tucked fishbones behind the cushions of the couch and considered a thorough housecleaning the tacking of another Japanese print over another spot of mildew. On stormy evenings, with a fire on the hearth and enough martinis, the apartment seemed rather desirable, but I shuddered when I thought of it in the daylight.

Then Don's roommate suddenly decided to take his fishbones to Algiers and Don asked me to marry him. We spent our weekend honeymoon (all that was allowed defense workers) in the apartment sans the roommate but avec the mildew, an eviction notice from the landlord who was tired of intellectuals, a shutoff notice from the gas company (gas had been roommate's responsibility, Don explained) and an old buddy of Don's who turned up in quite an unsteady condition and couldn't or wouldn't grasp the fact that "good ole Don" was married.

The eviction notice stated firmly that we were to be out of the apartment by the following Monday. From Monday to Friday I visited practically every real estate office in the city and was told by each that there was nothing to rent, there never had been anything to rent, there never would be anything to rent and "there's a war on!"

Sunday evening Don and Anne and Joan and I were sitting in front of the fire in his apartment feeling like people without passports, when the very charming Japanese professor, who with his wife lived in the top part of the duplex, came down and told us that they were being sent to internment camp and we could have their apartment. We thanked him fervently, but felt like grave snatchers as we piled into the car and raced over to see the landlord who was old and not friendly and brought out a list two miles long of applicants who he said were of *much* longer standing and *much* more desirable and *didn't* have children. Finally, grudgingly, the landlord agreed to let us have the apartment but he called after us in a loud voice as we were getting in the car, "I expect you folks to tend to business now. No wild parties and don't let the pipes freeze." Anne and Joan thought this hysterically funny and collapsed in the back seat in giggles. I was furious. I thought the landlord was rude and unfair and I wanted Don to do something manly and retaliative. I demanded it.

Don looked at me quizzically and said, " 'Hope not sunshine ev'ry hour. Fear not clouds will always lour.' " Don is a Scot.

Tuesday, Don and I moved in.

The upstairs apartment was light and airy, had a wood-burning fireplace, a view of Mount Rainier if you had good eyes, two large friendly gray squirrels who lived in the maple tree outside the bedroom window, and a studio couch in an alcove for Anne and Joan. We were very happy and quite comfortable. Then came warm weather and the normally quiet hillside around us suddenly exploded with shrieking children, barking dogs, yowling cats and yoohooing mothers. Peddlers followed each other up our stairs like ants and when they weren't banging on the back door they were leaning on the front doorbell. Don made a large sign: DEFENSE WORKER SLEEPING—PLEASE DO NOT DISTURB! which I hung on the door when I left in the morning. It didn't help at all. The peddlers pushed it aside and knocked under it. Don grew very pale and much dourer. I decided that I had better start looking for a house. Any house big enough for Don and me, Anne and Joan, Mother's dog Tudor, my cat Mrs. Miniver, our several thousand books and records, Joan's dried snakeskin and shell box of pretty rocks, Anne's collection of Sonja Henie pictures and Alma Gluck records, their bicycles, roller skates, ice skates and skis, my office dress, my other dress, Don's college bluebooks, his elk antlers, the brown suit he bought but could never wear because it had quite obviously been fashioned for a chimpanzee as the sleeves of the jacket were longer than the trouser legs, and the Jackie Coogan doll he had won at a carnival in Council Bluffs, Iowa, some twenty-two years before. The only trouble was that in Seattle, where we lived, there weren't any houses for rent and none for sale for nothing, which is what we had. We would have gladly moved into the police station if it had been for rent furnished. You see, in addition to no money, we had no furniture.

In the Pacific Northwest, there are several hundred islands, varying in size from small enough to be cuddled in the crook of your arm to over a hundred miles long. Five of the larger islands are within commuting distance of Seattle. They are all ringed with beaches both sandy and rocky, and homes, both permanent and summer, some of which might be for rent, we thought. But when I tackled a reasonably intelligent-looking real estate agent and asked him about these islands, he treated me as if I had bounded in and demanded a snap decision as to the exact number of female seals in residence on the Pribilof Islands. "Vashon Island?" he kept repeating incredulously. "Bainbridge? Whidbey? What ever give you the idea to move over there? My gosh, I've lived in Seattle thirty-one years and I never even seen them islands. Now we gotta little six-on-one dream for sale on Highway 99. . . ."

"We'd better look for ourselves," I told Don after the tenth try.

We were invited to spend the next weekend on Vashon Island. The Havers, whom we visited, had a charming house right on the beach, the tides were perfect for clamming; and Saturday night as Don and I lay in bed on their porch, listening to the slurp, splash, slurp of the waves against the sea wall, and watching the ferry gliding across the moonlit water, we decided that this was the perfect place. The beach was rich with clams and driftwood. The water was filled with salmon, sole, cod and Spanish mackerel. The soil was so fertile that syringa and alder grew twelve feet a season. The climate was warmer than Seattle, the ferry crossing took only fifteen minutes and it was walking distance from the ferry. The next morning, as we dug clams in the hot sunshine, we told George Haver, "We like this place. This exact spot. We want to live here."

George was glad that we liked his beach, but very discouraging about our finding anything to rent. He explained that all the people on that particular beach had been coming over there for thirty-five years and, even though there was no road and they had to walk in by a county trail and bring in all their provisions and possessions by boat or by wife, they were all very attached to their houses and never rented them. We were so downcast by this information that he took us for a boat ride around the point.

In the course of the ride he said, "As long as you're disappointed anyway, I'm going to show you a house that will spoil you for any other beach house."

He steered the boat to shore, pulled it up on a log and we climbed a small winding path to the house.

He had told the truth. It was the most attractive house we had seen and it certainly did spoil us for all the sagging built-by-Grandpa-designed-by-the-cat structures we had seen and were to see. Unfortunately, however, the Hendersons, who were living in it and who had bought it from the doctor who had built it, were very happy there.

"We are going to live here forever," they told us, smugly.

The house, built of hewn fir timbers, was snuggled on the lap of the plump green hillside. The roof was hand-split cedar shakes, each shake at least an inch thick. The rain and the salt air had turned it all a soft pewter color. The kitchen, which was small, had knotty pine walls with a bricked-in electric stove and a trash burner across one corner. Against the windows which looked at Puget Sound and Mount Rainier over an enormous window box filled with pink geraniums, was a Flemish blue drop-leaf table and four stools. The drainboard and insides of the cupboards were the same Flemish blue. The floor was pine planks put down with wooden pegs and calked. The living room, which opened from the kitchen by a swinging pine half-door, was about forty feet long, had the same plank floors (four by twelves), an enormous stone fireplace that went up two stories, a small rustic stairway leading to a balcony from which opened three small knotty pine bedrooms and a bath. At the south end of the balcony was the master bedroom. It had a beamed ceiling, pine walls and a fireplace with a copper hood. In all the rooms were hand-braided rugs and lovely pine furniture made by the doctor. There were two patios, one off the kitchen, one in the angle of the ell formed by the master-bedroom wing and the living room. They were made of rounds of cedar with flowering moss in between. Around the south patio was a rockery filled with heather. Above it on a knoll was a gnarled old apple tree. The ground under the apple tree was carpeted with blue ajuga and yellow tulips. Across the front of the house and available to the living room by French doors was a rustic porch overlooking the water and the sandy beach and facing Mount Rainier.

It was the house everybody dreams of finding. But it definitely wasn't for rent or for sale, so we finished our drinks, patted the dogs and said goodbye to Vashon.

Then my sister Dede found and rented a small beach house on Quartermaster Harbor at the other end of Vashon Island. For the next few weeks each Saturday morning we would load the car with groceries, the children, Tudor the dog, Mother and her sketching things, bathing suits, sun-tan oil and fifty pounds of ice because the house had that kind of an icebox, and go to Vashon.

In spite of having to stop the car every fifteen minutes for Tudor to be sick and so often not making it. In spite of my two dear little daughters acting as if we had put leg irons on them and were dragging them to the stocks because we were interrupting their regular Saturday and Sunday plans. In spite of the fact that the ice always leaked on something not improved by ice water, such as cigarettes or Cornflakes. In spite of the fact that the house was really very inconvenient with remarkably uncomfortable beds and a filthy little coal-oil stove that made even the orange juice taste like coal oil—we had a wonderful time. The water was warm for swimming. There were huge silvery piles of driftwood for beach fires. There were the mingled smells of fresh coffee and salt air. And there was sleep refreshing as only a sleep induced by too much sun, too much swimming and too much food, can be.

Don and I became revitalized and renewed our efforts to find a place on Vashon on the water. We looked at houses at the bottom of cliffs. We looked at crumbling houses furnished in sagging wicker and discarded pottery. We discovered that beach houses, no matter how attractive they are on the outside, are usually the catchalls for things not quite up to snuff or down to St. Vincent de Paul. Don and I got so that we could tell by the kind of fern in the abalone-shell hanging basket whether the rugs would be ragged Wilton or faded oriental.

Still we kept on.

Then one morning I was in a restaurant drinking coffee and dispiritedly leafing through the "For Sale—Waterfront" section of the paper when I saw what appeared to be an advertisement of the Henderson house on Vashon. The ad said: Lodge-type log house, huge stone fireplace, 400' of sandy beach—for sale $7,000 furnished.

I called Mrs. Henderson at the office where she worked and she told me that it was their house. That her husband had been offered a wonderful job in California and they thought he should take it. I asked her why she hadn't called me and she said, "Oh, I thought of course you had found a house by this time." I choked back an impulse to say, "Oh, sure and while I was at it I worked out a plan for world peace and a cure for cancer." Instead, I made arrangements to go over the next weekend. My hands were shaking as I hung up the phone.

The next Saturday, as Don and I swung along the trail leading from the dock to the Hendersons' house, carrying our share of the groceries and liquor for the weekend (unwritten law of beach Mrs. Henderson had said, but one obviously repealed the day we moved in) I said excitedly, "Don, I just know we are going to get this house. I feel it was meant to be. Won't living over here be wonderful for the girls?"

Don is not exactly an optimist. In fact, if I were to be absolutely truthful, and I wouldn't dare because we are so happily married, I would say that Don is a charter member, perhaps the founder, of that old Scottish brotherhood sworn always to bring bad news home even if it means mounting a rabid camel and riding naked over the Himalayas in winter.

I said again, "Don't you have that feeling, Don? That this house was *meant* for us?"

Don said, "I'd have more of that feeling if we had any money. There certainly is plenty of erosion along here."

But the house *was* for sale and the Hendersons had gotten it from the doctor who built it *with no down payment* because the doctor had to go in the Navy, and they were willing, really eager, to sell it to us the same way. We were to pay $150 a month until we had established a down payment, then we would go into the bank and have it refinanced. We were all terribly casual and gay, made more so by the fact that none of us had any money, didn't want the others to find it out and I kept my hand over Don's truthful mouth practically all day Sunday.

We made arrangements to come out the next weekend with two payments (which we intended to borrow) and the house would be ours.

"You see," I said to Don as we stood on the upper deck of the ferry on our way home. "It *was* meant to be."

Don pointed at the cars bouncing onto the ferry, each one denting its exhaust pipe because the deckhand hadn't lowered the ramp far enough, which he still doesn't, and remarked gloomily, "That ramp isn't down far enough."

If, like me, you have nurtured the idea that you have kept your possessions down to Deargrandmother's Satsuma tea set and a few first editions, then you should move to an island. Try mixing that minimum with water and see what you get. Deargrandmother's Satsuma tea set turned out to be three old trunks minus handles, filled with clothes and/or ingots, eight barrels of vases and dishes, stuff out of ten medicine cabinets, assorted boxes of canned goods, records, elk antlers, photographs, pillows, pots and pans, record players, bamboo rakes, skirt hangers, lamp shades, ironing boards and dog beds. My few first editions, supplemented by the contents of the trunk of Don's car, were mistakenly left to rise in the moving van overnight and when we unloaded them at Vashon they had swelled into eighty-seven cartons filled with lead.

My sisters Dede and Madge had married and moved into small apartments, Mother was to stay with my sister Mary while her husband was overseas, so I got the washing machine, the *Encyclopaedia Britannica*, Mother's portrait and the Christmas tree ornaments. There was also a gentleman's agreement that I would take my children, Mother's dog and my cat if Mary would take the assorted turtles, goldfish and canaries belonging to the household. The first step was to move out of our apartment into Mother's house. This was accomplished easily. We simply kept dumping things in the car and driving them to Mother's until the apartment was empty. I packed. Don carried and drove. I started out very methodically. "Books—reference" I marked on the outside of a carton. "Sheets—towels" I marked on another. "Silverware" another. When Don attempted to help I said kindly but firmly, "You had better let me do it, dear. I know exactly what I am doing and I want things to be orderly."

"Living room draperies" I wrote on a neat newspaper bundle. "Candles, vases, bric-a-brac" I marked a carton. Then somehow I began running out of enough of the same thing to fill a box—also out of boxes and newspapers—also out of strength. By the end of the day I was rolling a jar of mayonnaise, a heel of salami and a half-filled bottle of Guerlain's Blue Hour perfume in my tweed skirt and not even stamping the bundle "Perishable."

Next came getting the things to Vashon, which was easy too. Allison's husband borrowed a moving van, someone else solicited an unemployed musician to drive it, Don and the children and I loaded it and the car and we were off. One last sentimental look at the old brown house revealed that we had left Mother's portrait, the skis, and Tudor the dog, who didn't care for cars and kept oozing in one side and out the other. The rearranging to get these things in took just the right amount of time for us to miss the ferry and wait an hour on the dock.

Things weren't really going too badly, however, we kept saying loudly, hollowly. We *had* intended to get the ten-o'clock ferry, but, as is usually the case with expeditions of this kind, we weren't even packed by ten. The ferry we had just missed was the two-thirty.

Our new beautiful pewter-colored dream house had no road. This tiny flaw in its perfection, at first candidly spoken of and looked upon as a flaw but so insignificant compared to things like a salt water beach and hand-braided rugs, had during the summer somehow emerged as a blessing. No road meant no bores, the Hendersons said. No road meant privacy. No road meant nothing to run over the children and animals. Then came the day of reckoning and we were faced with the uncomfortable fact that walking the mile and a half from the ferry on a beautiful trail along the water carrying a pound of bacon and a quart of gin is one thing. Hauling in a van load of furniture and possessions is unquestionably another.

Thank God the civilization-ridden neighbors on the south side of us did have a road. They had a road that was steep and rutted and ended at least two hundred feet from the beach, but they generously offered to let us use it. They also let us use three rowboats and an outboard motor. Don and Harris tied all the boats together and we all loaded them. Harris insisted on steering the lead boat, which was unfortunate, as he seemed possessed with the idea that we were moving *from* Vashon *to* Seattle and kept heading out to sea, chairs, books and pillows spilling in his wake.

Harris, though confused, was eager and strong and by nightfall we had most of the stuff on our sea wall, a few things in the house and the washing machine in one of the boats. I invited Harris to dinner, but he pointed out that he had only six inches of beach left before high tide.

Then we all staggered wearily up the path to our beautiful new house, which was as cold as a crypt and piled high with junk. While Don and Joanie built roaring, quick-dying carton fires in the kitchen trash burner and the fireplaces, Anne and I pawed feverishly through boxes looking for the food. The night before, feeling just like Mamsie Pepper, I had baked a ham and a pot of beans and had wrapped the stuff for salad in a damp dishtowel, "so that everything will be ready and cozy for moving day," I told Don. But where were they? They certainly were not in this old box of pictures—or this one of vases or this . . . After almost an hour of fruitless search we decided that they might still be on the sea wall. I took Tudor and a flashlight and went down.

Even though my neck, my back, my arms, my legs and my palms ached and with each step on the path little jagged pains ran down my earlobes, I still experienced a wonderful feeling of security as I realized that this was *our* path and I was going down to look for *our* ham on *our* sea wall.

When I got down to the sea wall I had another surge of emotion as I listened to the waves slopping against the wooden pilings and realized that the tide was in and so these were *our* waves because Mr. Henderson had explained that we owned the tidelands too.

I flashed the light over the heaps of boxes and trunks piled higgledy-piggledy all over the sea wall, hoping against hope that I had marked the box of food or that, if I hadn't, in some mysterious way the ham would make its presence known. I hadn't and it didn't, so I called Tudor.

"Here, boy," I said kindly. "Here, Tudor, boy." As I have said, Tudor was my mother's dog and as I had heard my mother, who is a dog lover and a better-than-average veterinary, say a million times that a dog should be well trained, that it is not fair to the *dog*, and, as I hadn't been around Tudor too much, I presumed that I might get a little cooperation from him. A little of the man's best friend, old dog Tray stuff. I called again with even more kindness.

"Here, Tudor, old boy." Tudor, who was busy sniffing a rock, absolutely ignored me. "Tudor," I said rather sharply. Instantly he flattened himself on the ground, buried his head in his paws and awaited a blow.

I sweetened my voice again. "Tudor, old boy," I said, trying to speak just loud enough to be heard over the waves but not loud enough to frighten the little stinker. "Tudor, old boy, food! Good food! Find it, boy!" I patted the piles of boxes and trunks enthusiastically. Tudor raised his head, gave me a long disdainful look, then ran up the path to the house.

Tudor was no help but he had given me an idea. I began to sniff the boxes myself. It was not easy to get a true scent over and above the salt water and the rich rotten cabbage smell of the Tacoma pulp mill which occasionally rides in on the south wind, but I finally found the ham. It was under "Books—reference" and on top of "Living room draperies."

A fireplace in a bedroom is a very luxurious item. After we had turned out the lights, Don and I watched the leaping shadows on the pine ceiling and listened to Anne and Joan's childish trebles murmuring insults to each other through the walls of their adjoining bedrooms. The wind had freshened and was making small plaintive noises in the eaves. The bed was very comfortable. I sighed deeply, contentedly, and closed my eyes. Then suddenly I was aware that in addition to the crackle of *our* fire, the slosh of *our* waves, the moan of the wind under *our* eaves, the haggling of *our* children, I was listening to *rain* on our roof.

Fumbling for the bedlight I said wearily to Don, "Do you hear that? It's raining."

Don said, "Swhat?"

I said, "Rain. Listen, it's raining and the books and records are still down on the sea wall."

Sighing heavily, Don sat up and reached for his bathrobe. I got up and put mine on. Hearing sounds of activity from our bedroom the girls called out in the owlish way of children, "Who? What? Who? Where? Who? Who?"

I explained over my shoulder as I ran down the stairs and out onto the porch where we had dumped the tarpaulins. Snatching up a couple I started down the path—Don followed with the flashlight. The rain was brisk and wet. After we had tucked the tarpaulins over and around the boxes and trunks, Don flashed the light on the washing machine defiantly spraddled in the rowboat. The waves were almost washing over the stern. "Come on," he said without enthusiasm, "we'll have to try and pull the boat up the steps." I jerked on the rope and he jerked on the washing machine and we managed finally to get the prow onto the top step, the stern in the water, the washing machine veering dangerously toward the south. Grimly tying the painter to a slender maple tree Don said, " 'An' lea'e us nought but grief and pain, for promis'd joy.' "

Busy threading my bathrobe cord through the oarlocks and then over and under the wringer in the vain hope that I could keep the washing machine in the rowboat but knowing very well it was like trying to restrain a wounded buffalo with a piece of thread, I snarled and said, "And I used to wonder why they sold the house furnished."

By the time we got back to bed, the crackling fire in the fireplace had burned to coals, but it was still comforting and a delight after the chilly interlude on the sea wall in the rain.

From far across the water a freighter tooted. The rain on the roof sounded like millions of birds' feet. I said to Don, "Well, here we are, all together at last in our own house."

Don said, "Unk." He was very tired. With a snap the last piece of wood broke apart. The glow from the fireplace was very faint now. The noise of the Sound less of the slurp, slop, splash and more of a rhythmic thrummmmmmm, like a drum roll, showed that the little waves had matured to good-sized swells. A heavenly sound, I thought sleepily.

Then above the wind, the rain and the surf I thought I detected a heavy groaning scraping noise.

"The washing machine," Don said suddenly, loudly, in my ear. "The little bastard is still trying to get away."

We had moved Saturday. That gave us Sunday to unpack, put away, look around, plan ahead and get wood. Sunday morning when I got up later, tireder and nastier than I had planned, I found that the washing machine had gotten away after all. Joan and Don with their irritating early-morning cheerfulness and 20-20 vision had spotted it riding the waves halfway to Three Tree Point, directly across from us.

Don said cheerfully, "The water's awfully rough out there. I can see huge whitecaps. Let's row out now before breakfast."

"I'm not going anyplace until I have a cup of coffee," I said crossly.

"Im not either," Anne said. "Only I'm going to have cocoa. Let's start the fire."

"Ah, come on, Mommy," Joan said. "A boat ride before breakfast would be fun."

"Why don't you and Joan go," I said to Don, "and Anne and I will get breakfast."

"Yes," Anne said eagerly to Joan. "You and Don go and Mommy and I will have breakfast all ready when you get back."

"We'll all have to go," Don said. "Towing that washing machine in that rough water is going to be very ticklish business."

So we had breakfast first and after my second cup of coffee I became mildly enthusiastic about the boat trip. "Hurry with your cocoa, Andy," I said brightly. "We're going for our very first boat ride."

"Does Don know how to row?" Anne said suspiciously.

"Of course," I said. "Don't you, Don?"

"Well, I haven't had too much experience with boats," Don said truthfully, "but I can manage, I guess."

"Can you swim?" I asked him.

"I would be able to," he said, "if my bones weren't so heavy. I always sink."

I looked out at the Sound again. The water in the middle looked much rougher and several large dark clouds grumbled menacingly as they shoved and pushed each other around directly overhead. I poured myself another cup of coffee.

"Oh, Mommy," Joan said, "we'll *never* get started."

"This may be the last cup of coffee I'll ever have," I said, "and I intend to enjoy it."

"You may as well pour me one too," Don said, sighing resignedly.

"Well, I'm going down and get the boat in the water," Joan said.

"Go ahead," Anne said. "I'm going to make myself another piece of cinnamon toast."

"Why don't you get one of the neighbors to help you?" I said, peering past the pink geraniums in the window box toward the horizon. "If that speck I see out there is the rowboat with the washing machine in it, it's halfway to Alaska."

"Oh, nonsense," Don said. "People row across the Sound all the time. It won't take us long."

"I wish we had life jackets," I said.

"Oh, Betty," Anne said, suddenly switching loyalty in the irritating way children do, "don't be silly. Joan and I are wonderful swimmers. We could probably swim across the Sound. Anyway Don can handle the boat. Come on, let's go before it starts to rain again. I'll eat my toast in the boat."

When we got to the beach Joan had the big rowboat in the water and was splashily rowing up and down in front of the sea wall. We called to her to come in and after Don had pulled the boat onto the beach with a tremendous jerk that sent Joan, who was about to stand up, sprawling and lost an oar overboard, we all climbed in and began arguing about who was to sit where.

Don was not very adept at the oars. He blamed it on "these damned old oars which keep slipping out of the oarlocks," but Joan informed him tactlessly that he didn't hold the blades straight, he should dip deeper, he was rowing too hard with his right oar and he was getting everybody wet. She had learned *everything* about rowing at Aunty Dede's and she would be glad to help him.

Anne announced that she had learned *everything* about rowing on Lake Washington where she and Marilyn rowed the dinghy of Marilyn's father's "enormous speedy cruiser." She told Don he was dipping too deep, he was holding the blades too straight, but it was all right for him to row so hard with his right oar because it would turn us around and we could see where we were going. With set lips, Don continued to dip and pull and splash toward the washing machine.

Like a stout gray lady on an excursion boat, it had slid up and wedged itself in the prow of the rowboat, from which position it stolidly watched our maneuvers to ease alongside and get the painter. This was not too easy as the water was very choppy and the painter was tangled around the washing machine's legs. In his attempt to lift the washing machine and untangle the rope, Don leaned so hard on the side of our boat we dipped water.

Anne immediately began to shriek, "We're tipping over! We're sinking! Help! Help!"

Joan stood up and shouted, "Watch out, everybody, I'm going to get in the other boat!"

I yelled, "Don't get in the other boat, Joan! Shut up, Anne! Don, be careful!" and Don said, "EVERYBODY BE QUIET!" just as the black clouds above us released large wet raindrops, which began splatting on our heads.

Joan said, "Please, Mommy, let me get in the other boat. I can hand you the rope."

Don said, "Okay, Joanie, but wait until I steady the boat."

I said, "Don, *don't* let her! The washing machine will come loose and squash her and what if we can't get the rope and she drifts away?"

"Don't be silly," Don said. "Okay, Joanie, here you go." Nimbly Joan jumped into the stern of the other boat which was clear up out of the water owing to the weight of the washing machine, skipped down to the prow, crawled *under* the washing machine and fed the painter out the small opening between the wringer and the point of the prow. I grabbed the rope and yelled at her to "get out from under that washing machine right now!" She did, announcing unconcernedly as she jumped back into our boat, "It was caught on that faucet on the side and here's your bathrobe cord."

As soon as we started rowing back toward home, the washing machine became unwedged and slid down and leaned over the starboard side, thus making it as difficult as possible to tow. Of course Joan wanted to get back in the boat and try to push it into the prow again, but even Don vetoed this. We finally reached shore, the washing machine defiant and uncooperative all the way, and when we tried to maneuver it up the narrow trail to the house, it weighed just as much as possible and kept flinging its wringer around its head like a billy club.

When we had it comfortably installed in the service room, the girls insisted that I test it out. I filled it with water, threw in some dishtowels and turned it on and it swirled and swished very efficiently.

Joan said, "I'm certainly glad it works because I didn't pack anything but dirty clothes."

"How perfectly disgusting!" Anne said.

Don said, "I wonder if you'd rinse out a few pairs of my suntans."

Anne said, "Of course, all *my* clothes are clean, but I think I'll wash all my summer clothes again and put them away."

Joan said, "Can you wash coats in washing machines? My

school coat has mustard and a lot of hamburger juice on it."

I said, "Before we get too enthusiastic about washing, let's see if the wringer works." I turned off the washing part and turned on the wringer. The rollers began turning smoothly against each other, neatly pressing the water out of a piece of seaweed picked up on the trip.

"Okay," I said to Don and the girls. "Everything's working fine. Bring on your dirty clothes."

Then I reached in to get one of the dishtowels and the next thing I knew I was across the room, crumpled against the cement wall, and Anne and Joan were bending over me wailing, "Mommy, Mommy, are you hurt?", and Don, who understands electricity was saying soothingly from across the room, "Probably sand in the brushes."

Don finished the washing though, with Anne and Joan and me crouched in the doorway waiting for him to be electrocuted. Nothing happened except that he took all the buttons off Joan's blouses with a popping sound like shelling peas. Afterward he took the washing machine all apart, removed some seaweed and the sand from the brushes and a clamshell or two from the tub, oiled it and said he could not understand what had happened as he could find nothing basically wrong. He intimated that it must have been some careless action on my part.

19

God Is the Boss

IN THE CITY, as I remember, weather was a topic passed around with the salted peanuts and not expected to hang around much past the introductions. In the country, weather is as important as food and sometimes means the difference between life and death. Discussions of it can branch out into all sorts of interesting directions, such as Mrs. Exeter's baby which was almost born on the beach because of the storm that took out the dolphins (those bruised bunches of pilings at the end of docks without which the ferries cannot nuzzle into the slip) so the ferry couldn't land, and a call to the Coast Guard delayed because of a prune upside-down-cake recipe dictated over an eighteen-party telephone line, or that summer we didn't have any rain from May until September.

In the twelve years since we moved to Vashon Island we have experienced the most rain, the driest summer (that wonderful one), the coldest winter, the most snow, the severest earthquake, the worst slides, the highest tide, the lowest tide, the strongest winds, the longest unceasing period of rain, the densest fog, the hottest day, the earliest spring, the latest spring, the coldest summer, the warmest fall, the dreariest winter (this one), the wettest Christmas, in addition to a total eclipse of the moon, a total eclipse of the sun, and a flying saucer on the Oregon coast.

We have also come to expect, in times of great emergency, no cooperation from the elements.

Christmas Eve we went in to my sister Mary's as we always do. It was raining hard, but we were very gay with our carload of presents (mostly bought at the Vashon drugstore)—anyway in the city rain is merely shiny black pavement, blurry street lights and using the windshield swipes.

The entire family was at Mary's. Mary's house looked beautiful and very Christmasy and there was a delicious supper and magnificent Christmas spirit. We had a wonderful time. Then as we sang "Silent Night" for the last time Don announced suddenly that we had only twenty-seven minutes to get the last ferry.

By taking back streets and going through Chinatown, we made it and the next thing we knew we were on the Sanders' sea wall looking down at the tide which was slapping playfully at the *top* step. The trail was dark with an impenetrable darkness like oily smoke, wet and very slippery. By the time we got home it was two-thirty and our Christmas presents and our spirits (even mine so homemade and old-fashioned) were like yesterday's dumplings.

Don cheerfully built the fires while I put Christmas carols on the record player and made oyster stew. The girls' reaction was tepid.

Christmas morning, rain was still lashing the windows and gurgling in the downspouts, but we managed a semblance of gaiety as we opened our partially dried-out presents in front of a roaring fire. The sagging atmosphere was leavened still further by the girls' getting just what they wanted (I believe it was men's sweaters, deep purple lipstick and a reasonable facsimile of a peignoir that year) *and* Mother and Alison and her husband, who had been invited to dinner, loyally appearing.

Then came January and the big snow. We are not used to snow in this country, are never prepared for it and, even when it is actually flittering down and lying on the ground and the sky is leaden and the weatherman predicts twelve inches, we keep talking gamely about those winters when the nasturtiums bloomed straight through.

I remember how surprised I was at ten o'clock that morning when I left my office building to go across the street for coffee and found that it was snowing hard—small dry flakes that powdered my hair and were still unmelted when I looked in the mirror behind the coffee urns.

By noon the snow was three or four inches deep on the downtown sidewalks and the radio reported six inches and more in the residential districts. Everyone in the office began calling home and excitedly relaying reports of six, eight, even twelve inches of snow, stuck cars, and no bus service. I tried to call the Russells, the only other year-rounders on the beach, to ask them to look out for Anne and Joan and keep them at their house until Don got home at four or thereabouts. The operator said the lines to Vashon were temporarily out of order. Every once in a while I went to the window and looked out. In spite of the wind, a thick white curtain of Lux flakes had turned the early afternoon into dusk and made the street lights wan and ineffectual. The roofs of the parked cars on the street below were heaped with snow which was pulled by the wind into peaks like seven-minute icing.

About three o'clock the "big boss" announced reluctantly that he was closing the office. He said that most of the city busses had stopped running and many of us would have to walk. There was a portentous germ-warfare atmosphere about the place. Even those most ardent "get-in-good-with-the-companys" (the ones who had *asked* to work on Thanksgiving) were hustling into their coats and hurrying out. I tried to call Vashon again but the lines were still out. I put on my raincoat (white poplin and stylish but no warmer than cellophane) and galoshes and started for the Vashon bus stop five blocks away. The wind, apparently fresh off a glacier, had gathered great momentum on the north-and-south streets and came whining down between the buildings with an armload of snow that made each crossing a little nightmare of streaming eyes and frozen legs. Everybody was walking huddled with their heads down, their coats pulled around them like bathrobes.

When I got to the Vashon bus stop, an unprotected corner by a furniture store, I found most of the commuters already there. Apparently every office in Seattle had closed early. While we crowded in the small doorway waiting for the bus, I heard that the lights always went off on Vashon during a snow—the telephone was already out and probably would be for weeks—the ferries probably wouldn't be running—this looked like a *big snow*—big snows always caused terrible slides—a wind like this would certainly take out a lot of sea walls—they hoped the local grocers (five all told—two very small) had plenty of food on hand because it certainly looked as if we were going to be marooned for a long time.

I became almost frantic with worry. What if I couldn't get to the island? Poor little Anne and Joan would be there all alone. I tried to inventory the supplies we had on hand. All I could accurately remember was a case of Frisky dog food, part of a case of Pus'n Boots cat food, and three cartons of Camels. I remembered stories Gammy, my grandmother, had told us when we were children and wouldn't eat something she had cooked (wise precaution), of the starving Armenian children who were grateful for willow twigs and cow dung. I thought of pictures I had seen of Swiss people digging the bodies of their loved ones out of avalanches. I wondered if smoking was really harmful for children. All those cigarettes and nothing to do day after long dark day. I wondered where Don was. I thought of our huge virgin firs, so black and majestic against a summer sky, now loaded with snow, leaning, leaning and finally crashing down on the house where two tiny matchstick figures shivered by a fire made out of the last chair.

Then the bus came. We all squeezed on board and drove to the dock, where we were informed the ferry, in the clutches of the wild north wind, had crashed into the dolphins and knocked them down. The ferry was now leaving from another dock in downtown Seattle. We drove back to Seattle and down onto the dock. There was a long line of waiting cars, but the bus had priority and went right to the front. There was no Vashon ferry in the slip nor in sight on the troubled waters. I got out of the bus and walked up and down the line of cars, talking to people I knew and even ones I didn't know because disaster does much to break down the barriers of reticence.

Going from car to car I learned that the lights always went off on Vashon during a snow—the telephone was already out and probably would be for weeks—the ferries probably wouldn't be running after this trip *if* they made it—this looked like a *big snow*—big snows always caused terrible slides—a wind like this would certainly take out a lot of sea walls—they hoped the local grocers had plenty of food on hand because it certainly looked as if we were going to be marooned for a *long long* time—had I seen the size of the waves—they were *enormous* and would be much much *more enormous* out in the middle of the passage—certainly made a person wonder if these boats were really seaworthy—after all they were old to begin with—had been discarded by San Francisco. . . .

The ferry finally left at eight o'clock. The waves *were* enormous, the ferry creaked and groaned and writhed in pain. In the restaurant where I sat out the trip, the coffee cups slid off the counter and one quite sensible-looking woman pushed away her apple pie and sobbed, "We'll never make it. We'll all be drowned!"

We landed at the Vashon dock about nine-thirty. At the store,

Bob Russell and I were told the trail was impassable and we would have to go by the beach. The tide, for some strange cooperative reason, was out. We started out. The wind was at our backs, but the rocky beach was like walking on frosty billiard balls and our flashlights were futile against the driving snow. It took us almost an hour to reach the point where Bob lived. He wanted me to come in and warm up a little before going on, but I was too worried about the children. I stumped on. My nylon-clad legs were numb. My face felt as if it had been sandpapered. I recognized our sea wall, but the path from the beach to the house was completely obliterated.

On my hands and knees I crawled where I thought the path should be. I reached the kitchen door just as Don and the children came down the steps. They helped me to my feet, dragged me into the kitchen and gave me a big drink of whiskey by candlelight.

"The lights are off, the telephone won't work, and the pipes are all frozen," Don told me cheerfully.

"The school's closed," Anne caroled. "It'll probably be closed all winter."

"Isn't this snow keen?" Joan said.

We were snowed in for two weeks. At first I was happy because I couldn't go to work and could be with my family. Anne was hysterical because of no school, Joan loved the snow and Don was very cheerful about hauling water from the spring and wood from the beach.

Then came the *second* day and cooking on the trash burner without an oven, by candlelight, lost a little of its hilarity; Don didn't leap to his feet eagerly when I called WOOD, and the girls began quarreling the minute they opened their eyes. At night I dozed off to something murmured by Joan and answered by Anne's shriek, "Mommy, Joan's caught a mouse" (or a fly or a spider) "and she's going to put it in my room! Stop her!"—to Don's, "Peace! All I want is a little peace! Do something, Betty!"

By the sixth day I began to wonder what all those delightful things were that I had been planning to do when I stopped working. By delightful I didn't mean cooking, washing dishes, scrubbing, washing clothes, mending, making beds, refereeing quarrels, carrying wood or sweeping. I had faint recollections of dreams of long country evenings spent in front of a roaring fire reading Shakespeare, each of us taking a part, the way we used to do when Daddy was alive, listening to symphonies on the record player, braiding rugs.

Of course, the first drawback was the fire and Don's attitude toward the woodpile which had become that of a mother puma guarding her young. If I had more than two matches and a sliver going at once, I had to listen to moans about waste and lectures on not looking ahead. Naturally, during this period the beach was as clean as a plate—the tide didn't even bring in seaweed.

Another thing was the matter of light. We had one kerosene lamp and one kerosene lantern but we had no kerosene. We had quite a few candles but we learned that a wick is a wick even if a candle is three feet tall and bayberry. We couldn't play the record player because it was electric—I hadn't learned how to braid rugs —the Shakespeare was in one of the hundreds of boxes in the back hall (the house had only three small bookcases) and the last thing I wanted to do was to look for it.

Finally our life boiled down to reading, eating, sleeping, getting wood and getting on each other's nerves. Even eating lacked its customary fillip, and when I was asked what I was fixing for lunch or dinner and I told them, I was almost certain to hear at least one "Ugh!" This was partly induced by ennui and partly by the fact that our only really ample supplies were the dog food, the cat food and noodles, of which we seemed to have about a thousand pounds.

One bleak morning toward the end of the siege, I was shuffling around the kitchen contemplating a casserole of noodles, Puss'n Boots and candle stubs, when Don announced, "My God, we have run out of *whiskey!*" and offered to mush up to Vashon and get some supplies.

Of course at this point the girls rushed in with demands for absolutely vital things such as hormone cream, movie magazines, Firecracker Red nail polish and bobby pins. After a great deal of discussion and a few tears, Don said firmly he would not forget the kerosene. He *would* get some candy and gum. He *would* get bobby pins. He would *not* get movie magazines, hormone cream or nail polish. He *would* get the mail. He would *not* forget the matches.

We bundled him up and waved him off and, as he crunched down the beach past the spring which was a frozen waterfall and the big logs in their white fur scarves, I could almost hear the enclosing howl of the wolves and smell the cow dung burning in our sod hut.

Don came back at dusk with the kerosene, several cans of beef stew, very heavy and tasting like dog food, candy, gum, movie magazines, nail polish, mail, whiskey, steaks, bacon, eggs, canned milk, matches, lettuce, coffee and noodles.

He brought the noodles, he said, because, although I hadn't said anything, he noticed the supply was getting low.

There were times during that first long, dreary, wet, dark winter when I wondered what I had ever seen in this nasty little island. When I longed to pitch a tent in, say, the lobby of a downtown movie theater—a stifling hot downtown movie theater.

The fireplace in our living room is very large. Its maw will hold, without crowding, eight large logs or three sacks of bark or ten big cartons squashed or three orange crates whole or sixty-two big magazines rolled up. Before we moved in, when we were just visiting, I noticed that the Hendersons had tiny fires in only one corner of this great friendly fireplace. I thought this niggardly and uncozy of the Hendersons and I called any little fire an "Emmy fire" after Mrs. Henderson. That was when we first moved in, before we realized that *wood*, the getting and burning of, was going to dominate our entire existence.

At first, getting wood seemed fun. An excursion. A gay family enterprise. And it was free. No fourteen dollars a cord any more. All we had to do was to go down to the beach in front of the house and pick it up, or go to the woods in back of the house and roll it down. We had alder and fir and cedar just for the cutting or picking up and we were lavish with it. We kept great big eight-log MacDonald fires burning in both fireplaces and the stove (no "Emmy fires" for us) from early morning until late at night and the house became warmed all the way through. If we had been less enthusiastic and more observant we might have noticed the cracking and snapping of the pine walls and beams warning us that such heat was unaccustomed.

But we were so happy in our new life and it was still October and there were many bright days and many bark tides and we considered a six-by-twelve-foot woodpile on the sea wall a big supply and kept the fires roaring until the chimneys were hot and we could eat in comfort at the dining room table with only one sweater and without heating the plates until they had to be passed with tongs. Then the days began getting shorter. At the same time the bark tides were fewer and the weather wetter and colder. Don and Joan, our wood-getters, began to speak of Emmy Henderson as a pretty smart little lady. Three toothpicks, a broomstraw and a rolled-up copy of *Quick* centered on one firebrick became their idea of a dinner fire. Anne and I took to heating the dinner plates until they turned brown and the food sizzled on them. We all wore two or three or four sweaters all the time. We filled hot-water bottles with boiling water right out of the teakettle and put them in our beds before dinner. We never had colds, but we didn't have much fun either. It was like living in a mine. Dark and damp and cold when we got up. Dark and damp and cold when we went to bed. We let the animals sleep on all the couches and chairs because they warmed them.

Then one morning it was spring. The willows blew in the sunshine like freshly washed golden hair. The white hyacinths bloomed. The cherry trees were frothy with blossoms. We had our first steamed clams and fell in love with Vashon all over again.

Digging clams on your own beach is a special thing. An unexpected dividend, like having a beautiful daughter who can also divine water. I remember that first Saturday morning in April when we were awakened by the sun pouring in the window and lying on our bedroom floor in golden pools. I remember the sea gulls playing tag against a delphinium-blue sky and the Sound glittering in the sun like a broken mirror. The tide was far out, past the eel grass, and the sand steamed in the sunlight and was warm on our bare feet.

"Wait until they squirt," Don cautioned Anne and me, but we couldn't. We dug huge holes in the wrong places and found only cockles or "Indian clams" as they are called around here. Don and Joan wisely waited for squirts and got big sweet butter clams.

I believe that steamed clams should be served hot with melted butter and only melted butter. The flavor of freshly dug clams is very delicate and is ruined by the addition of Worcestershire Sauce, garlic or vinegar. With steamed clams we like only hot buttered toast and adults. It takes an almost fanatical affection for children or clams to put up with the "What's this little green thing, Mommy? Do we eat this ugly black part? Do you think this is a worm?" that always accompanies any child's eating of clams. In addition to the company of adults we advocate plenty of clams—at least half a gallon per person.

By the way, the way to get the sand out of clams is to let them stand in sea water for an hour or so. A good recipe for a quick delicious *Clam Chowder* which we have evolved over the years is:

At least four cups of butter clams cut out of the shell and washed thoroughly.

Grind with the clams:

>1 green pepper
>1 bunch green onions
>6 slices of bacon
>2 large peeled potatoes
>1 bunch parsley

Put everything in a large kettle, add one cube of butter and enough water to cover. Cook slowly until the potatoes are done. Add two or three large cans of milk, salt and coarse ground pepper to taste. Serve, as soon as the milk is hot, with buttered toast.

I learned that first spring how riotously things grow here on Vashon. We cleared land in January and by June it was a jungle again. I sent away for a dwarf white buddleia because it was unconditionally guaranteed not to exceed thirty inches, stuck it in what we considered a very poor spot at the top of the rockery in the white garden and it grew ten feet that first year and bore blossoms eight inches long. Right now it is twenty feet high and I cut it to the ground every time I go past it. There are also millions of little dwarf (hah) white buddleias flourishing around the mother plant for a radius of one hundred feet. The blossoms are a pure white, lilac-shaped and lovely if you can see them without tipping over backwards.

Then there are the Empress trees I bought that first spring. "Very rare!" the nurseryman told me, pretending in the crafty sure-fire way all nurserymen do that he didn't really want to sell them, that he was only letting me buy them because his wife was at her sister Cora's. As he dug me up *five* he told me that they were so terribly rare, "Sacred tree of the Empress of China," that there were only two in Seattle. Don and I planted the Empress trees and I hovered over them and stroked them and was awed by their rareness and wondered how they were going to display it.

They then started to grow. Wow! The one by the kitchen door is over forty feet high and by Empress tree standards is still only a little tiny baby. Empress trees have lovely, sweet-scented, periwinkle-blue blossoms in spikes like foxglove. The buds, formed at the ends of the branches in the fall, stand up against the winter sky like brown velvet buttons unless Don happens along with his pruning saw and decides to "shape the trees" by cutting off a limb four inches in diameter.

Empress trees have enormous, loosely attached leaves which drop off all summer long and lie around on the patios and flower beds like palm-leaf fans. We have found that the best, well really the only, way to enjoy the Empress tree blossoms is to go out in the rowboat and look in at them against the sky.

That is really the best way to view all of my gardening. One hundred yards from shore in the rowboat it looks marvelous. Up close there is the embarrassing sight of horsetail, wild morning-glory, dock, wild cucumber, blackberries and nettles, busily choking out the tender planted things.

The best vegetable garden we ever had was our first, planted in an old cesspool. An old cesspool that didn't work exactly right, the Hendersons told us with a chuckle, intimating that the not working was a temporary thing like rheumatism caused by the damp weather but would clear up in the spring.

When spring came it was not necessary for us to go down to the sea wall to see how the old cesspool was not working. We could tell by just opening any door. Joan said with some pride, "Gosh, you can smell our cesspool clear up at the bus stop." So one Saturday morning Don and I went purposefully down and began poking around. It took us about five minutes to deduce that for years and years the cesspool had not been emptying into the sump, or whatever was planned, but had been viciously seeping into an area about fifty feet long and fifteen feet wide along the sea wall. Don drilled drainage holes in the sea wall, cleaned out the intake and outgo pipes, remarking bitterly that standing in an old cesspool was not his idea of a day off, dug up the sump when the tide was right and he could get at it, and finally had the whole system working again.

Though all the seepage had been drained off and that part of the sea wall smelled better, it looked forsaken and untidy. Don suggested buying clover seed and scattering it around, but as this is his stock remedy for anything not curable by whiskey in hot milk, I decided instead to plant a vegetable garden there. I cleared out all the syringa and horsetail and wild blackberry vines, Don dug up the ground and, as it was pure clay, I drafted the girls into helping us scoop up and dump on about fifty (they still say a thousand) buckets of beach sand. For the next two weeks I raked and smashed clay lumps until my hands were reduced to flapping blisters with fingers but I had a fairly friable soil.

I made neat, short, north-and-south rows and we all planted radishes, romaine, carrots, ruby Swiss chard, New Zealand spinach, salsify, cucumbers, summer squash, zucchini, garlic, onions and tomatoes. I marked all the rows carefully with the seed packages stuck on little sticks, but I needn't have bothered. Those vegetables shot out of the ground like rockets and grew so enormous that even nearsighted Anne and I could look north from the old dock and tell our salsify from our carrots.

Because of the fast growth, some of the things were hollow like gourds, but we had enough for the whole Northwest. I was terribly proud and planned sharing, until the afternoon when Anne and Joan came breathlessly in and told me with relish that the whole beach was talking about my garden and waiting hopefully for us all to get hookworm or Shigella. "Does hookworm start with a sort of pain in your ribs?" Joan asked.

"No," I said shortly, "that is the direct result of seven peanut butter sandwiches and three Cokes before lunch and not making your bed."

Then I called Mary's husband who is a doctor and asked him if we were doing a dangerous thing. He said wistfully that he certainly wished he had some of that fine fertilizer for his garden.

Don loves trees—I suspect sometimes that he had a dryad ancestor, because he will never willingly part with any tree and suffers actual physical pain when I chop one down—even the wild cherry that was choking out his favorite weeping pussy-willow. When we began landscaping he rushed feverishly to town and bought out the entire evergreen output of a small nursery. It was fine when they were itty-bitty. Now they have taken hold and though Mother and I secretly slash them back all the time, it doesn't even show and you should see the Sequoias which were about six inches high when Don brought them home. "Zowie!" they said, after he had turned them out of their tiny pots and tucked them into our black leaf mold. "This is a place we like!" and they began beating their chests and springing toward heaven in dark green leaps and bounds.

It is satisfactory, though, to plant things and have them thrive. To celebrate our first Valentine's Day on Vashon, Anne and Joan brought me a pale pink single camellia in a little pink pot. It was a sallow trembly little thing about four inches high with one bloom. I stuck it in the bed with the espaliered apricot tree, even then apparently dedicated to pushing in the south wall of the house. The little camellia grew very well and the next year had four blossoms. After a while we put in a gas furnace. "The exhaust has to come out here" (right by the camellia), the furnaceman said sternly. I was worried. "Shall I move it?" I asked Mother.

"Move that damn wisteria first," Mother said. She hates wisteria because it is vigorous and heedless and its little clutching hands had choked the life out of a rare French lilac before it had time to settle its roots or learn the English for "Cut that out!"

So I moved the wisteria over by the guesthouse where there were no foreigners and where we wanted it to clutch and choke, and forgot about the camellia. I just went out and looked at it to make sure I was not dreaming and the camellia is taller than I am, five feet, six and three-quarters inches in my stocking feet and I have on shoes (just for a lark, of course), it is well branched and loaded with blossoms. Either it likes gas fumes or this is Shangri-la.

20

Why Don't You Just Relax, Betty?

IF YOU LIVE on the salt water, I am informed by the old-timers, you can expect everything you own, even a great big stone fireplace, to break down eventually. This, they say, has something to do with the corrosive effect of salt air. My private opinion, solidified by experience, is that it has more to do with the corrosive effect of the eight million houseguests attracted by the salt air. Anyway, in addition to the icebox, beds, stove, etc., that were in the house when we bought it, we added, as fast as we could gather up the down payments, dishwashers, automatic washers, dryers, freezers, gas heaters, electric heaters on thermostats, chafing dishes, plant sprayers, septic tanks and more toilets with bowls eager for charm bracelets and little celluloid ducks, and with handles that must be juggled *ad infinitum* unless we want the toilets to run ditto. At inconvenient intervals each of these machines has stopped doing the thing it was hired to do and by means of smoke signals, grinding noises and pungent smells of burning rubber has indicated that it desired the evil eye of the local handyman.

The local handyman, always referred to as "Nipper" or "Gimpy" or "Mrs. Walters' Harry," will fix anything but, like a room that is tidy except for the underwear hanging out of the bureau drawers, the repair job is invariably left with tag ends. "The dishwasher's okay, now, Betty," Mrs. Walters' Harry told me the time the dishwasher insisted on using only dirty cold water which it was apparently sucking up from the septic tank, instead of the nice clean hot water so handily piped into its abdomen. "But remember *no soap* and keep that big screwdriver of Don's handy to pry the lid up."

In my early island days I cuddled a cozy little notion that our country repairmen might not be as dextrous or have as big tool kits as their city brothers but they were a *lot* more willing and *much* cheaper. The willing part is true enough. Nipper, when you can find him (which he has not made easy by marrying an Estonian girl who speaks only one word of English, "hello," which she screams into the telephone before immediately hanging up), will attempt anything. Need your rowboat calked, your *Pittisporum tobira* transplanted, your Stradivarius tuned? Nipper will gladly take on the assignment, but *first*, and I mean before one broken fingernail or big rusty tool touches the job, he must send to Seattle for the most recent rate schedule for boat calkers, landscape gardeners or Stradivarius repairment. Your alternative is portal to portal pay from Seattle and maybe the lights are off and they are grinding the ramp of the dock down by hand.

Of course the pipes froze during the big snow and of course as soon as the weather warmed up we intended to put in new pipe. However, while the snow was still on the ground a delegation from the Spring Committee called on us. They were our neighbors on the beach, mostly summer people whom we had not met as yet, all male, the delegation, that is.

"The spring," they told us with great seriousness as they stamped the snow off their boots at the back door, "is on your property, but it is a community thing. We *all* have water rights. We *all* work together. We will *all* fix the frozen pipe. *Do not do anything yourself!*"

"What darling people," I said to Don after we had all had coffee and they had admired the way we had arranged the furniture and I had wished fervently I had washed the windows. "I just love community spirit. I adore people working together. I am so glad we live on an island."

Don said, "Did they say *when* we were *all* going to fix the pipe? I'm not exactly dedicated to carrying water."

"I don't think they said when exactly," I said, "but I imagine it will be this afternoon. After all, nobody else has any water either."

But it wasn't that afternoon or the next or the next. Finally Don and Anne and Joan went back to the spring (I regret to say I protested this breach of community spirit and would take no part in the undertaking) wound rags and friction tape around the worst places in the pipe and that is the way it stayed until late spring.

The spring had a cement tank into which it flowed and from which the houses on the beach got their water supply. This tank was supposed to be cleaned once a year. "Don't you touch it," the Spring Committee had warned us. "Community project. We *all* get together and clean it." The tank was not mentioned again until one Sunday afternoon two summers later after a grueling weekend of fourteen adolescents, seven boys and seven girls, since Friday. It was about five-thirty in the afternoon and the houseparty had been up and eating (four more stacks of hotcakes and some more sausages, please Mrs. MacDonald) since dawn (more hamburgers—one without lettuce and lots of relish on mine but Mary Jean says she doesn't like onions) but were at long last on their way to the ferry and Don and I were wearily sitting down to a pitcher of martinis and some fried chicken, served on a cardtable on the front porch.

Don said, "I don't understand kids these days. When I was fourteen or fifteen if I had had a chance to spend a weekend at the beach I wouldn't have spent the whole time lolling around in the house giggling and listening to records. *I* would have been out in the boat fishing or hiking through the woods or digging clams."

I said weakly, "Oh, it's just that Anne and Joan seem to have so many good records. Have another martini. I'm on my third."

Then Tudor began to bark, which is a mild way of saying that he rushed between our legs, hurled himself off the porch and ran shrieking down the path to the beach. After an interval a neighbor appeared.

"Say, Don," he said ignoring the chicken cooling on our plates and our haggard faces, "we don't have any water. Haven't had any all day. Let's go up and take a look at the tank. Must be something wrong."

With an accusing look at me, Don got to his feet and followed Neighbor up the path to the spring. Tudor and Neighbor's dog came up from the beach and followed them. I gazed across the horizon and thought longingly of the Deep South where girls marry at fourteen. Don and Neighbor returned.

Neighbor said, "Tank needs cleaning. I'll get a bunch together and we'll all pitch in. Now, don't you touch it, Don. The spring's a community project. We *all* take care of it."

Don said, "Have a martini."

Just then Tudor and Neighbor's dog started a fight under the cardtable. I will say that the fight was undoubtedly started by Tudor who even now at fifteen still attacks great Danes and small females. I jumped up and Don and I both yelled at Tudor to "stop—stop it—stop it you naughty dog—stop it you little bastard!" As always Tudor ignored us and continued to hurl himself at Neighbor's dog's throat until the cardtable tipped over and our martinis and chicken were tossed over the railing and down the bank.

As I scrambled down after the silverware and pieces of plates, I heard Neighbor calling from the path, "Remember, Don, community project. We'll all get together."

For a while after we moved to the island the Puget Sound Power and Light Company had an electrician who knew what he was doing and did it. When the roaster lid got caught in a little spring in the oven element and filled the kitchen with lightning, when the pump was clogged with silt, when we had no water pressure and somebody was hammering inside the hot-water tank, when I tried to unplug the vacuum cleaner and one prong came off and stuck in the wall socket—any of those little womanly emergencies—I called the Puget Sound Power and Light and they sent this nice man who located the trouble and also knew lots of interesting stories of buddies who grabbed live wires without their gloves.

Then for some reason the power company stopped this fine unselfish service and we were left with Orville Kronenburg who hated everybody in the whole world and whose wife wore her bedroom slippers downtown. Orville knew about electricity I guess, but he didn't consider looks important and, unless you stopped him, he would run wires across doorways and over pictures. Also he didn't measure when he cut holes for wall plugs and when he had finished putting the new wall plug in our bedroom, Don said bitterly, "It looks like a small raft in a large quarry." Orville also had a special kind of wall plug that even when just installed wiggled dangerously and made the lights flash on and off like beacons.

The time my Bendix shrieked and jumped up and down when I put anything bigger than a washrag in it, I called Orville and he came sullenly down and told me there was sand in our hot-water tank. I told him to take the sand out and he did but after he had gone I tried out the Bendix and it didn't scream but it whirled like a transport propeller and threw a geyser of water out the soap hole. I called Orville and he said, "That's just the fledamora plankstaff. It will slow down after a while." It didn't, but I got used to it. Then after a time Orville went back to South Dakota and the Bendix began shrieking again and jumping up and down when I put anything bigger than a handkerchief in it so I called Newmotor Marvin, and guess what the trouble was?

Anybody who has girl children over the age of ten knows the necessity of either having two bathrooms or learning to comb your hair and put on your lipstick by looking in the dog's pan.

Don and I decided to make the small bedroom next to our room into a combination dressing room and bath for us and to put a tub in the other bathroom and give it to the girls—which was certainly locking the barn after . . .

This was still during the war and basins and bathtubs were impossible to get, to say nothing of carpenters and plumbers. We had a friend around the Point who was a good amateur carpenter and who offered to do that part of the work for us in the evening and on the weekends. Through the ferry-commuters' grapevine we heard that there was a plumber living at the other end of the island who also sold plumbing supplies and could get us the fixtures and install them. Don immediately contacted this phenomenon, a Mr. Curtis, and one evening he came to the house and we showed him the bathrooms and he drank brandy, and the deal was made including a large septic tank which Mr. Curtis was going to install in the south patio with a sump down on the beach. We were also at that time putting in a road which was at the deep-cut, knee-deep-mud stage but which, Mr. Curtis assured us, after some brandy, would make bringing in the pipe and fixtures a cinch. Just a cinch!

The carpentering of the bathrooms went along very rapidly. We bought hand-wrought black strap hinges and knotty pine and in no time at all our friend turned them into closets and drawers and shelves.

The plumbing seemed to be at a standstill. Don called Mr. Curtis and called Mr. Curtis and called Mr. Curtis, and Mr. Curtis said his back hurt, he couldn't work in the rain, he was using his secret powerful influence to get the fixtures, was the road paved yet (it was barely bulldozed), he would let us know.

Weeks later, about eight o'clock one evening, Mr. Curtis and his wife appeared. Mr. Curtis wore a light polo coat and a brown Fedora. His wife had on jeans and a mackinaw. This was not too unusual a combination in a place where husbands go to the city while wives dig clams and get wood, but in the case of the Curtises it had a special significance, we learned. We offered them a drink which he readily accepted in the cause of his back and she refused, rather wistfully I thought. Don threw another log on the fire and we prepared to settle down and discuss the current ferry strike. To our amazement Mr. Curtis downed his drink in one gulp, leapt to his feet and said, "Sorry, Don, but we must get to work." Firmly he took his wife's arm, led her into the service room and handed her a pick. She chipped where he pointed.

They worked pretty steadily after that. She did all the heavy work, chipping cement, digging the hole for the septic tank, laying the sewer pipe, and so on, not done by Don and his carpenter friend who also dragged all the pipe and the fixtures down the road and set them in place. Mr. Curtis, who never once removed his polo coat or Fedora, in addition to directing the job, did a little screwing on of different things. He performed this rite delicately with his tapering fingers.

We had quite a celebration when the job was finished. Two bathrooms, wheeee! Then the girls reported that if they wanted to take a bath in their new tub they had to fill it with the shower because the faucets wouldn't turn on. Don said, "Nonsense!" and went masterfully upstairs with his pipe wrenches. He came out in a minute soaking wet and told me to call that "fellow Curtis."

There was no answer at the Curtis house. I called every day for a week but there was never anyone home.

Then one very rainy morning Don and I were getting dressed to go to town. I finished first and was downstairs drinking a cup of coffee when I heard an agonized howl from upstairs. I ran up and found Don on his knees by the washbasin, his forefinger in a hole in the floor shouting, "The shutoff—find the shutoff!"

"What's the matter?" I asked.

Don said, "I was shaving and suddenly my shoes were full of water and the pipe came apart and dropped down below the floor and water was spurting up. I finally found the pipe and put my finger in it but for God's sake hurry and shut the water off."

"Where is the shutoff?" I asked reasonably.

"How in hell should I know," Don shouted. "Curtis put it in."

Then, Joanie who was home from school with a sore throat and/or history test, said, "I think it is outside my window. I'll go and see."

In a few minutes she announced that it was the shutoff and she had turned the water off. Don took his finger out of the dike and stormed down to call Curtis. Mrs. Curtis answered the phone and apparently told Don that Mr. Curtis was lying down. Don yelled, "Get him up. Get him to the phone." Apparently she told

Don it was Mr. Curtis' back because Don yelled, "His back'll hurt a lot worse after I get hold of him." So Mrs. Curtis finally said she'd have him come right up.

Don and I explained to Mother, who was visiting us but had as yet not experienced all of the pleasures of island living, about Mr. Curtis, his weak back, need for brandy, loose connections, and so on. I actually believed that Mother thought we were exaggerating, but she promised to see to everything. That night when we got home Mother said, "Well, Mr. Curtis came. He limped in, introduced himself and asked me if I had any brandy. I said no so he said he'd have to go to Vashon and get some as his back was hurting. He came back after a while with a strong breath and two pints. I took him upstairs, pointed out the trouble in both bathrooms and went downstairs. In about three minutes he came down and told me everything was fixed. I said, 'How about that pipe in Betty and Don's bathroom?' He said, 'All fixed. But say, Mrs. Bard, tell them not to *brush* against it.'"

Mother asked him if he had fixed the shower in the girls' bathroom and he said yes and so Mother asked him to test it. He said sure so he and Mother went into the girls' bathroom and he pointed at the bathtub and said, "See, everything's okay here now."

Mother said, "Turn on the faucets, I want to see if they work."

"Well, sure," said Mr. Curtis, sitting down on the edge of the tub in his polo coat and Fedora. "But it's not necessary. I put in bell top crossers and street elbows." (I think those are the terms, but of course it might have been California trap crosses or flow flanges.)

Mother said, "Turn on the faucets."

"Well, okay," said Mr. Curtis reaching over and turning on both the hot and cold water full force, "but it's not necessary." Just then the shower, on fine spray, went sssssssssssss all over Mr. Curtis' polo coat and Fedora.

Mother said Mr. Curtis looked very hurt. "I can't understand it," he said. "Everything is tight as a drum. Maybe it's the sissom joints." He took a drink of brandy out of the bottle he had in his right coat pocket.

Why Don't You Just Relax, Betty? 319

Mother said, "I'm going to stay right here in this bathroom while you fix those faucets."

Mr. Curtis said, "My coat's all wet, I might catch cold and I've got a bad back."

Mother said, "It must be the valve that releases the shower."

"Say, you got something, Mother," Mr. Curtis said, taking another drink of brandy for his bad back.

Mother said, "Fix it," and he did finally so that anybody equipped with a wrench could have a shower *or* a tub as they wished.

When I contemplate my own household and our way of life with fountain pens washed in the Bendix, candy bought for the raccoons, the small fireplace tongs burning up in the cedar tree, my greenhouse devoted to little sailboats, big plastic alligators and suntan oil, twenty-four sheets to the laundry on Mondays, and $183.50 long distance phone bills, I think longingly of a neighbor who always has her cuticle pushed back and buys her ground roundsteak one pound at a time.

"Well, one reason I'm glad we have this house," Anne said, "is because now I can invite all my friends to visit me."

Joan said, "Who am I going to invite? I don't have any friends."

Don said, "I think before anybody invites anybody we should talk things over."

Anne said, "Of course I'm not sure any of my friends would care to come *way* out here?"

Joan said, "Who'll I invite? I don't have any friends."

I said, "Anne and Joan, you can invite your friends, Don can invite his friends, I can invite my friends and if *we* feel like singing 'The Star-Spangled Banner' at three in the morning *we* can."

Don said, "I think we should talk things over. I think I should be consulted."

Anne said, "Of course I'm not sure any of my friends . . ."

But as it turned out everybody had friends and relatives and they were all glad to visit, especially in good weather and nobody ever talked things over until the guests had gone and then often in loud voices, and I learned right away that the big difference between island entertaining and any other kind is that on an island guests stay all night or for two weeks or a couple of years. Even the few rare good sports who try to go home usually miss the last ferry or the ferry company hears you are having people to dinner and knocks down the dolphins or stops running the ferries just for the hell of it.

The point being, if you are not an "I always defrost on Wednesday" kind of housekeeper, but still enjoy having people in for dinner, you can stuff that four gallons of half-finished and a little scorched currant jelly under the sink; tuck the large stack of *Popular Mechanics*, *The Farm*, and *Country Gentleman*, which Don insists on keeping on the kitchen window sill so that he can get at them easily, in with the ironing; toss the beach coats, the dog dishes and my manuscripts in the back hall with the vacuum cleaner; light the candles; put some good music on the record player; mix up a pitcher of very dry martinis and you are ready.

But when people stay all night too, such slap-dash methods will not pass muster and there are the items of the so-revealing morning sunlight, the medicine cabinets, and the jam cupboards in the back hall where we also keep old magazines, the Christmas candles, the coloring books and the weed killer.

Of course, there is the thing about staying up until two or three or four A.M. If we have congenial people and they are having a good time, it is easy to stay up most of the night, especially when it is a houseparty and some of the guests are slightly hysterical at being out of their traps, away from clawing little sticky hands for a change. I like to stay up late too and I like to have a good time, but four o'clock in the morning is not a time to make decisions. Shall I clean up before I go to bed and perhaps not get to bed until dawn or let it go and probably be just as tired in the morning and the house will still look like a saloon.

In the meantime, all the guests have popped off as has Don, who keeps calling hoarsely, "Betty, come to bed. Why don't you come to bed, Betty?" Another thing, I love children and almost always have some tiny friend with me. Some tiny friend who goes to bed at seven and gets in my bed at six. Oh well, sleep is just a habit, the psychologists say.

Why Don't You Just Relax, Betty?

There are all kinds of guests. Fun, no-fun, hard, bores, nasty, crazy, alcoholic, religious-fanatic, old pals who have gotten fat and dull, old pals who have gotten rich and dull, old pals who haven't succeeded and are on the defensive, relatives, babies, foreign friends who know no English dumped on you by Mary, adolescents who play the record player from 7 A.M. to 3 A.M. and paint their toenails while I wash the dishes, bright young friends of Anne and Joan's who are fun, bright young friends of Anne and Joan's who are no fun and don't help, foreign men who light my cigarettes lingeringly and tell me "Youth is so gauche, so raw," then try to lure Anne or Joan out on the porch.

My idea of heaven would be an enormous house, preferably one with twenty-four bedrooms and twenty-four bathrooms, thousands of guests, a great many excellent unobtrusive servants, and no work to do. As my alternative is a house with four bedrooms, a guesthouse, three davenports, a lawn swing, three chaise longues and the floor, thousands of guests, many of them under four years old, and no servants, I often go six months without getting to the beach. Don says that my problem is that I don't relax. He usually says this to me early in the morning after I have been up until three o'clock anyway and then gotten up again with somebody small who has thrown up in the upper bunk.

Of course I'll *never* forget the summer I took care of my sister Alison's three- and five-year-old boys because she was expecting a new baby, and Joanie invited her steady to stay with us because she was so sorry for him because she didn't love him; I invited a dear friend who was an alcoholic but didn't feel that she was quite ready for psychiatry; a couple whom I had met somewhere in the Southwest and carelessly asked to "come and see us any time —we have plenty of room" took me at my word and dropped in for the month of August; my Norwegian cleaning woman's husband had a heart attack; and Anne, who was leading her own life in town being a model, kept bringing home for the weekends and recuperation another model who looked like a Madonna but whose husband was everlastingly blacking her eyes and knocking her against "our new twenty-seven inch TV set" because she was so attractive to other men.

The weather was fair and by that I mean gray and cold, but I forced everyone to eat supper on the beach every night—paper plates, no dishes. Things might have worked out after a fashion if my alcoholic friend had not been deeply suspicious of the woman from Arizona, who had one of the first chic short haircuts, and if the woman from Arizona had just once gotten up before three in the afternoon. Her husband was disgustingly hearty and arose and went swimming in the icy Sound at five-thirty A.M. and was lathering around in the kitchen ready for a *big* breakfast at six.

Then of course there was the Saturday afternoon when Don and the girls and I came staggering along the beach with our loads of groceries and a male voice yelled "Yoohoo!" at us from the *roof* of our house and it was Don's old buddy, the very same old buddy who, refusing to believe that "ole Don" had finally taken the step, spent our weekend honeymoon in Don's apartment *with* us.

Although he did not come down off the roof, we drew closer to home and finally could see clearly that Old Buddy's face was suspiciously flushed and that he was crawling around loosening the shakes in none too steady a fashion. I sent Don out to "talk" to him while the girls and I put the groceries away. Mary and some Navy people were expected on the next ferry and I still had a great deal of rapid stuffing and tidying and flower arranging to do and I didn't intend to be hampered by Old Buddy.

I set Anne to making clam and cream-cheese dip and Joan to filling little dishes with nuts and sunflower seeds and olives. When I had finished my tidying I opened the back door and called to Don to start the fire. Don didn't answer, but Buddy peered at me over the edge of the roof on the steep water side and said, "Heigh-ho!" I slammed back into the house and into Don who was making two drinks.

"You've got to get him out of here," I said.

"Why?" Don asked mildly. "He's up on the roof out of the way."

"I don't think you're funny," I said. "Mary and those Navy people are coming on the next ferry and anyway think of the girls."

"Yes, think of us," the girls said.

"Why don't you all relax?" Don said. "Everything will work out. Let's all be sweet."

He went out the door carrying the two drinks.

Leaving Anne and Joan with the hors d'oeuvres I dashed upstairs, washed my face, put on my tight black slacks and a white sweater and was splashing on perfume when from my open bedroom window I heard Mary and the Navy people crunching along in the sand, and then from overhead I heard Buddy calling out to them "Heigh-ho!"

Anne, who had come in to inspect my makeup and borrow a handful of perfume, said, "Oh, Mommy, honestly, I think he's perfectly disgusting. Can't Don get rid of him?"

I said, "He's Don's oldest friend, Andy, we'll just have to be understanding."

It really wasn't too hard as Mary and her friends were fun and Old Buddy stayed on the roof all evening only asking for occasional favors in the way of drinks and the binoculars so he could examine the crevasses on the moon.

One of the Navy officers (there were three) had brought a guitar and after dinner we went out on the porch in the moonlight and he played sad songs and sang to us. It must have been after three when I was stumbling around emptying ashtrays and brushing potato chips off the mantel while Don hissed at me from the upper hall, "Why don't you come to bed?" that I remembered about Buddy and realized that we had not heard from him for some time.

"What are you going to do about Old Buddy?" I whispered hoarsely. "He's still out on the roof."

"Nothing," Don said. "His responsibility. Now come to bed."

"I'll be along in a minute," I said, sweeping the hearth.

As I put the glasses in the dishwasher and put away the liquor and the enormous amount of equipment Don uses for fried-egg sandwiches, I thought again about Buddy out there on the roof in the cold night air. What if he rolled off and broke his neck? What if the raccoons, who favor our roof as a playfield, clawed him?

Humming happily, I went to bed.

The next thing I knew there was sunlight dappling the rug, Don was handing me a silver fizz and up from the patio floated the cheerful thrumming of a guitar.

"What happened to Old Buddy?" I asked Don as I patted the silver fizz off my lips with the sheet. "I was so worried about him last night I couldn't sleep."

Giving the cord that pulled back the draperies a yank, Don said, "Take a look."

Draining my gin fizz, I got warily out of bed, walked to the window and looked out. Below me, spread-eagled in the lawn swing, a white goatskin rug clutched around his throat, was Old Buddy. One of the Navy officers was kneeling beside him strumming his guitar, the other was propping up his head, feeding him a gin fizz.

Anne and Joan and Mary came in with coffee. Anne said, "You'd better hurry and drink this, Mommy, that Lieutenant Commander and I have breakfast almost ready. We are making buttermilk hotcakes and sausages."

Joan said, "What's that one's name with the guitar, Aunty Mary?"

"Johnny," Mary said.

"Well, Johnny and I are going out sole spearing right after breakfast."

Lighting a cigarette, Mary said, "It's heavenly out here, Betty. So relaxing."

21

Adolescence, or Please Keep Imogene Until She Is Thirty

THE TRICKY THING to remember about adolescents is that they seem so miserable doing what they are doing that you, their loving and bewildered parents, assume that they would be happier doing something else. They wouldn't. Adolescents are going to be miserable no matter what they are doing but they would rather be miserable doing the things *they* choose. This is all so easy for me now that Anne and Joan are twenty-four and twenty-five, charming, intelligent, beautiful, companionable, adult and married. Don and I adore them and can't see enough of them, even if Don did design a Christmas card showing him on the roof shooting at the stork.

But during that long pull between fourteen and twenty (they were both married at twenty) it came over us with a flash, well really more like a punch in the stomach accompanied by the splash of tears, that the English are truly more civilized than we are and they know what they are doing when they send Imogene away to school—and by "away" I mean from Rangoon to England or vice versa—at age seven and bring her home reluctantly when she is thirty.

The summer Anne and Joan turned fourteen and fifteen and both bolted themselves in the bathroom for hours at a stretch and wore lipstick to bed, Don and I sent away for the catalog of a fine school in Canada. It had the splendid English approach, we could tell, because the catalog said, "No need for them to come home for any of the holidays—we will keep them all summer." Anne and Joan found the catalog and cried, not because we didn't want them home in the summer but because the school demanded that all pupils have their hair chopped off even with the ear lobes and wear black oxfords with Cuban heels.

Frankly I do not know any easy answer to adolescence. About the only thing to do is to try to hang on to your sanity and pray much as you would if you were lost in a blizzard without a compass or were adrift in a leaky canoe and could hear the roar of the falls just ahead.

While you are hanging on I will reach down into the black pit of my experience and give you a few things to think about, in case they aren't already glaringly apparent:

1. Adolescents do not hate their parents. They merely feel absolute contempt, occasionally coated with condescending pity for them, their tiny brains, ridiculous ideas, unfair rules and obvious senility. They all refer to their father as "oh him" and their mother as "she": "*She* won't let me go, naturally. *She's* scared to death I might have a little fun for a change." "Who was that on the phone? *Oh him!* What did he want, his overcoat again?"

2. All adolescents are masters of the double- even triple-cross. This does not mean that they will grow up to be either Communists or politicians—it is merely an indication that in adolescence, loyalty is no long-term emotion, and best friends can turn brown quicker than gardenias.

3. All adolescents "go steady." Daughters with boys who appear to be oily, weak-chinned and untrustworthy. Sons with girls who appear hard-eyed, brazen and, if not downright immoral, certainly not wholesome sister types. No parent gets anywhere combatting these great romances. How can anyone as stupid as "oh him" evaluate a big wheel like Billy? (A big wheel who lies on the couch more than the dog and has a vocabulary of thirty words.)

"It just so happens that Billy is left half on the football team and president of SqueeGees, *the* high school fraternity."

What can "she" possibly know about a wonderful girl like Charlene (with her skin-tight skirts, fuchsia lipstick apparently put on with a putty knife, and scintillating conversation of "Gollee, Anne, Johnny may have the mind of a boy but he sure has the *body* of a man!"). "*She* is just jealous because Charlene was voted sweetheart of the SqueeGees *four times*" (no wonder).

The thing that is so difficult for fathers to remember is that very few, if any, of the brilliant lawyers, bankers, doctors, architects or statesmen, a facsimile of which they desire for a son-in-law, ever took out girls when they were in high school. They were too shy and too busy studying to be brilliant lawyers, etc. Big Wheels in high school are, always have been, and undoubtedly always will be the smooth, shifty-eyed, self-confident non-studiers.

The thing that comes as such a blow to the mothers is the fact that little Conroy is not attracted to Ermingarde Allen, who "has such pretty manners and will be very nice-looking when her skin clears up and after all her mother was my classmate at Bryn Mawr." Conroy, who is shy and unsure, refers to Ermingarde, who is shy and unsure, as "that pimply creep," and spends all his time trying to get a date with Carmen Smith who is reputed to let the boys take off her sweater in a parked car. If it is any comfort, isn't it really better for Conroy to satisfy his curiosity about Carmen Smith at sixteen rather than, say, forty?

4. All adolescents telephone. This is part of the cohesive quality that makes them all eat in the same beanery, walk in bunches, knot up in hallways, keep in constant touch. United we stand—divided we might learn something. (You will not solve anything by having two telephones, "Wow, *two* telephones!" Anne and Joan's friends said, and kept them both busy.)

5. All adolescents intend to have the family car all of the time. To accomplish this they resort to the gentle nag or water-on-stone method, the smooth lie, or the cold tearful silence. They will always win if you try to reason or appeal. They have the least resistance to the cheerful impersonal "no."

6. Adolescents are not careful of their own possessions, but they are absolutely reckless with anything belonging to their parents. Don's gray flannel slacks, Don's shoes, my small radio, my

toast-colored cashmere sweater, Don's bathing trunks (about four pairs), my jeans, our sweatshirts, our beach towels, hit the adolescent trail and were never seen again.

7. All adolescent girls would prefer to live in a bathroom.
8. All adolescent boys would prefer to live in a car.

Examining in retrospect that first long wet difficult winter when daylight was only on weekends and keeping warm was the motivating force, I am overcome by how wonderful Anne and Joan were. How cooperative and uncomplaining and hard working and dear. Of course, viewing things in retrospect does blunt corners and point up bright places, but they were such little girls to be getting wood, cooking dinner, making beds and smiling, and I repeat again they were such little girls and they did smile. I wondered if they were happy living on an island and leaving for school in the dark. After all, they were used to my large family and our hordes of friends, I told Don.

He said cheerfully, "Look at the Brontës, Saki, Ruskin, Lincoln. All great people who thrived on isolation."

I said, "When I was a little girl I always came home to a house smelling of gingerbread and filled with people."

Don said, "I always came home to a house smelling of funerals and filled with Methodists. I think Anne and Joan are lucky."

I said, "Perhaps we should have waited until they were older before moving to the country."

He said, "Living in the city doesn't solve everything. Think of all the city children who are alone because their parents are in Palm Springs or down at the Athletic Club getting pie-eyed or in New York attending the National Convention of the Juvenile Delinquency Prevention Society. Anyway there weren't any houses for rent in the city. Remember?"

One stormy night Don met on the ferry and brought home to dinner a widower who lived by himself on the other side of the island. Anne, home from school with one of her fleeting unlocalized ailments, had stuffed and baked a salmon and made an apple pie. The man couldn't get over it. "That little girl, that wonderful little girl!" he said over and over again as he passed his

Adolescence, or Keep Imogene Until She Is Thirty 329

plate for more salmon and watched Anne swishing competently around making boiled coffee and cutting the cheese.

Joanie said, "I'm wonderful too, aren't I, Mommy? I rowed out and bought the salmon from the fishing boat and I carried up a root so big Don can't get it in the fireplace."

"You don't know how fortunate you are," the old widower told Don and me, with tears in his eyes. "I've never seen anything like it." Anne and Joan glowed like little fireflies and in his honor after dinner, when they were doing the dishes, kept their fighting down to quiet slaps, hissed insults and one broken saucer.

Sunday morning the girls always climbed in our bed, Don lit the fire in the fireplace and we took turns going down and getting coffee, orange juice and the Sunday papers. After we had read the papers, accompanied by a great deal of shoving and spilling and jerking of the covers Anne and I got up and cooked a big Sunday breakfast. Kippered herring and scrambled eggs or clam fritters and bacon or shad roe or eggs scrambled with Olympia oysters no larger than a thumbnail. While Anne and I cooked, Joan and Don got wood and built the fires. We never bothered with Sunday dinner, preferring soup and sandwiches whenever we got hungry.

Sunday afternoons we took walks, gathered bark, wrote and acted out plays, popped corn, made fudge, sang into the recording machine, read aloud, helped with homework, took trips in the rowboat with the outboard motor, cleared land, fed the deer and played with the kittens. In spite of my occasional misgivings, we were a very happy, enthusiastic family and I was delighted that Anne and Joan had accepted Don so easily as my husband and their friend.

Then Satan, in the form of adolescence, entered the Garden of Eden and turned it overnight into a jungle. A jungle filled with half-grown, always hungry, noisy, emotional, quarrelsome, rude, boisterous, snarling animals.

The first manifestation was the hair. Anne had bright copper-colored curly hair which she wore shining clean and hanging shoulder length. Joan had pale blond curly hair which she wore shining clean, if I caught her, and hanging shoulder length. One early evening Anne began rolling her pretty hair into small wet snails, about six hairs to a snail, secured tightly with bobby pins crisscrossed like swords.

I said, "What are you doing to your hair?"

Sighing heavily she said, through a mouth filled with bobby pins, "Oh, you wouldn't understand."

"Why shouldn't I?" I said.

"Because you don't know anything about style and anyway you want me to look ugly."

"Your hair looks lovely just the way it is," I said unwisely.

"I knew you'd take that attitude," Anne said, beginning to cry. "I knew you'd get furious if I tried to fix my hair the way *everybody* is wearing it."

Joan said, "That's right, Mommy, *everybody* puts their hair up in pin curls. They all think we look like hags."

"And bags."

"And scrags."

"I'm not furious," I said, getting a little furious. "But I don't see much point in curling curly hair."

"You don't see any point in *anything!*" Anne sobbed. "You don't know anything about anything! You even like to live on this godforsaken island."

From then on Anne and Joan and all their little female friends spent at least one third of their lives rolling their hair into the small snail curls. Over the snails they tied bandannas of different kinds—one year dishtowels, one year men's bandannas, one year woolen scarves, one year enormous silk squares. The strange thing was that except for special occasions such as the Friday night dances, SqueeGee formals and Junior Proms, we never ever saw these curls unfurled. Their hair was pinned up when they left for school, it was pinned up again the minute they got home.

Of course everybody knows that adolescents, in spite of a repulsively overconfident manner, are basically unsure. We read it in books. It is pointed out to us in lectures. There are even articles about it in the newspapers. But you have to live with an adolescent to realize that in this half-ripe, newly hatched, wet-feathered stage they are not aware they are unsure. They consider themselves wise, tolerant, responsible adults. Adults so mature they have a phobia against anything childish. Thus the pleasant Sunday mornings in our bed came to a sudden end. Instead Anne and Joan rushed down and got the papers, fought over them shrilly for a while, then came into our room, sat on the bed, drank the coffee which we had gotten ourselves, and complained. "Gosh, you look hideous in that nightgown, Betty," was one form of greeting, followed quickly by, "Raining again!" heavy sigh. "It seems like it has been raining for years and years." Another heavy sigh. "Do you think Tyrone Power's going to marry Lana Turner, Mommy?" They were both wearing Don's pajamas, their hair was of course in pin curls, their faces smeared with calamine lotion, their fingernails were long, ruby-colored and chipped, their eyes sad.

I said, "Let's get dressed, have breakfast, build a big fire in the fireplace and play charades."

"Charades? You mean that baby game where you act out words?" Anne said.

"It isn't a baby game," I said. "You remember we played it last summer."

"I don't want to play," Joan said. "It's too much like school work."

"I wish I had a pink Angora sweater," Anne said. "Marilyn has two. A pale blue one and a pale pink one."

"Two?" Joan said. "Are you sure? They're twenty-five dollars, you know."

"Marilyn's rich," Anne said. "She gets thirty-five dollars a month just to spend on clothes."

Don said, "I can't understand why we let the Russians into Berlin."

Anne said, "Marilyn's going to spend Christmas in Palm Springs."

I said, "Palm Springs is the last place I would want to spend Christmas. Who wants hot weather and palm trees for Christmas?"

"I do," Anne said wistfully. "I'm so sick of rain I could die."

"Me too," Joan said. "Marilyn's going to get her own car when she's sixteen."

Don said, "Of course Russia had the world bluffed and our policy of appeasement, uncertainty and double-talk isn't fooling anybody but ourselves."

I said, "Possessions don't bring happiness. Happiness is something you must find in your own self."

"Well, it would be a lot easier to find if I had a car of my own," Anne said.

Joan said, "If we had a car of our very own we could drive to California next summer."

"You could not," I said.

"Why?" they said together.

"Because I don't believe in young girls' driving around the country by themselves. It's not safe."

"Well, next summer we'd be fifteen and sixteen."

"That's not old enough to take a trip by yourselves."

"It certainly seems funny to me that we are always old enough to do what *you* want but never old enough to do anything *we* want."

Don said, "Listen to this, 'Peace is largely beyond the control of purpose. It comes as a gift. The deliberate aim at peace passes into its bastard substitute, anesthesia.'"

I said, "Why don't you girls get dressed?"

Don said, "You never listen to anything I say."

I said, "I do too. But it's hard to concentrate on Russia when the girls are leaving for California in their own car."

Anne said, "Don't you think Joan and I are old enough to drive to California, Don?"

"What about South America?" Don said. "It's farther away."

"Who'll go down and get me a cigarette?" I asked.

"You go," Anne said.

"You go," Joan said.

Don said, "Here, smoke one of mine."

Anne said, "Gosh, I hate Sunday. Nothing to do but damned old homework."

"Don't swear," I said.

"Why not?" Anne said. "You do."

"You swear all the time," Joan echoed.

"Let's get dressed," I said, getting out of bed.

To be sure they weren't missing out on any new vital beauty aid, Anne and Joan studied *Glamour, Mademoiselle, Charm, Vogue, Harper's Bazaar*, as well as all the movie magazines. They knew instantly if Burnt Sugar was the latest color in lipstick and they pled and bled until they got it. When they got it they wore it out in about two hours because they put on a new complete makeup when they got home from school (this one was for getting wood), another for eating dinner and of course another before doing the dishes because "somebody might come over." On occasion they would experiment with different blemish removers.

One night when they both came in to kiss us good night coated entirely with some pure white stuff that smelled like creosote and made them look like plaster casts, I said mildly, "Are you sure that is good for your skin?"

Anne, her voice throbbing with bitterness, said, "If it's deadly poison it's better than having to go to school with a face that is always just one big running sore."

"Where are all these running sores?" I asked.

Bending down so that the lamp shone on her face, she said, "Look."

I looked, but all I could see was one small red lump on her chin. I said as much and she stamped up to bed.

Joan said, "Look at my face. My pores are so enormous I look like a cribbage board."

I examined her face as well as I could through the white paste and said, "Your skin looks fine to me."

"Naturally you'd say that," Joan said. "Because you don't care. You cook rich foods all the time because you want us to break out and look ugly."

Don said, "What have you got on your hair?"

"Straightener," Joan said. "It's not stylish to have curly hair. Nobody has it any more. It's corny."

"White stuff on your face, straightener on your hair, what are you trying to do, pass over?" Don asked.

I thought it was very funny and laughed. Joan flounced upstairs.

No matter what garment I bought Anne and Joan the grass was always greener in somebody else's closet. They and their schoolmates exchanged clothes constantly. Anne and Joan would leave for school in one outfit, come home in another. It was hard for me to understand this because all the skirts, blouses, sweaters and coats were exactly alike and all made the girls look like figures in faded photographs of long-ago picnics.

Next in importance to clothes were eating and dieting. For weeks everything would be so-so. The girls would come home from school with their accompanying wake of Jeanies, Lindas, Ruthies, Sandys, Bonnies, Chuckies, Normies, Bills and Jims, go directly to the kitchen and the icebox door would begin to thump rhythmically like the tail of a friendly dog, as they devoured everything not marked with a skull and crossbones or frozen. During those intervals any old thing I cooked, stew, spaghetti or deep-fried pot holders, was greeted with "Is that *all* you made? We're starving."

Then one morning I would decide to get up early and cook something very nice for my growing girls and their long chain of Ruthies, Jeanies and so on, who apparently didn't care if they slept six in a bed or in the fireplace just so it was every night at our house. "I'll make French toast," I said fondly to Tudor as I flitted happily around getting out the real maple syrup and crowding another place on the table each time another gruesome little figure in a torn petticoat, bobby pins and calamine lotion appeared and asked me where the iron was.

When I had a stack of golden French toast about two feet high, ordinarily a mere hors d'oeuvre, I called loudly that breakfast was ready and sat down in my corner with a cup of coffee and a cigarette. After an interval the girls began straggling in, dripping with my perfume and, of course, wearing each other's clothes.

"Hurry and drink your orange juice," I said proudly. "I've made French toast."

"I hope you didn't cook any for me," Anne said loftily, sitting down at the table and unscrewing the top on a bottle of nail polish. "I'm dieting and all I want is one hard-boiled egg."

"Why do you always fix orange juice?" Joan said. "Tomato juice only has fifty calories."

The various Ruthies and Jeanies said to my offers of French toast, "None for me, thanks, Mrs. MacDonald. I'm just going to have black coffee"—or warm water and lemon juice, or a hard-boiled egg.

After they had gone I grimly dumped the lovely golden brown French toast into the raccoons' pan and decided that this was the last time I would ever get up and cook breakfast for my disagreeable little daughters and their ungrateful little friends.

After school the locusts arrived on schedule, but only the boys ate. The girls sipped tea and smoked. Then came dinner and no matter what I cooked, rare roast beef, brook trout, ground round-steak broiled, it was never on their diet. Also I could count on either Anne or Joan or both of them saying, "So much! Why do you always cook in such enormous quantities?"

Of course you can't examine adolescence without getting on the subject of sex, the discussion of which occupied a prominent place in our dinner table conversation during those years. Don and I tried to be very frank with Anne and Joan and encouraged them to be very frank with us. We answered their questions with medical terms, as many as we knew, and, we hoped, the correct casualness. The result was that no matter who came to dinner, the conversation was dappled with rather clinical discussions of sex in which Anne and Joan and their friends seemed to be extremely interested. Adolescents enjoy, in fact will go to most any length to get, the center of attention. In our quiet little home this was accomplished rather easily. We sat down to dinner, Don began to carve, I took a bite of salad and Ruthie said, "Did you know that Ellen broke up with Bob?" There was an excited chorus of No! When! Why! Where! Then Anne remarked in a very conversational tone, "It was bound to come, after all they have been having sexual intercourse every five minutes for years."

Dropping my lettuce into my lap, I said, "Anne MacDonald, what a dreadful thing to say!"

Reaching for another biscuit, Joan said, "Don't get so worked up, Betty. It's common knowledge."

Putting down my salad fork I would launch my standard, worn-to-the-fraying-point lecture on reputations, their preciousness, their gossamer fragility and so on, and so on. The girls waited impatiently but politely for me to finish, then Anne said, speaking patiently, slowly, the way you discourse with mental defectives, "But, Betty, we're not hurting Ellen's reputation."

Ruthie broke in eagerly, "That's right, Mrs. MacDonald. Yesterday she told the whole botany class about Bob and her."

Sighing heavily Don said, "Can't we change the subject?"

Sitting up straight, I began an interesting discourse on the new book I was reading.

I learned after a while, a long while, that if I displayed shock or any other interesting reaction during these discussions they went on and on and on. So I became able finally to toss it off—to say casually, "Please pass the gravy," right in the middle of the gory details of the story about Murdene Plunkett, who didn't wear panties to the spring formal. . . .

I encouraged Anne and Joan to read from the time they first learned how. Our library is large and varied, and beyond casual suggestions I made no attempt to monitor their selections. One rainy school morning Anne asked me for a piece of wrapping paper. I asked her why she wanted it, merely to determine the kind and size, and she said she wanted to wrap up a book so it wouldn't get wet. I offered to wrap the book for her and she handed me *Lady Chatterley's Lover*. I said, trying very hard to speak casually, "Why are you taking this book to school, Andy?"

"Because I'm going to give a book report on it," she said just as casually as she adjusted her bandanna.

"Have you read it?" I asked.

"Part of it," she said. "It's awfully dull, but D. H. Lawrence is supposed to be a good writer, isn't he?"

I tactfully substituted *The Turn of the Screw* by Henry James, as a little more suitable for high school English, just as dull and a lot easier to carry in the rain.

They loved all movies except the ones depicting Hollywood's conception of college life. They were wildly enthusiastic about any stage play or musical, but only Anne and I enjoyed the symphony or concerts.

Anne and Joan and their friends talked a great deal about

sophistication, tight strapless black evening dresses and long cigarette holders, but when boys appeared they screamed like gulls, laughed like hyenas and pushed one another and the boys rudely. One day I came into the living room and found Anne lifting a chair with two great big boys in it. I was horrified and that night I gave the girls lectures # 10874-98734 on Being a Lady —Nice Manners—Charm—Womanliness. They listened with half-closed cobra eyes until I had finished, then yawned and stretched rudely, shoved and pushed each other up the stairs, and locked themselves in our bathroom. The thing that troubled me the most was that none of Anne and Joan's friends were as rude as they were. All the Ruthies and Jeanies, etc., said please and thank you, stood up when I came in the room and wrote their bread-and-butter letters. I wondered what magic their mothers used and when, as they were at our house most of the time.

Then one day Don and I were at a cocktail party and a strange man came up to us and said, "So you're the parents of Anne and Joan. They go skiing with us quite often, you know, and Mrs. Alexander and I think they are the *most charming girls* we have ever met. They are also very witty and very bright but, right at this point, it is their *manners* that impress us the most. You see, Carol," (I realized all of a sudden that this was one of the mysterious parents of Carol, quiet, exquisitely mannered Carol, who had been with us off and on, mostly on, for over a year) "ever since she entered adolescence has apparently been taking a behavior course from Al Capone." Of course we told him about Carol and how beautifully she behaved at our house and he went on and on about Anne and Joan, and then he said, "I can't keep this to myself," and rushed off and got Mrs. Alexander, and we went over the whole thing again. We all left the party looking years and years younger.

Anne and Joan had always been to my prejudiced maternal eyes, normally truthful children. Joan told me when she broke the windshield of the Alcotts' car. Anne told me when she spilled nail polish on my new bedspread. Joan told me when she cut off her eyelashes. Anne told me when she drank the cherry wine. They both told me when they took the candy out of the ten-cent store. Perhaps they each told me what the other did, but anyway I got the truth one way or another, most of the time.

Then came adolescence and the birth of the wilful, deliberate, bold-faced lie. The lie, told, I finally decided, to test parents out, to see what kind of fools they really were.

It began with the lost wallet. Anne and Joan were each given five dollars a week allowance. This was to cover carfare, school lunches, Saturday movies and occasional shopping trips. One Saturday Anne told me that she had lost her wallet with her "whole allowance in it." She cried a little when she told me and I felt niggardly and probing when I asked her for details. She was remarkably definite.

"It was in Frederick and Nelson's at the hat bar on the first floor at eleven in the morning last Saturday. I put the wallet on the counter right beside me while I tried on a hat and when I looked for it, it was gone. Probably taken by a shoplifter." While she was telling her story, Anne and Joan both fixed me with large innocent guileless blue eyes. Of course I believed them and gave Anne another five dollars. She snatched it eagerly but I was not suspicious.

The next Saturday the same thing happened. Almost the same story only this time it was Joan and the Vashon drugstore and the culprit probably "some poor starving farmer who needed the money."

I shelled out another five dollars.

Monday morning Velma, my cleaning woman, brought me Anne's green wallet which she had found behind the bed. In it were two one-dollar bills and the stubs of four loge seats in the Fifth Avenue Theatre.

When Anne came home from school I showed her the wallet and the theater tickets and said sorrowfully, "You lied to me."

"I know it," Anne said cheerfully.

"Why?" I asked, my voice hoarse with emotion.

"I don't know," Anne said. "I guess I just wanted to see if I could. All the kids lie to their mothers."

"Very well," I said. "You owe me five dollars. You can pay me back two dollars a month. Did you lie to me too, Joan?"

Joan, who had her mouth full of apple, nodded brightly, vigorously.

"I'm very very disappointed in you," I said.

"Well, my gosh," Joan said, "Carol's been lying to *her* mother for months and months—she *never* catches on." She made it sound as if I had taken unfair advantage.

"Then why does Carol always borrow money from me?" Anne said furiously. "She owes me about a million dollars."

I said, "You can pay me back two dollars a month too, Joan."

Anne said, "I'm going to get my money back from Carol if I have to choke her to death."

A few nights later, at dinner, Anne announced, "Gosh, we had a hard geometry test today."

"We had an algebra test," Joan said, taking a tiny uninteresting sip of her milk.

"The geometry test was hard but I think I got an awfully good grade," Anne said, as she pushed her peas into a string of green beads encircling her mashed potatoes.

"How do you think you did in algebra, Joanie?" I asked.

"All right, I guess," Joan said. "I despise Miss Gantron but she's so senile she can't think up very hard tests."

"What did they have for lunch at school?" I asked conversationally.

Anne and Joan glanced at each other quickly, then said together, "Spaghetti—macaroni and cheese."

"Make up your minds," I said levelly. "Which was it—spaghetti or macaroni and cheese—surely they wouldn't have both?"

"The food at school gets more revolting every day," Anne said, taking a tiny bite of avocado. "Absolutely tasteless and always cold."

"The macaroni and cheese tastes just like Kem-Tone," Joan said.

"It's better than their vegetable soup," Anne said. "It tastes just like perspiration."

I said, "Speaking of perspiration, Aunty Mary saw you coming out of the Paramount Theatre this afternoon."

Ruthie said, "Oh, it couldn't have been us, Mrs. MacDonald. We were all at school. Weren't we, Jeanie?"

Jeanie said, "Sure they were, Mrs. MacDonald. Ask Kathy."

I said, "I don't have to ask anybody. I *know* you weren't at school and I *know* you aren't hungry for dinner because you have spent the day stuffing down popcorn and ice cream and candy and Cokes. Now CLEAR THE TABLE, WASH THE DISHES, DO YOUR STUDYING AND GO TO BED!"

Later on when Don and I were lying in bed reading and trying to take our minds off adolescence, I heard Ruthie say to Anne, who was of course taking her bath in our bathroom, "Gee, Anne, your mom's sure sweet. I wouldn't dare tell my mom I skipped school. She'd kill me."

Anne said, "Oh, *she's* all right, I guess. Do you think Bill really likes me?"

There was also the music—the loud, blatting, tuneless music that boomed out of the record player from the minute the girls opened their eyes in the morning until they closed them at night. Listening required that they be draped over some piece of furniture surrounded by a litter of Coke bottles, apple cores, candy wrappers, cigarette stubs, cookie crumbs and shoes. Nobody ever wore shoes except outside. Even at formal dances the girls kicked off their shoes and got holes in *my* nylons.

And perfume with names such as Aphrodisia, Quick Passion, Come Hither, Lots of Sin—all with a heavy musk base. I am not at all partial to heavy perfume, preferring light flowery scents, but I'm particularly not partial to heavy perfume slopped on by the handful at seven o'clock in the morning when I'm tentatively taking my first sip of coffee. Anne would come downstairs immaculate, pressed and perfect to the last hair but with the husky scent of Quick Passion hovering over her like smoke over a genie. Once or twice I remarked mildly, "Andy, darling, don't you think that perfume is awfully, uh, well, penetrating for school?" She and Joan, who by that time had also made an appearance quite obviously pinned in many places but drenched in Aphrodisia, exchanged long-suffering looks and sighed heavily. Any further mention of the stench in the kitchen I knew would

Adolescence, or Keep Imogene Until She Is Thirty 341

bring forth a torrent of "You don't *want* us to smell nice. You'd like it if we had B.O. or used Lysol perfume. *Everything* we do is wrong. *All* you do is criticize." Keeping as far away from them as I could and drawing heavily on cigarettes, I put their breakfast on the table and thought with pity of the teachers who had to put up with perhaps thirty-five, all smelling like that.

Of course Anne and Joan treated Don and me as if we were tottering on the edge of senility. We weren't even thirty-five but if we danced (never exactly a spontaneous outburst of animal spirits on Don's part) we became the immediate objects of a great deal of humorous comment. "Oh, look at them! Do you mean to say they really used to dance like *that*? He, he, he, ha, ha, ha, you look so funny!" If I occasionally came back at them and reminded them how funny *they* looked when *they* danced they wailed, "You're so crabby all the time. You're never any fun any more."

I don't know how or when Anne and Joan learned to drive, but I do know that each one, on the day of her sixteenth birthday, demanded to be taken to town so she could go through the ridiculous routine of a driving test and be given a license to drive her steady's father's car and to lend our car to any bonehead friend who wished to back it onto a busy street without looking, run it into a tree, turn a corner without seeing "that dumb truck," or put it in reverse by mistake when going very fast. After a time I became rather accustomed to answering the phone and having a small quavering voice say, "Mrs. MacDonald, this is Joanne and I've had a little trouble with the car, your car I mean, and there's a policeman who wants to speak to you."

Once when we had been up very late listening to "then I said to Ted and Ted said to me" and then were kept awake further by the music of Morks and Doggo and further still by the pattering of big bare feet and shrieks and giggles and the thump of the refrigerator door and finally by my bedside light being switched on and Joan demanding, "Where have you put my down quilt? We're making up a bed for Evelyn and Ruthie on the porch," Don remarked with feeling, "What are we running here, a youth hostel? That Ruthie hasn't been home for two years. How come nobody wants to go anywhere but here? Why should we be the only ones with Coke bottles and shoes on the mantel? Where are the other parents? What are they doing?"

Yawning, I said, "Probably sitting around in their uncluttered houses saying, 'What is all this talk about the problems of adolescents? I don't find them any trouble at all.' "

Anne burst in and said, "Do you care if Carol smokes?"

"I don't care if she bursts into flame," Don said.

"Very funny," Anne said witheringly, "and *very old*." Taking our only package of cigarettes she went out, slamming the door.

"Never mind," I said to Don, "someday they will marry and leave home."

"Are you sure?" Don said, as he sadly sorted over the butts on his ashtray, finally selecting a pretty long one. He examined it critically for a minute or two then, with a sigh, struck a match and lit it.

22

Bringing in the Sheaves

I DON'T KNOW why I ever entertained such a ridiculous idea, but it was undoubtedly the fruit of misery and desperation—could even have been nature's way of keeping me from becoming an alcoholic or cutting a main artery or taking any other coward's way out. As I remember, the dream came to light first, the time I was called to school to learn that Anne, who had almost finished three years of high school, had accumulated exactly six and one third credits in required subjects. All the others were cooking, sewing, basket weaving, leather punching, mural painting and so on. I didn't even know they had so many courses for those "better with their hands," as the principal explained kindly. I told him again about Anne's very high IQ and he said without enthusiasm, "Yes, I've checked with her junior high school principal, but the problem is that unless you want her to graduate with a *certificate* instead of a *diploma* she will have to buckle down." That night after dinner when we were having a discussion of Anne's buckling down and Anne wasn't, Joan said finally, "Oh, why don't you just send her to Opportunity School" (a local school for the retarded) "that's where she belongs."

Anne said calmly, "I hate school. I've always hated school. I always will hate school. You'll never change me, so you might as well not upset yourself trying."

"But, Andy," I said, "you won't be able to get into any college unless you take science and languages and math."

"College!" Anne laughed derisively. "I wouldn't go to college if you slashed my wrists and beat me with a steel cable and cut off my allowance. I loathe school and I loathe all teachers."

"The feeling appears to be mutual," Don remarked dryly from behind *Time* magazine.

I said, "But, Andy, you don't know how different college is from high school. In college you're treated as an adult and the professors are brilliant and stimulating and you realize for the first time the importance of knowledge—the reason for studying."

Yawning elaborately, then inspecting her long red nails, Anne said, "I'm sorry, Betty, but you are just wasting your time. Anyway you seem to forget that I've seen some college students. Look at Evelyn Olwell. She's a sophomore in college and she thinks Villa Lobos is a sport like handball. And Martha Jones—she's a junior in college and last summer she told me her mother was 'alternating' her dress. And Catherine Morton—she's never read a book—not a single one—her family doesn't even own a book and her mother and father are both college graduates."

After a time we reached a sort of agreement, or hard-eyed, shouted compromise. Anne would change her courses, go to summer school and graduate with a *diploma*, but whether or not she went to college would be her decision.

I had the dream next when Joan, who for two or three Sundays had been singing at a local USO, suddenly decided that she was going to leave school and sing with a band. The first inkling Don and I had of this splendid plan was when we went in to check on Anne and Joan who were in town weekend baby-sitting with the two small children of a friend of ours. It was Sunday afternoon and we dropped by to see what time they expected the parents and what time they wanted us to pick them up.

I remember the nice feeling of pride I had as I ran up the steps of the Morrisons' house. "Anne and Joan solicited this baby-sitting job all by themselves," I told Don, who was morosely inspecting a broken downspout. "And I think it shows encouraging signs of maturity for them to take care of two little children and stay in a house all by themselves from Friday afternoon to Sunday night."

Stepping up on the porch railing so he could take a look at the eaves trough, Don said, "We'll probably get a blast from Jim and Mary when they get the grocery bill."

"The trouble with you is that you don't want to see any improvement in the girls," I said crossly.

"Not at all," Don said, his chin on the roof. "I just like to face facts. I'd better tell Jim this eaves trough is rotten."

I rang the doorbell. There was no answer, but I thought I detected giggling and scuffling from somewhere in the house. Then Anne came to the door, wearing a dishtowel tied low over her forehead like an Arab's headdress. She was flushed and nervous. "How come you're so early?" she asked, ungraciously barring the door.

"We came to visit," I said cheerfully. "To see how you are getting along."

"We're getting along all right," Anne said, trying to shut the door.

"Where's Joanie?" I asked.

"Oh, she's around," Anne said evasively.
"What do you mean," I said firmly, moving her out of the way and going into the house.
"She's upstairs."
"Joanie," I called loudly. "It's Mommy. Where are you?"
"I'm up here," answered a muffled voice.
"You'd better not yell," Anne said. "The baby's asleep. Come out in the kitchen and I'll make you a cup of coffee."
Patty, the Morrisons' four-year-old, came down the stairs, slowly one step at a time. The front of her dress was quite wet.
We all went out to the kitchen. Patty settled herself in a chair by the kitchen table with crayons and a coloring book. Carefully choosing a white crayon she announced companionably, "This is just the color Joanie's hair is going to be when she finishes bleaching it!"
"You be quiet," Anne hissed at her.
"Why?" asked Patty, whose shoes were on the wrong feet.
"Because you promised," Anne said.
"I promised not to tell about *your* hair," Patty said. "I didn't promise about Joan's."
I got up, walked over to Anne and jerked the dishtowel off her hair. She stood paralyzed, the coffee pot in one hand, the can of coffee in the other. Her hair exploded from under the dishtowel like a deep old rose chrysanthemum.
"Anne MacDonald," I shrieked. "What have you done?"
She began to cry, using the dishtowel as a handkerchief. Through her tears and the dishtowel, she said finally, "Well, Joan thought that her hair would look better platinum if she was going to sing with a band and so she bought a bottle of triple-strength peroxide and we both tried it and if you think I look awful just wait till you see Joan."
Then Joan appeared pale and trembling. Her head was swathed in a bathtowel. I told her the jig was up and jerked off the towel. Her normally ash-blond hair was the bright egg-yolk yellow of highway signs.
"We don't know what to do," Anne sobbed. "We can't go to school like this."

"You could have your heads shaved," Don suggested helpfully.

"Or you can let it grow out," I added heartlessly. "It will take at least six months."

"It's all Joan's fault," Anne said. "She's the one that wanted to sing with a band."

"You're a double-crosser," Joan yelled. "You're the very one that told me to bleach my hair."

"But you bought the peroxide," Anne screamed.

"Only because you didn't have any money," Joan shrieked.

Don and I tiptoed out. The girls were so busy fighting they didn't even notice.

When we retrieved the girls about six, Anne's hair was a pinkish brown and Joan's a yellowish brown. "Don't we look keen?" Joan asked cheerfully as she squeezed past me into the back seat.

"Watch what you're doing with that suitcase," I said irritably as she dragged it past my ear and clunked it down on Anne's foot.

"Ouch," Anne shrieked. "You clumsy dope!"

"Don't call me a dope," Joan said calmly. "Remember I'm the one that figured out how to fix our hair."

"What did you do?" I asked, turning around and taking a closer look at their dusty rose and ochre heads.

"I went up to the drugstore and bought a bottle of light brown dye," Joan said proudly. "I dyed Anne's hair and she did mine. Don't we look keen?"

I said, "You don't look keen, but you don't look quite as awful as you did."

Joan said, "Gosh, you're crabby. I'll certainly be glad when I leave home. Everybody in this family is a big crab."

"Where are you going and when?" Don asked.

"Joe Charteris told me that if I quit school I could travel with his band and I'm going to," Joan said.

I said firmly, loudly, "You're not going *anywhere* and you are *not* going to sing at that USO any more."

"Okay," Joan said cheerfully, "but you don't have to get so worked up. Let's get Chinese food."

"Oh, please, Mommy," Anne said. "Let's go to Won Ton's."

"What about your hair?" Don asked.

"Oh, the Chinese don't care about our hair, anyway we brought our dishtowels," Anne said.

"I won't take you anyplace in those hideous dishtowels," I said.

"Oh, Betty, do you have to be so disagreeable *all* the time," both girls said, sighing. "You never say a civil word any more."

So we went to Won Ton's and while the girls argued about what they were going to have and Don intently studied the Chinese side of the menu, I lapsed into this familiar soothing daydream. It was Anne's eighteenth birthday and her presents were heaped by her place at the breakfast table, and Don and Joan and I were in the kitchen waiting for her to come downstairs. Then she appeared, my little girl, my own dear little serious-eyed Anne, all soft and sweet and loving, kissed us all, including Joan (this part of the picture was really far-fetched), and said, an amused smile tugging at the corners of her mouth, "Well, Betty and Don, you can start living again. One of us is out of adolescence." The dream faded as Don announced happily, as he always does, that he thought he'd just have the pressed duck and the waiter said as he always does, "Press dock take two day. Have to odah day befoh."

It was the night before Anne's nineteenth (I had adjusted my dream a little—after all there is no point in being just plain ridiculous) birthday, but as I sat on our bed wrapping the presents, a white cashmere cardigan, an album of Bidu Sayao and a triple strand of pearls (Japanese), I had an unhappy presentiment, bordering on certain knowledge that there wasn't going to be any Santa Claus. The morning of the birthday confirmed it. Anne and Joan had a furious quarrel over who was going to get the car before they even got out of bed. When she finally came shuffling down to breakfast with a bad case of hay fever, Anne tripped over Tudor who was lying in the kitchen doorway and when she kicked him "with only my soft old bedroom slipper" he nipped her ankle and Don heartlessly refused to drive her into Seattle for rabies shots and so she stamped upstairs without opening her presents.

Oh, well, she had graduated from high school and she did have a job in the advertising department of a large department store, even if the only apparent changes wrought by her new adult status were that she wore what she termed "high style" clothes (Don said she could call them what she liked but they looked to him like Halloween costumes), more and heavier perfume and eyeshadow in the daytime. However, she didn't seem to actively dislike Don and me as much as formerly. She still treated us like lepers, but good old lepers. The faithful non-irritating kind, who are so dumb they don't know they don't know *anything*. Her attitude toward Joan was that of a high caste Hindu forced to associate with an untouchable. Her friends were all models. She went steady with a boy Don referred to as "that sneaky Bradley."

Joan was a senior in high school. When she wasn't fighting with Anne over clothes or the car, she was going to sorority meetings which were every night in the week at our house, and going steady. Going steady meant that there were always two pairs of shoes on the mantel and twice as many Coke bottles under the couch. Joan didn't treat Don and me like anything, because we still weren't anything—just "she" and "oh him."

Then Joan was in college living at her sorority house but coming home quite often because she was "starving to death." College had wrought no appreciable change in anything except her laugh which was now a bleat accompanied by a wide open mouth and tightly squinted eyes. Her best friends all laughed the same way. It seemed to be something they were teaching at the University that year. Don and I thought the new laugh very unattractive and one day I tactlessly said so. Joan blew up like a defective hot-water tank. "I can't do *anything* right," she shrieked. "You don't like my hair, you don't like my clothes, you don't like my friends, you don't like the way I drive. The real trouble of course is that you haven't any sense of humor and you're terribly neurotic." She and her friends slammed out of the house—then slammed back in for two quarts of garlic dill pickles and a large bundle of ham sandwiches they had made earlier.

Stifling a strong unmotherly desire to pick up the refrigerator and hurl it after them, I poured myself a cup of coffee, sat down at the kitchen table and lit a cigarette. What was wrong? Where had I failed? Were all adolescents like Anne and Joan? What had happened to our happy home? Who had erected this great big spiky impenetrable wall between us and our children? Would it always be like this? Would things be like this if we hadn't moved to the country? It was Saturday and I hadn't vacuumed the living room or thrown out the dead flowers or changed the sheets on the bunkroom beds and I didn't care. All I wanted to do was to throw myself face down on the brick floor, beat my heels and scream.

After a time I heard a car door slam. I jumped up guiltily. I had almost forgotten that Anne and a model friend were coming for the weekend.

Her appearance set me back just a little. Anne was wearing a charcoal-gray *costume*, spats, a black-and-white-checked man's cap and about twenty pounds of pearls. I could smell her perfume clear from the kitchen door to the wild cherry tree. The model, who had such little hips I didn't see how she was going to sit on them, was all in black and heavy gold jewelry. I was pretty sure I was going to catch hell about my blue jeans (Vashon grocery store) and white blouse (Sears, Roebuck). "Really, Betty, you *are* getting older—you do have other clothes," and so on, and so on, and so on. I could feel the old familiar defensive wariness take over as I kissed Anne and said, "I'm just going to make fresh coffee."

Anne said, "It's wonderful to be home. It smells so good over here on the island."

"The model said, "No wonder you rave about this house so much, it's dreamy."

Putting down her suitcase, taking off her man's cap and getting out a long black cigarette holder into which she carefully inserted one of my cigarettes, Anne said, "I love it here on the island. Being here gives me a different perspective. The right things are important over here." She smiled at me and then said briskly, to hide her moment of weakness, "Here, you sit down and I'll make the coffee."

I did sit down, with a thump of astonishment, opposite the model who smiled at me with her lips pulled out at the corners and her teeth all touching each other. She was very very pretty with the impersonal perfection of a Swedish crystal pitcher. I said, "You are certainly pretty, Renée."

She said, "Thanks, but I don't think black does much for me. I like black, I think it's real chic, but white's really my color."

Anne, who was pouring the coffee, said, "As soon as we drink our coffee, let's put on our jeans."

Renée said, "I didn't bring jeans, honey, I can't get them small enough around the waist, my waist is only nineteen inches, but I brought my leopard skin slacks. Gee, they're dreamy. Shall I go put them on now?"

"Yes, do," Anne said, winking at me. "They sound terribly smart."

After Renée had taken her suitcase upstairs, Anne said, "I realize that Renée's brain is the size of a proton, but I feel sorry for her—she's really very sweet and her husband beats her to a pulp practically every half hour. She is always coming to work in dark glasses to cover a black eye or in high collars to cover finger marks on her neck."

"Why does he beat her—is he insane?"

"Oh, no, just jealous and a drunk. Last week he blacked both her eyes and cracked a couple of ribs so she moved in with Janet and me. As she brought at least $150,000 worth of clothes, her husband may have some reason for his jealousy. Anyway she lets me borrow anything I want and she's a wonderful cook."

As we drank our coffee Anne asked me about Joan and I told her and even though I was all braced and ready for the usual "*Why* won't you realize Joan and I are grown up, *why* do you always nag?" it wasn't forthcoming. Instead, Anne said, "Poor Mommy. Never mind, she'll grow out of it. I did and nobody in the entire universe was ever such a revolting adolescent." I guess I must have lost consciousness for a moment or two because, when I came to, Anne and Renée in her leopard skin slacks were saying, "We've got to do something about your hair, Betty. The way you're wearing it isn't smart at all." They both had their hair peeled back from their faces and pinned with huge gold barrettes. I wore my hair in a medium bob with bangs. After surveying me for a while from all angles through squinted eyes and a cloud of cigarette smoke, they decided I should wear my hair skinned up into a sort of whale spout on top of my head, secured with the red elastic band from the stalk of celery on the drainboard. When they had finished with me and I was very wet around the shoulders and felt as though my eyebrows were up by my hairline, Anne said, "Now, you look smart." Renée said, "God, you're a doll, Mrs. MacDonald."

I went into the lavatory off the kitchen and looked in the spattered mirror of the medicine cabinet. I finally decided that the light must be wrong. When I came back into the kitchen, Anne said, "You don't like it, I can tell." She laughed, took off the elastic and combed my hair back into its normal do. Sunday night, as I kissed Anne good-bye, I realized that her adolescence really was over, that she was an adult. What is more important I felt I had a new friend. One who was witty, intelligent, loving, beautiful and *liked* me. My little Anne, my serious-eyed little girl whom I had mourned and longed to bring back, was gone as surely as yesterday's rainbow, but I was really happier with my new friend. The heavy perfume, high style clothes, eyeshadow in the daytime that had been major irritations in my little girl, were now just the small lovable eccentricities of a friend.

The following summer Joan got a job as a saleslady in an exclusive dress shop. The sorority laugh was gone, but she began wearing high style clothes and the haunted look of the bill-ower. However, she was a tiny bit of fun sometimes and, anyway, Don and I had Anne to help us understand her. In January Anne was married—not to Sneaky Bradley—and during the hectic preparations for the wedding, Joan suddenly emerged as an easygoing witty slapdash affectionate sympathetic adult. Now they are both married and each has three babies. They are loving wives, marvelous mothers, divine cooks and excellent housekeepers. Don and I are very proud of them, but, more important, they *like* us. Their husbands *like* us. We are *friends*. Sometimes we are such good friends I get all six of the babies—the oldest is four—but I love it and it is awfully good for my figure.

Of course there have been times when I have wondered if we

did do the right thing in moving to an island. If it was fair to Anne and Joan. If it was fair to me. Once I asked Don and he said:

"Guiding children through adolescence is no joyride no matter where you live. At least here on Vashon we had something to take our minds off it. Fun things such as sawing wood or cleaning out the storm sewers."

Then I foolishly said, "And how do you think it has been for us? For instance, how do you think I compare to other women my age?"

Giving me a long, fond husbandly look, Don said, "Well, you don't look as tired as you did yesterday."

Printed in the USA
CPSIA information can be obtained
at www.ICGtesting.com
LVHW011212141123
763823LV00006B/213

9 781013 522130